Adobe® Premiere® Elements

FOR

DUMMIES®

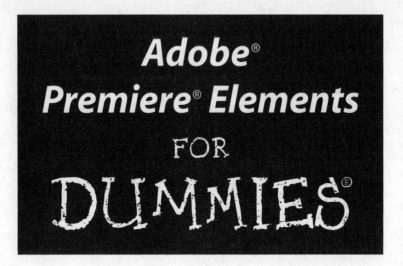

Adobe® Premiere® Elements FOR DUMMIES®

by Keith Underdahl

Author of *Digital Video For Dummies*, 3rd Edition

Wiley Publishing, Inc.

Adobe® Premiere® Elements For Dummies®

Published by
Wiley Publishing, Inc.
111 River Street
Hoboken, NJ 07030-5774

WILEY

About the Author

Keith Underdahl is a digital-media specialist residing in Albany, Oregon. Professionally, Keith is an electronic publishing specialist for AGES Software, where he serves as program manager, interface designer, multimedia producer, graphic artist, programmer, customer support manager, and resident Portable Document Format (PDF) guru. At the end of the day, he even sweeps up the place. Mr. Underdahl has written numerous books, including *Teach Yourself Microsoft Word 2000*, *Microsoft Windows Movie Maker For Dummies*, *Macworld Final Cut Pro 2 Bible* (co-author), *Digital Video For Dummies,* 3rd Edition, and *Adobe Premiere Pro For Dummies.*

Dedication

My beloved brethren, let every man be swift to hear, slow to speak, slow to anger.

— *James 1:19*

Author's Acknowledgments

So many people helped me complete this project that I hardly know where to begin. First and foremost I wish to thank my family for allowing me to work two full-time jobs as I completed *Adobe Premiere Elements For Dummies*. My wife, Christa, has been my entire support staff, head cheerleader, creative advisor, and inspiration throughout my entire writing career. She was the one who urged me to start writing for a small motorcycle magazine in 1995, and that endeavor has led to so many great adventures and challenges in the years since. I owe everything to Christa.

My undying gratitude also goes out to my two very favorite movie subjects, Soren and Cole Underdahl. Not only do my boys take direction well, but they are also incredibly intelligent and look great on camera! I also received help both on-screen and behind the scenes from Brian and Darlene Underdahl.

I wish I could take full credit for the quality and content of *Adobe Premiere Elements For Dummies,* but many other kind folks contributed to this work to make it what it is. I'd like to thank Steve Hayes for hiring me once again to write this book, my project editor Nicole Haims, my technical editor Dennis Short, and the many other folks at Wiley who toiled to make this one of the best references on Adobe Premiere Elements to be found.

I had help from some industry people, including Andy Marken, Pete Langlois, and Rick Muldoon. And finally, thanks to Christine Yarrow, Mark Wheeler, Stephen Inoue, Abhay Sarup, and all the folks at Adobe for inviting me to help develop this excellent video-editing tool. I've been on the user side of Adobe software for a long time, and I am honored to contribute to their testing and development programs as well.

Publisher's Acknowledgments

We're proud of this book; please send us your comments through our online registration form located at www.dummies.com/register/.

Some of the people who helped bring this book to market include the following:

Acquisitions, Editorial, and Media Development

Project and Copyeditor: Nicole Haims

Senior Acquisitions Editor: Steven H. Hayes

Technical Editor: Dennis Short

Editorial Manager: Carol Sheehan

Media Development Manager: Laura VanWinkle

Media Development Supervisor: Richard Graves

Editorial Assistant: Amanda Foxworth

Cartoons: Rich Tennant, www.the5thwave.com

Composition

Project Coordinator: Maridee Ennis

Layout and Graphics: Andrea Dahl, Joyce Haughey, LeAndra Hosier, Lynsey Osborn, Heather Ryan, Julie Trippetti

Proofreaders: Joe Niesen, Brian H. Walls, TECHBOOKS Production Services

Indexer: TECHBOOKS Production Services

Publishing and Editorial for Technology Dummies

    Richard Swadley, Vice President and Executive Group Publisher

    Andy Cummings, Vice President and Publisher

    Mary Bednarek, Executive Acquisitions Director

    Mary C. Corder, Editorial Director

Publishing for Consumer Dummies

    Diane Graves Steele, Vice President and Publisher

    Joyce Pepple, Acquisitions Director

Composition Services

    Gerry Fahey, Vice President of Production Services

    Debbie Stailey, Director of Composition Services

Contents at a Glance

Table of Contents

Introduction

· ·

*B*ack in the Dark Ages — a little over a decade ago — most video editing was conducted in specialized TV and movie production facilities staffed by professionals working on equipment that cost millions of dollars. Then in 1993, Adobe released a program called Adobe Premiere. Premiere allowed people to edit video on conventional desktop computers, a revolutionary idea at the time.

Years went by, and new technologies entered the picture. More and more video professionals switched to editing on desktop computers. This switch created a growing market of users — and new competition for software manufacturers to produce programs like Adobe Premiere, Apple Final Cut Pro, Avid Xpress, and Pinnacle Edition, all of which cater to professional-consumer (or *prosumer*) users.

Meanwhile, "regular" consumers started editing their own movies too, using low-cost (or even *no*-cost) programs like Apple iMovie, Pinnacle Studio, and Windows Movie Maker. These programs, combined with high-quality, afford-able digital camcorders, created an explosion in moviemaking as a hobby enjoyed by many rather than a profession practiced by only a few.

Adobe kept updating Premiere over the years, and when the name changed to Adobe Premiere Pro in 2003, we knew it was only a matter of time before they also released a more affordable non-Pro version. Adobe Premiere Elements is that version. Adobe Premiere was a pioneer in desktop video editing, and Adobe's many years of experience shows in the high quality of Premiere Elements.

Now that there are two versions of Adobe Premiere — Pro and Elements — you must decide which version is for you. When I spoke with one of Adobe's marketing people during the development of Premiere Elements, he sug-gested that the difference boils down to this: If you are getting paid to edit video, you should use Premiere Pro. If you're editing video for fun, use Premiere Elements.

This way of looking at things seems a little too simplistic to me for two rea-sons. First, even a video hobbyist can appreciate some of the extra features in Premiere Pro. But second, and more important, in my opinion, Adobe Premiere Elements is so powerful that you probably can use it to make movies that others would buy. In fact, I can think of several professional movie production projects on which I've worked (using Premiere Pro) that could have just as easily been produced using Premiere Elements.

Ultimately, the choice of whether to buy Adobe Premiere Pro or Premiere Elements boils down to price. Adobe offers Premiere Elements at a remarkably low retail price of about $100 in the U.S., and Premiere Pro costs about $700 more. Although Premiere Pro does offer some extra features, it is not eight times better than Premiere Elements.

Adobe Premiere Elements allows you to get serious about your video-editing hobby without having to spend serious money. When it comes to video-editing programs, Premiere Elements truly gives you more for less.

Why This Book?

Despite the low price, Adobe Premiere Elements is an advanced program. *Adobe Premiere Elements For Dummies* is an advanced reference to this program, but like Premiere Elements itself, this book doesn't come with an advanced price tag. I realize that you want to get right to work with Premiere Elements, so I've written this book with the goal of providing you easy-to-follow instructions, as well as real-world tips and tricks to help you work smarter and better.

Needless to say, you're no "dummy" — otherwise, you wouldn't be reading this book and trying to figure out how to use Adobe Premiere Elements correctly. Video editing is fun, and it is my hope that you'll find this book fun to use as well. I have included instructions on performing the most important video-editing tasks, and I've included lots of graphics so that you can better visualize what I'm talking about. You'll also find tips and ideas in this book that you just won't find in the dry, cryptic help files that Adobe delivers with the program.

Adobe Premiere Elements For Dummies doesn't just help you use the Premiere Elements program. If you're relatively new to moviemaking, you'll find that this book helps you choose a good camcorder, shoot better video, publish movies online, and speak the industry techno babble like a Hollywood pro.

Foolish Assumptions

I've made a few basic assumptions about you while writing this book. First, I assume that you have an intermediate knowledge of computer use, and that you are ready, willing, and able to take on the challenge of movie editing, which is one of the more technically advanced things a person can do with a computer.

Because you're an intermediate user, I assume you already know how to locate and move files around on hard drives, open and close programs, and perform other such tasks. I also assume that you have Windows XP, because that is the only operating system in which Adobe Premiere Elements will run.

Premiere Elements will not run in Windows Me or Windows 2000. And I'm sorry to say it, but there's no Macintosh-compatible version of Premiere Elements either.

Another basic assumption I've made is that you might not (at least not yet, anyway) be an experienced video editor. I explain the fundamentals of video editing in ways that help you immediately get to work on your movie projects. Most of the coverage in this book assumes that you're producing movies as a hobby, or you are just getting into professional video editing by doing wedding videos and such, but you can't yet afford a professional-grade program like Premiere Pro. Typical projects might include vacation travelogues, weddings, birthday parties, or even amateur fictional movie productions.

Conventions Used in This Book

Adobe Premiere Elements For Dummies helps you get started with Premiere Elements quickly and efficiently. The book serves as a reference to this program, and because Premiere Elements is a computer program, you'll find this book a bit different from other kinds of texts you have read. The following are some unusual conventions that you encounter in this book:

- ✔ File names or lines of computer code will look like THIS or this. This style of print usually indicates something you should type in exactly as you see it in the book.

  The display format for the *timecode* (the unit for measuring time in video) is hours;minutes;seconds;frames. The timecode 01;33;20;03 represents 1 hour, 33 minutes, 20 seconds, and 4 frames (the frame count begins with 0).

- ✔ Internet addresses will look something like this: www.dummies.com. Notice that I've left the http:// part off the address because you almost never have to actually type that into your Web browser anymore.

- ✔ You will often be instructed to access commands from the menu bar in Premiere Elements and other programs. The menu bar is that strip that lives along the top of the Premiere Elements program window and usually includes menus called File, Edit, Project, Clip, Timeline, Marker, Title, Window, and Help. If (for example) I tell you to access the Save command in the File menu, I will use arrows that look like this: Choose File⇨Save.

✔ You'll be using your mouse a lot. Sometimes you have to click something to select it. This means you should click *once* with the left mouse button after you've put the mouse pointer over whatever it is you're supposed to click. I'll specify when you have to double-click or right-click (that is, click once with the right mouse button).

✔ Another mouse-related task you'll often have to perform is the classic click-and-drag. For example, I often ask you to click-and-drag a video clip from one window to another. To click-and-drag an item, hover the mouse pointer over the item and then hold down the left mouse button. While holding down the button, move the mouse pointer to a new location. Release the mouse button to drop the item on the new location.

How This Book Is Organized

I took all the chapters of *Adobe Premiere Elements For Dummies* and put them in a bucket. I stirred that bucket with a stick and then poured the chapters out on the floor. This was how I decided which order to place things in, and I think that it has yielded a book which is pretty well organized. The chapters of *Adobe Premiere Elements For Dummies* are divided into five major parts, plus an appendix. The parts are described in the next section.

Part 1: Presenting Adobe Premiere Elements

Adobe Premiere Elements is an advanced program, and if you're new to video editing, many parts of this program may seen unfamiliar. Part I helps you get started with your moviemaking adventure by introducing you to Adobe Premiere Elements. You'll begin by touring the Premiere Elements program and getting familiar with its tools and basic features. If you've never edited a movie before, Chapter 1 gets you started right away on your first movie project — you can complete it from start to finish in the first chapter.

Because Premiere Elements is just one of many tools that you will use to make movies, I spend some time helping you prepare your production studio. I also show you how to prepare Premiere Elements for use with a variety of media formats. Chapter 4 introduces you to the fundamentals of video technology, which you'll need to be familiar with as you create your movies.

Part II: Basic Editing in Adobe Premiere Elements

After you're comfortable with Adobe Premiere Elements, you are ready to get right to work. The first chapter in Part II shows you how to start new projects in Premiere Elements. Next, I show you how to capture video from a digital camcorder onto your computer, and I show you how to import and manage other kinds of media as well. Chapters 7 and 8 take you through the most common and important video-editing tasks, and in Chapter 9, I show you how to add fancy transitions between video clips.

Part III: Advanced Editing in Premiere Elements

Adobe Premiere Elements is far more advanced than any other program in its price range. The chapters in Part III show you how to use the more advanced features that come with the software. I show you how to improve colors and lighting in video images, how to create compositing effects with blue screens, how to add and customize special effects, and how to work with audio and titles in your movies.

Part IV: The Finishing Touches

Moviemaking is a highly expressive art form. The chapters in Part IV show you how to share your artistic expression. First, I show you how to put the finishing touches on your movie projects, and then I show you how to make sure they're ready to share with others. Next, I show you how to share your movies on the Internet, how to burn your movies to DVD, and how to record your movies onto videotape.

Part V: The Part of Tens

I wouldn't be able to call this a *For Dummies* book without a "Part of Tens" (really, it's in my contract). Actually, the Part of Tens always serves an important purpose. In *Adobe Premiere Elements For Dummies,* this part gives me a chance to show you ten advanced video-editing techniques that you can use in Premiere Elements, ten moviemaking tips and secrets used by the pros, and ten gadgets and programs that will help you make better movies.

Appendix

Video editing is a technical subject with a language all its own, so at the end of Part V I've provided a glossary to help you quickly decrypt the alphabet soup of video-editing terms and acronyms.

Icons Used in This Book

Occasionally, you'll find some icons in the margins of this book. The text next to these icons includes information and tips that deserve special attention and some of them may warn you of potential hazards and pitfalls you may encounter. Icons you'll find in this book are easy to spot:

Although every word of *Adobe Premiere Elements For Dummies* is important, I sometimes feel the need to emphasize certain points. I use Remember to occasionally provide this emphasis.

Tips are usually brief instructions or ideas that aren't always documented but can greatly improve your movies and make your life easier. Tips are among the most valuable tidbits in this book.

Heed warnings carefully. Some warn of situations that can merely inconvenience you; others tell you when a wrong move could cause expensive and painful damage to your equipment and/or person.

Computer books are often stuffed with yards of techno babble, and if it's sprinkled everywhere, it can make the whole book a drag, and just plain difficult to read. As much as possible, I've tried to pull some of the deeply technical stuff out into these icons. This way, the information is easy to find if you need it, and just as easy to skip if you already have a headache.

Where to Go from Here

If you've always wanted to be in pictures, this is your time. Video editing is *the* hot topic in computer technology today, and you're at the forefront of this multimedia revolution. If you still need to set up your movie studio or need some equipment, I suggest that you start off with Chapter 2, "Equipping Yourself for Moviemaking." If you aren't quite ready to start editing yet, you may want to spend some time in Chapter 4, "Introduction to Moviemaking." Otherwise, you should go ahead and familiarize yourself with Adobe Premiere Elements, beginning with Chapter 1.

Part I
Presenting Adobe Premiere Elements

The 5th Wave   By Rich Tennant

©RICHTENNANT

"Mary Jo, come here quick! Look at this special effect I learned with Adobe Premiere Elements."

In this part . . .

*V*ideo-editing programs have been around for a few years now, but the programs on the affordable end of the price scale have tended to lack features and provide an almost cartoonish interface. Adobe Premiere Elements has changed this, making truly pro-caliber editing power affordable for almost anyone.

This part of *Adobe Premiere Elements For Dummies* begins your moviemaking adventure by exploring Adobe Premiere Elements and finding out just what this program can do. It also looks at what's needed for your personal video-production studio and helps you configure Premiere Elements do help you with your moviemaking magic.

Chapter 1

Feeling at Home with Adobe Premiere Elements

· ·

· ·

A few years ago, video editing was only practical for people with a lot of fancy editing equipment and piles of cash. But a revolution has been happening for a few years now, a revolution that is putting the moviemaking art within reach of almost anyone. The revolution has occurred in three phases:

1. The creation of mega-powerful computers with huge hard drives that are unbelievably affordable has changed the rules of video editing. Such computers incorporate technologies like IEEE-1394 FireWire, which make working with video easy.

2. The advent of affordable digital camcorders has made collecting high-quality video a snap. These camcorders interface easily with computers.

3. The clincher is software. High-end video editing programs like Adobe Premiere Pro and Apple Final Cut Pro brought pro-caliber video editing to desktop computers, and simpler programs like Apple iMovie and Pinnacle Studio made editing software affordable.

I hesitate to call Adobe Premiere Elements the next step in the video editing revolution, but it's definitely a step forward. Premiere Elements delivers about 90 percent of the video-editing power of high-end programs like Final Cut Pro for an astoundingly low retail price of just $100. I cannot think of another program that costs less than $300 and offers anywhere near the level of features of Premiere Elements.

This chapter introduces you to Adobe Premiere Elements by showing you what this program is designed to do and what it has to offer. You also get a tour of Premiere Elements to help you find your way around this feature-packed program; I even guide you through your first movie project in Premiere Elements.

What Is Adobe Premiere Elements?

You already know that Adobe Premiere Elements is a video-editing program. But what does that mean? It means that using Adobe Premiere Elements, you can quickly take video from your digital camcorder, delete and rearrange scenes, add some special effects and credits, and within minutes export your movie to a DVD or the Internet. Just a few years ago all of this required equipment and software that costs thousands — if not tens, or even hundreds, of thousands — of dollars.

You can find lots of video-editing programs on the market, even at the $100 price point of Adobe Premiere Elements. But several important features set Premiere Elements apart from the others:

- Make use of up to 99 separate video tracks that can be composited and combined to make a single image.
- Add and edit audio soundtracks to your program. Up to 99 separate audio tracks can be added to the program.
- Add animated elements. For example, you can create advanced, professional-style titles and add still graphics to your movie projects. Then you can animate these titles and graphics in a variety of ways.
- Apply one of over 70 different transitions to video. Transitions can be used in any video track.
- Modify your movie with over 70 video and more than a dozen audio effects.
- Fine-tune color and lighting in your video images and improve audio quality.
- Preview edits immediately, in real time, without having to render effects first.
- Record movies to videotape at full broadcast quality.
- Export tightly compressed movies for the Web in QuickTime or Windows Media formats.
- Output movies directly to DVD and easily create DVD navigation menus.
- Integrate Premiere Elements with Adobe Photoshop Elements to quickly burn your still-image collections onto slideshow DVDs.

Even these hefty capabilities are only a smattering of what you can do with Adobe Premiere Elements. It's one of the most versatile programs you'll ever use.

Where's the Mac?

Older versions of Adobe Premiere (version 6.5 and earlier) were available for both Macintosh and Windows computers. Adobe's announcement that Premiere Pro (technically Version 7 of Premiere) would run only in Windows XP was met with some shock and surprise, especially considering that only a few years ago, Adobe was considered a very Mac-oriented software company. Adobe Premiere Elements is based heavily on Premiere Pro, so like the Pro version, Premiere Elements only runs on computers using Windows XP. And by the way, Adobe really means it when it says that Windows XP is required. Premiere Elements will not run on older versions of the Windows operating system such as Windows 2000 or Windows Me.

If you have a Macintosh, you might be considering running Premiere Elements on your Mac using a program that emulates the Windows operating system. I do not recommend this workaround: As I describe in Chapter 2, Premiere Elements relies heavily on a technology called *SSE* — a set of multimedia instructions only found in the latest computer processor chips from AMD and Intel. If those exact instructions are not present, Premiere Elements will crash hard and crash often — and as of this writing, no Apple processors include the SSE instruction set. If you use a Macintosh and are looking for a powerful yet somewhat affordable video-editing program, consider Apple's Final Cut Express, which retails for about $300.

Taking the Grand Tour

Adobe developed Premiere Elements on the foundations of Premiere Pro, and one of their primary design goals was to make Premiere Elements much easier to use, especially if you don't have any prior experience with video-editing programs. Still, even though the user interface has been simplified, I would not call Premiere Elements a "dumbed down" version of Premiere Pro. Little has been left out — you are probably going to have more options than you even need. And the quality of the tools is great; the basic aspects of a high-quality video editing program are all there. In short, I think that video newbies and veterans alike will feel right at home using Premiere Elements.

Launching Premiere Elements for the first time

To launch Premiere Elements, click the Start button to open the Start menu and choose All Programs⇨Adobe Premiere Elements. For more information on using Windows XP, see "Commanding the Interface," later in this chapter. When you first launch Premiere Elements, you see a welcome screen that looks like Figure 1-1. The area under Recent Projects gives you quick access to any projects you've been working on recently. (If this is the first time you've launched Premiere Elements, you probably won't have anything listed under Recent Projects.)

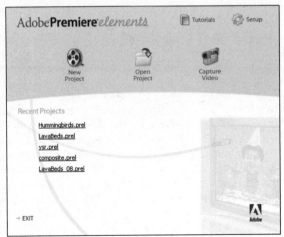

Figure 1-1:
Adobe
Premiere
Elements
welcomes
you with this
screen.

If you don't have a previous project to open and continue work on, you have
to start a new project if you want to see Premiere Elements in action. Click the
New Project button in the welcome screen. A dialog box like the one shown
in Figure 1-2 appears. Enter a name for your project — the exact name isn't
important for now — and click OK.

Figure 1-2:
Give your
new project
a name.

When you give your project a name, Premiere Elements opens (at last) to the
editing workspace.

The exact appearance of your workspace depends upon the current screen
resolution setting on your computer, but the basic appearance should resem-
ble Figure 1-3.

Although the *exact* appearance varies, you still see at least the four fundamental windows that make up the Premiere Elements interface — the Media
window, the Monitor, the Timeline, and the How To window, as shown in
Figure 1-3. These windows are explained in greater detail in the following
sections.

Media window   Monitor   How To window

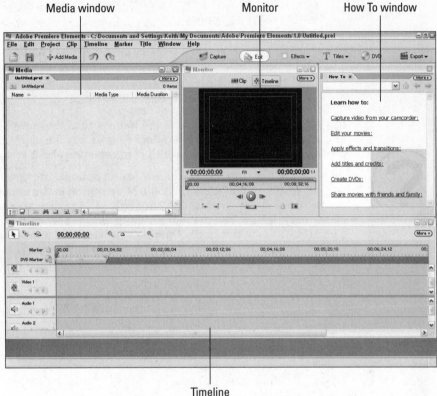

Figure 1-3:
The
Premiere
Elements
interface
consists of
several
important
windows.

Timeline

Getting to know the Media window

Think of the Media window as a sort of filing cabinet that helps you organize the various video clips, audio clips, and other pieces of media that you use in your project. Whenever you capture video from your camcorder, import still graphics, or capture audio from an audio CD, the files show up in the Media window. If you're working on a big project, you'll end up with many different files in this window; a full Media window looks similar to Figure 1-4. You can create new folders in the Media window to help organize your files. Folders in the Media window work just like folders in your operating system. To create a new folder, follow these steps:

1. **Click in the Media window to select it and make it active.**

2. **From the menu bar at the top of the Premiere Elements screen, choose File⇨New⇨Folder.**

   A new folder appears in the Media window with the name highlighted.

3. **Type a name for your new folder and press Enter.**

Your new folder now appears in the Media window. Click the folder to view its contents. To add items to a folder, simply click-and-drag them into the folder from elsewhere in the Media window. Figure 1-4 shows a Media window for a project I'm working on; as you can see, I've imported and captured a lot of files into it.

Although the Media window is primarily a storage place, you can also use it to

✔ **Review data about a file.** What's the frame size of the image? Is the file an audio clip, video, or a still graphic? How long is the clip? Columns in the Media window provide a wealth of information about your files.

✔ **Preview the file.** The Media window has an optional preview area that you can display if you wish. Click the More button in the upper-right corner of the Media window and choose View⇨Preview Area from the menu that appears. The preview area appears, as shown in Figure 1-4. If you click a file in the Media window, a preview of it appears in the preview area. If you click the little Play button next to the preview, you can play audio and video clips to get a better idea of what's in them.

Preview   More menu

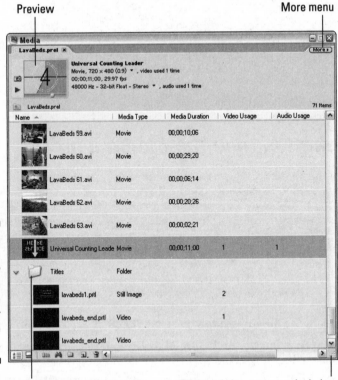

Figure 1-4:
The Media window stores the files you use in your movie projects.

Use folders to organize media. Click-and-drag to expand window.

Reviewing the Monitor window

Try to imagine editing video without being able to look at it. Would it be possible? Perhaps. After all, Beethoven composed his epic Ninth Symphony while completely deaf. But most of us aren't Beethoven and we need to be able to directly experience our work. Thankfully, Premiere Elements makes sure you can always see exactly what your movie looks like as you work on it. The Monitor window is where you view your work. It has controls for playing video and audio clips and for performing other editing tasks.

In the Monitor, you can

✔ Play through clips you plan to add to a movie project. As you play each clip, you decide which portions to add to the movie by setting *In points* and *Out points*. When you set In and Out points, only the portions of the clip between those two points will be added to your movie program.

✔ Play through the edits you have already made in your project.

The Monitor has two modes:

✔ **Clip mode:** In Clip mode, shown in Figure 1-5, the Monitor window lets you preview clips before placing them in your project. If you double-click a clip in the Media window, it automatically opens in the Monitor in Clip mode.

✔ **Timeline mode:** In this mode, the Monitor shows you the contents of the Timeline, which is where you assemble your movies. To switch between Clip and Timeline modes, simply click the buttons labeled Clip and Timeline at the top of the Monitor window. I explain what the Timeline is in the next section.

Trying out the Timeline

The Timeline could be considered the heart and soul of Adobe Premiere Elements. As with virtually every other video-editing program, the Timeline in Premiere Elements is the tool that enables you to craft your movie by putting its pieces in the desired order. You assemble clips, add effects, composite multiple clips on top of each other, and add sound with this bad boy. As you can see in Figure 1-6, the Timeline shows audio tracks on the bottom and video tracks on top. You can have up to 99 video tracks and 99 audio tracks in the Premiere Elements Timeline.

I can't completely explain the Timeline here. That would fill a chapter all by itself. (In fact, it does — Chapter 8.) However, I do want you to know that by using the Timeline, you can

✔ Figure out where you are in the project by using the Timeline ruler.

✔ Use the CTI (Current Time Indicator) to set the current playback and editing location in the Timeline.

Figure 1-5:
Preview and
edit clips in
the Monitor
window.

✔ Control aspects of a clip directly. For example, you can adjust the timing of video effects or adjust audio levels. (See Chapter 12 for more on working with effects; Chapter 13 shows you how to work with audio.)

✔ Use the Zoom control to zoom your view of the Timeline in and out.

Current timecode   Zoom control   CTI   Timeline ruler

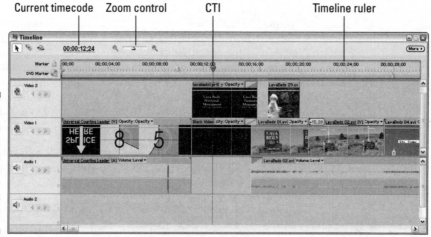

Figure 1-6:
The Timeline
is where
your clips
come
together
to make
a movie.

✔ Move clips by simply dragging-and-dropping them to new locations in
the Timeline. If your clip calls for some effects and transitions, you can
add them by dragging them to the Timeline as well.

Saying howdy to the How To window

Admittedly, the Media window, the Monitor, and the Timeline are the three
primary components of Adobe Premiere Elements. An introduction to Adobe
Premiere can't stop there, though. A new feature in Premiere Elements is the
How To window, which is shown in Figure 1-7. If you don't see the How To
window, choose Window⇨How To. Adobe created the How To window as
part of an effort to make Premiere Elements easier to use. The idea is that the
How To can quickly provide help and tips on whatever it is you happen to be
working on at any given time. Click blue links in the How To window to view
help articles and tips.

The menu at the top of the How To window allows you to choose a general
help category. In Figure 1-7 the How To window displays help tips on basic editing. If you're working on Titles or a DVD, for example, choose a different option
from the menu. Or if you find that you get all the help you need from *Adobe
Premiere Elements For Dummies*, and the How To is just a big waste of screen
space, click the red X in the upper-right corner to hide the How To window.

Figure 1-7:
Need help?
Consult the
How To
window.

Meeting the Effects and Effect Controls windows

As you work on your movies you'll eventually get to the point at which you'll
want to do more advanced editing. That means adding transitions and special
effects. Adobe Premiere Elements stores all of its transitions and effects in
the Effects window, which is shown in Figure 1-8. To view the Effects window,

choose Window➪Effects. Effects and transitions are arranged into folders and subfolders. For example, if you want to create a transition that dissolves one clip into another (this one of my favorite effects), simply open the Video Transitions folder to reveal the Dissolve subfolder as well as other subfolders.

Just as important as applying transitions and effects is the ability to fine-tune and control those effects. Premiere Elements offers the Effect Controls window, shown in Figure 1-9, to help you control your effects. Choose Window➪Effect Controls to open the Effect Controls window, and then click a clip in the Timeline to view the effect controls for that particular clip. I show you how to work with video transitions in Chapter 9. In Chapter 12, I show how to work with video effects and I describe audio effects and transitions in Chapter 13.

Figure 1-8:
Premiere
Elements
stores all
effects and
transitions
in sub-
folders like
this.

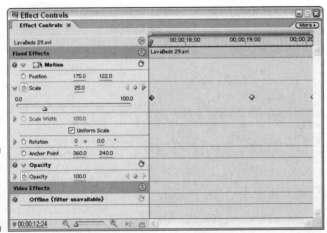

Figure 1-9:
Fine-tune
your effects
here.

Understanding floating palettes

If you have ever used other Adobe programs like Photoshop or Illustrator, you're probably familiar with the small floating windows called *palettes*. Like most other Adobe creative programs, Premiere Elements stores some of its advanced features and effects in floating palettes. Premiere Elements offers just two palettes, the History palette, and the Info palette. The History palette (described in Chapter 7) shows a record of all the edits and changes you've made, and the Info palette displays detailed information about clips and other items in Premiere Elements. To view them, do this:

1. **Choose Window⇨History.**

2. **Choose Window⇨Info.**

Two floating palettes that look something like Figure 1-10 appear on-screen. You can move these palettes around by dragging the title bar, or close them by clicking the little Close (*X*) button in the upper-right corner. Use the Window menu to re-open the palettes. To resize a palette, click-and-drag an edge or corner of the palette.

Figure 1-10:
Premiere
Elements
stores some
commands
on floating
palettes.

Commanding the Interface

As I mention in the "Foolish Assumptions" section of the Introduction, one of the assumptions I make about you is that you already know how to open and close programs on your computer. You probably also know how to open menus, click buttons, and even resize or minimize windows.

That said, Adobe Premiere Elements is so advanced (and video editing is so demanding of a computer's resources) that I suspect you've recently bought a new computer — and there's a good chance you've recently "switched camps" from Macintosh to your first Windows PC. To help ease your transition, I want to provide a brief overview of the basic Windows interface controls in Adobe Premiere Elements.

Adobe Premiere Elements requires Windows XP. Any edition — Home, Professional, or Media Center — of Windows XP will suffice. You can't run Premiere Elements in Windows 2000, Windows Me, or any previous version of Windows. If you're new to Windows XP and are feeling a bit discombobulated, I suggest you purchase a book with more detailed information on using and managing the system. I recommend *Windows XP For Dummies,* by Andy Rathbone (Wiley). For more advanced Windows XP tips, check out *50 Fast Windows XP Techniques* by Yours Truly (Wiley).

The fundamental look and feel of the Microsoft Windows interface has not changed significantly since Windows 95 was released in (ahem) 1995, although the cosmetics were modernized a bit with the release of Windows XP. Figure 1-11 shows a typical Premiere Elements screen.

To launch Premiere Elements, click the Start button to open the Start menu and choose All Programs➪Adobe Premiere Elements. If you use Premiere Elements a lot, it will show up in the list of commonly used programs that appears when you first click Start.

Basic Windows XP controls include

- ✔ **Start menu:** Use this menu to access programs on your computer, as well as to shut down and restart controls. The Start menu is similar in concept to the Apple menu on a Macintosh.

- ✔ **Taskbar:** All currently open programs have a button on the Taskbar. Click a program's button on the Taskbar to open it. The Taskbar is similar in concept to the Mac OS X Dock.

- ✔ **System Tray:** Memory-resident programs like antivirus programs and other utilities often show an icon in the system tray. In Chapter 6, I show you how to prepare your computer for resource-intensive operations such as video capture, and part of that preparation includes temporarily disabling a lot of your system tray icons.

- ✔ **Minimize:** Click this button to minimize a window. When a program is minimized, it becomes a button on the Taskbar. Use this button like you would the Collapse or Minimize buttons on a Mac.

- ✔ **Restore/Maximize:** Use this button to change the window size. Restore/ Maximize works like the Zoom button in the Mac OS.

- ✔ **Close:** Click this to close a program or window.

Close

Restore

Minimize

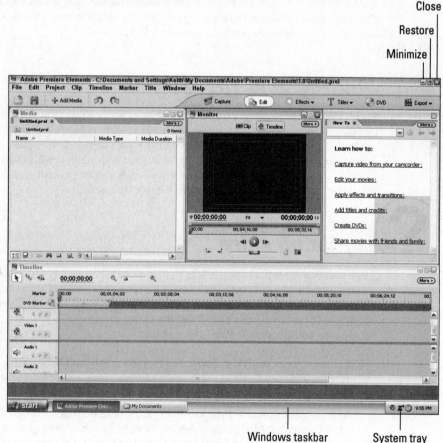

Figure 1-11:
If you're
new to
Windows
XP, never
fear. It's
not *too*
different.

Windows taskbar   System tray

TIP

If you don't like digging through the Start menu every time you want to launch
Premiere, you can launch it from a desktop icon created by the Premiere
Elements setup program. If you don't see a Premiere Elements desktop icon,
right-click the Adobe Premiere Elements link in the Start menu and choose
Send To⇨Desktop (create shortcut) from the menu that appears. Doing so cre-
ates a desktop icon that you can double-click to launch Premiere Elements.

Making Your First Movie

Sometimes the best way to get to know a program is to just dig in and get
your hands dirty with it, actually putting its features to use as the designers
intended. If you have a digital camcorder handy with some video already
recorded on the tape, and you have installed Adobe Premiere Elements on
your computer, you're ready to start making movies. The following sections

walk you through the basic steps of making a movie, and if you've never used Premiere Elements before or even edited a movie on your computer, the following sections should serve as a good introduction.

Starting your first project

Your first step in making a movie is perhaps the most obvious one. Launch Premiere Elements, and when the welcome screen appears (refer to Figure 1-1) click New Project. Enter a name for your project in the New Project dialog box — any old name will do, as long as it's something you will remember later — and click OK. Premiere Elements creates your project and opens to the basic Premiere Elements screen. Wasn't that easy?

Capturing video

After you've created a new project in Premiere Elements, you need some source footage to work with. For now I assume you have a digital camcorder and you've already recorded some video that you want to edit. The process of getting video from the camcorder into your computer is called *capturing*. To capture some video, follow these steps:

1. **Connect your digital camcorder to your computer's FireWire (IEEE-1394) port.**

   If you're not sure whether your computer has a FireWire port, or if you need to add one, see Chapter 2. Premiere Elements can only capture video from a digital camcorder connected to a FireWire port; if you have an older analog camcorder, you'll need to use special analog video capture hardware and probably some different video capture software. See Chapter 6 for more on capturing analog video. See Chapter 4 for information on the differences between digital video and analog video.

2. **Turn the Camcorder on to VTR or Player mode.**

   If Windows automatically opens a window stating that a digital video device was detected, click Cancel to close the window.

3. **In the toolbar and the top of the Premiere Elements window, click Capture.**

   The Premiere Elements Capture window appears as shown in Figure 1-12. You should see the words `Capture Device Online` at the top of the window. If you see a message that says `Capture Device Offline`, see Chapter 6 for more on video capture.

Figure 1-12:
The Capture
window is
where you
capture
video from
your digital
camcorder.

4. Rewind the tape in your camcorder to the beginning of a section that you want to capture.

You may notice that as you play and rewind your camcorder tape, the video image from the camcorder appears in the Capture window.

5. Click the Play button in the Capture window to begin playing the tape, and click the Capture button to start capturing some video.

6. After you've captured a few minutes of video, click the Stop Capture button.

7. Close the Capture window when you're done capturing video.

You now see a collection of video clips in the Premiere Elements Media window, as shown in Figure 1-13. These are the video clips that you captured from the camcorder, and they are ready to be used in a movie project.

Capture problems are usually caused by a computer that hasn't been properly prepared for video capture. If you have any trouble capturing video, I show how to prepare your computer for capture in Chapter 6.

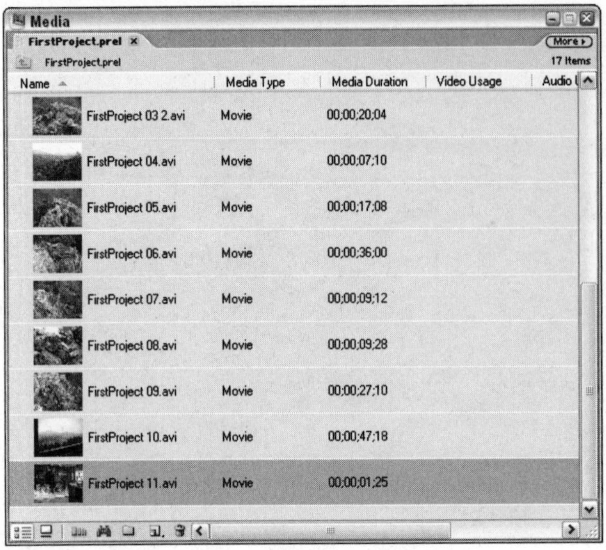

Figure 1-13:
Captured
video clips
show up in
the Media
window.

Assembling the movie

After you've captured some video, turning your footage into a movie is easy. (Of course, I am skipping the fancy stuff that you can do using later chapters in this book.) Follow these steps:

1. **If your Premiere Elements screen doesn't look something like Figure 1-11, click Edit on the Premiere Elements toolbar.**

   If the workspace seems stubborn and won't change to the basic editing layout, choose Window⇨Restore Workspace⇨Edit. For more on setting up your Premiere Elements workspace, visit Chapter 3.

2. **To preview a clip, double-click it in the Media window.**

   The clip loads into the Monitor window, where you can click the Play button to play the clip. For more on previewing clips and selection portions of clips to use in movies, see Chapter 7.

3. **Click-and-drag some clips from the Media window and drop them on the Timeline as shown in Figure 1-14.**

   For now, just drop each clip on the track labeled Video 1, and drop the clips one after the other in the Timeline in the order in which you want them to play. Chapter 8 gives more detailed information on putting movies together using the Timeline.

4. **Click the Timeline button at the top of the Monitor window, and then click Play to preview the movie you have put together in the Timeline.**

Drag clips from here.   Click to switch from Monitor to Timeline mode.

Figure 1-14:
Drop clips in
the Timeline
to assemble
your movie.

Drop clips in Timeline.   Click to play.

Saving your movie for the Web

After you've put together a basic movie in the Timeline, Premiere Elements lets you quickly save it in a Web-friendly format. One of the formats you can choose is the Windows Media format. Check out Chapters 15 and 16 for more on preparing movies for online use in either the Windows Media or Apple QuickTime formats. To quickly export your movie in Windows Media format:

1. **Click Export on the Premiere Elements toolbar, and choose Windows Media from the menu that appears.**

   Alternatively, you can choose File⇨Export⇨Windows Media.

2. **In the Export Windows Media dialog box that appears (see Figure 1-15), choose Cable Modem/DSL in the menu on the left and click OK.**

   The exact format you choose isn't important right now. For more on what the different formats mean, see Chapters 15 and 16.

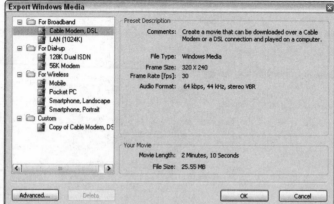

Figure 1-15:
Exporting
your movie
in a Web-
friendly
format is
easy.

3. In the Save File dialog box that appears, choose a location in which to save the file, enter a filename for the movie file, and click Save.

A Rendering dialog box appears. *Rendering* is the process that Premiere Elements goes through when it applies your edits and compresses a movie project into its final output format. Rendering may take a few seconds or minutes, depending on the length of your movie and the speed of your computer. When rendering is complete, locate the movie file, and double-click it to open it in Windows Media Player. Congratulations! You've just made your first movie!

Chapter 2

Equipping Yourself for Moviemaking

*N*ot so long ago, the price of a good video-editing system could have bought you a pretty nice home in the suburbs. But thanks to programs like Adobe Premiere, many of those suburban homes now *have* good video-editing systems — and the owners of said homes didn't have to take out second mortgages to purchase the equipment. For several years now, Adobe Premiere has been revolutionizing video by providing professional-grade editing capabilities in a software package that runs on affordable computers. Now Premiere Elements is so affordable that even video hobbyists on the tightest of budgets can afford near-professional level editing capabilities.

Another revolution has been the recent affordability of digital video (DV) hardware. Amateur videographers can now shoot near-broadcast-quality video on cameras that cost as little as $500. Apple created the IEEE-1394 FireWire interface a few years ago, and that technology — which works on both Macintoshes *and* Windows PCs — makes it easy to save the high-quality videos you shoot on your computer. These three things — video-editing software, digital camcorders, and FireWire — have come together and created a synergy that is changing the way people think about and use moving pictures.

When you have the software (Adobe Premiere Elements), you need the hardware to go with it. This chapter guides you through the process of finding a computer to serve as a video-editing platform. You also get a look at digital cameras and other hardware that you may need or want as you get serious about video.

Choosing a Computer for Video Editing

Although ultra-powerful computers have certainly become affordable, you should be aware that you can't expect to edit video on just any old PC. That PC your parents bought you for college ten years ago, for example, won't cut it. In fact, almost any computer that is not fairly new or has not been significantly upgraded for a couple of years is probably barely adequate for use with Adobe Premiere Elements. The following sections help you identify what kind of computer you need, including specific system requirements.

Macintosh computers have long been favored by video professionals, but as of this writing, Adobe Premiere Pro and Premiere Elements are both Windows-only programs. This is a departure from earlier versions of the software, which were both Mac and Windows compatible up through Adobe Premiere 6.5.

Identifying your needs

First, you need a computer that is capable of running Adobe Premiere Elements without crashing. Beyond that, your computer should run Premiere efficiently without making you wait for hours on end while it performs a simple action. You need lots of storage space for your video files. And you need special hardware tailored to video editing. The next two sections describe the computer that you need.

Minimum system requirements

Like virtually all software programs, Adobe Premiere Elements has some minimum system requirements that your computer must meet. You'll find them emblazoned on the side of Premiere's retail box, as well as in the INSTALL READ ME file located on the Premiere Elements installation disc. The minimum requirements are

- Pentium III processor, 800 MHz or higher
- Windows XP
- 256MB of RAM
- 24-bit video display and a monitor capable of displaying a screen resolution of at least 1024 x 768
- DirectX compatible sound card
- IEEE-1394 / FireWire adapter
- 1.2 GB of free hard-drive space for program-installation files

Can I run Premiere Elements in a Windows emulator?

No.

When Adobe released Premiere Pro, one of its most important features was the ability to preview complex video effects and edits in real time. This was a big improvement over older versions of Premiere, as well as most other video-editing programs, which required you to spend minutes or even hours rendering effects, transitions, and other changed before you could preview them. Adobe was able to incorporate this powerful new feature into Premiere Pro by designing the software to take advantage of specific advanced graphics and processing features in Windows XP and modern Intel and AMD central processor chips.

Premiere Elements is based on Premiere Pro and it has the same basic requirements. One of the processor technologies that Premiere Elements relies on is called SSE, which is short for *Streaming SIMD Extensions*. This is a multimedia instruction set found only in certain processors from Intel and AMD. These processors include the Intel Pentium III and Pentium 4, as well as the AMD Athlon XP. The 1 GHz+ "Morgan" versions of the AMD Duron processor also support SSE, but not the older 600-950 MHz "Spitfire" versions of the Duron. Any new PC sold today that runs Windows XP should have a processor that supports SSE.

The point of all this technical central processor stuff is that if your computer doesn't have an AMD or Intel processor which supports SSE, Adobe Premiere Elements will not run. So, for example, if you have a Windows XP emulator program running on your Macintosh, the PowerPC processor in your Mac won't be able to run Premiere Elements no matter how powerful it is or how much RAM you have installed. If you want to use Premiere Elements, you'll have to do it on a regular PC running Windows XP.

You must be logged in to Windows XP with administrator rights to install the software. You must also be able to restart and log in again to Windows with administrator rights to complete installation.

The real system requirements

You've seen the *minimum* system requirements, but I think you'll find that you can work a lot easier and faster if you use a computer that well exceeds those requirements. Video editing puts unusually high demands on a computer. Video files require massive amounts of disk space, as well as special hardware to capture video and lay it back to tape or burn it to DVD — and the computer's memory and processor are utilized to their maximum capabilities when you render video for playback. Premiere Elements works computer hardware especially hard as it displays effects and other complex edits in real-time.

Whether you are buying a new computer or upgrading, you really need some relatively souped-up capabilities:

- ✔ **A seriously powerful processor:** Think of the *central processing unit* (CPU) as the brain of the computer; a faster processor affects how well everything else runs. The faster the processor, the less time you spend twiddling your thumbs as your video renders, and the better real-time previews play. Adobe recommends an Intel Pentium 4 3GHz (or better) processor, but an equivalent AMD Athlon XP processor works just as well. Any processor you use with Premiere Elements must support the SSE instruction set, a set of CPU instructions that helps the processor handle multimedia data. This means that you should stick with a Pentium III, Pentium 4, or Athlon XP processor. Older AMD Athlon processors (without the XP suffix) and Duron processors may cause system crashes or other stability problems during certain video-editing operations.

  You will find the very best editing performance with an Intel Pentium 4 because that processor includes an even more powerful instruction set called SSE2.

- ✔ **Lots of memory:** Your CPU uses *random-access memory* (RAM) as its working space. The more RAM that is available to the CPU, the more programs and processes (like video rendering and real-time previews) you can run. Although Adobe says that 256MB is the bare minimum, they recommend at least 1GB of RAM for use with Premiere Elements, and I think that is a good recommendation.

- ✔ **A big, fast hard drive:** Video requires *lots* of storage space. You can get a good start with 80GB (gigabytes) of disk space, but more is always better. If your computer uses IDE hard drives (it probably does; check the spec sheet), always choose 7200 RPM drives over 5400 RPM drives. I recommend installing a second internal hard drive in your system, and dedicating it solely to video storage.

  Many interesting hard-drive alternatives have appeared in recent years. These include external hard drives that plug into FireWire or USB ports. I recommend against using such drives for video storage when you're editing in Premiere Elements. External drives are seldom fast enough to keep up with video's demands, meaning that you may experience *dropped frames* (that is, some frames of video are skipped and lost) and other problems when you try to output your video.

- ✔ **A good video card:** Many new PCs have the display adapter built into the motherboard. When you're reading the spec sheet, you may see something like "32MB on-board video" or "Shared VRAM." If you see something like this, run away! On-board video cards almost always use up some system RAM and they tend to make the whole PC perform quite slowly. The better solution is to buy a system with a separate video card in an expansion slot. This is the way PCs have been built for over a decade, and the separate card is still the way to go. I recommend a video adapter card with at least 64MB of video RAM.

✔ **A large monitor (or two):** Premiere takes up a lot of screen real estate. Unless you want to spend half your life scrolling back and forth in the Timeline and moving windows and palettes this way and that, I recommend a monitor that can display a screen resolution of *at least* 1280 x 1024. Premiere Elements runs at a screen resolution of 1024 x 768, but you may find that your workspace seems cramped. I recommend a high-quality CRT monitor of at least 19 inches or larger. Thankfully, big monitors are pretty affordable these days.

You may also want to consider a dual monitor setup if your budget and desk space allows. Some advanced video display cards support dual monitors, meaning that you have two monitors connected to your computer. Placed side-by-side, these dual monitors behave like one giant desktop that basically doubles your digital workspace. Windows XP and Premiere Elements work quite nicely on a dual monitor setup. You can seamlessly move the mouse and various Premiere program elements back and forth between each monitor as you see fit.

✔ **FireWire (IEEE-1394) interface:** FireWire ports are essential for working with digital video, and Premiere Elements can only capture video from a FireWire port. Even if you don't currently have a DV camcorder, you will probably need a FireWire port before long. Many new PCs come with FireWire adapters built-in, but double-check before you buy. FireWire adapters can be added to most PCs for less than $100. If you're not sure whether your computer already has a FireWire port, see the "Capture Hardware" section later in this chapter for a more detailed explanation of FireWire.

✔ **A DVD recorder:** Many Windows PCs now include DVD recorder (also called a DVD *burner*) drives. For video editing, a DVD burner is virtually mandatory these days. As you shop around you'll notice that some DVD burners are called DVD–R drives, whereas some others are called DVD+R drives. The use of a minus sign (–) or a plus sign (+) actually denotes unique, competing recordable DVD standards, each one supported by a list of manufacturers. Neither format has a clear technical advantage over the other, except perhaps that blank DVD–R discs seem to be a little cheaper than DVD+R blanks. Whichever format you choose, make sure you buy blank discs that match your recorder. DVD–R blanks won't work in a DVD+R drive, and vice versa. Many newer drives support both –R and +R formats, so if you buy one of these drives, blank disc format is less of a concern. If you haven't yet purchased a DVD burner I recommend that you choose a DVD+/–R drive. DVD–RAM is a third recordable DVD technology that is of limited value for digital video work, so I don't recommend paying extra for it.

✔ **A clean installation of Windows XP:** Adobe claims that Premiere Elements has been optimized for Windows XP. You can run Premiere Elements on a computer running Windows XP Home, Windows XP Pro, or Windows XP Media Center. Premiere Elements is *not* recommended for systems running Windows 2000, Windows Me, or any earlier version of the Microsoft operating system. I further recommend that you only

> run Premiere on a system where Windows XP was installed *clean*. That is, Windows XP should have been installed on a blank, freshly formatted hard drive. If you bought your computer new with Windows XP preinstalled, this shouldn't be a problem. But if you have upgraded your computer to Windows XP from Windows Me or Windows 2000, you may encounter stability problems. Check out a book such as *Windows XP All-in-One Desk Reference For Dummies* by Woody Leonhard (Wiley Publishing, Inc.) for more on installing Windows XP.

Some of the most powerful computers built today are designed as gaming systems. Modern computer games require massive amounts of disk space, memory, CPU power, and powerful graphics capabilities. So if you see a computer advertised to gamers ("The Ultimate Gaming System — this thing will blast your socks off!"), you can bet that system will probably make a great video-editing computer as well. Just make sure you get that FireWire option, the DVD burner option, and if possible a second hard drive!

Building your own PC

When considering a new Windows PC, you can either buy a complete system or build your own from parts. Building PCs from scratch (or upgrading an older PC) has been a vaunted geek tradition for years, and many people — myself included — still practice it. Components are available from mail-order companies, Web sites, and some retail electronics stores.

For most PC users, building a computer from scratch doesn't make a whole lot of sense anymore. You must purchase a case, power supply, motherboard, processor, RAM, sound card, video card, modem, network card, FireWire card, hard drive, DVD-R drive, floppy drive, keyboard, mouse, monitor, some cooling fans, speakers, Windows software, various cables, and plenty of coffee to sustain you through a long night of PC wrenching and tweaking. Expect to go back to the computer shop at least three times to get the things you forgot. Now you have a pile of parts that you must put together, and that pile probably cost hundreds of dollars *more* than a pre-assembled unit from a PC maker like Dell or Hewlett-Packard. And unlike your homebuilt computer, that affordable pre-made PC from Dell or H-P comes with a pretty good warranty and technical support.

But for some maniacs — like me — building your own PC can be a lot of fun. Besides, if you need a video-editing system, building your own can help you ensure that you're getting the best possible components. A pre-assembled unit is bound to include some cost-cutting measures to give it more mass-market appeal. Furthermore, because mass-produced computers usually use proprietary case and motherboard designs, gutting them for an extensive upgrade in the future may not be practical.

If you have never built a computer from scratch, this probably isn't a good time to start. I couldn't possibly tell you how to do it in this section, because the topics of PC building and upgrading fill many books. (May I recommend *Building a PC For Dummies* by Mark L. Chambers, from Wiley?) But if you are comfortable with PC upgrades and construction — and want to build your own video-editing system — follow the system-requirements guidelines listed earlier in this chapter when you pick out your components. And remember, get as far above the minimum system requirements as you can afford.

One of these days you'll unplug your FireWire cable from your camcorder, only to have the loose cable fall down behind your desk. Then you'll have to get down on the floor and fish around behind your PC to retrieve the stray cable. Not fun. To address this eventuality, I like to have FireWire connectors right on the front of my computer case. If you are ordering a computer, contact the builder to find out if this feature can be added. If you are building your own, check your local PC parts retailer for a front plate kit for your FireWire connectors.

Selecting Video Gear

So you have a fantabulous new computer that is ready to edit video at blazing speeds. Don't worry: You're not done spending money just yet. You still have a lot of cool — and really important — gear left to buy. Some of the gear covered in the next few sections is pretty mandatory — a camera, for instance. Video can be kind of hard to record without a video camera. Other gear — video decks, audio recorders, and capture cards — may be less mandatory, depending on your needs and budget.

Cameras

No single piece of gear is more precious to a budding videographer than a good video camera. Most modern video cameras are actually *camcorders* because they serve as both a camera and a recorder. Older video cameras used to connect to separate VCR units which recorded the video. Often these VCR units were hung by a strap from the videographer's shoulder. Bulky.

When buying a new camcorder, go digital. The quality of digital video is very good, and it is a lot easier to transfer video from a digital camcorder into a computer. And these days you don't have to take out a second mortgage to afford a digital camcorder — consumer-grade digital camcorder prices start at under $400.

Of course, if you *want* to spend more money, plenty of high-end camcorders are available as well. The best digital camcorders have three *charged-coupled devices* (CCDs) — the eyes in the camera that actually pick up light and turn it into a video image. These include camcorders like the Canon GL2, Panasonic PV-DV952, and the Sony DCR-TRV950. These cameras provide superior color and resolution, as well as features that the pros like — such as usable manual controls and high-quality microphones. Be prepared to spend $2,000 to $5,000 for these high-end digital camcorders.

When you're shopping for a new digital camcorder, check the following:

- **Audio:** For the sake of sound quality, the camcorder should have some provisions for connecting an external microphone. Most camcorders have a standard mini-jack connector for an external mic, and some high-end camcorders have a 3-pin XLR connector. XLR connectors — also sometimes called *balanced* audio connectors — are used by many high-quality microphones and PA (public address) systems.

- **Batteries:** Make sure that spare batteries are readily available at a reasonable price. I recommend buying a camcorder that uses Lithium Ion or NiMH (nickel-metal-hydride) batteries — they last longer and are easier to maintain than NiCad (nickel-cadmium) batteries. Buy plenty of extra batteries when you buy your camcorder. If you'll be doing long "on location" shoots, also consider a battery charger that plugs into a car's accessory power socket.

- **Digital Video connections:** Virtually all digital camcorders use a FireWire port for capturing video from the camcorder onto your computer. FireWire is also called IEEE-1394 or i.Link by some camera manufacturers. Some camcorders also have USB connectors, although this isn't terribly useful to you because Premiere Elements can only capture video from a FireWire port.

- **Manual controls:** Auto focus and automatic exposure controls are great, but as you get more serious about shooting video you may want more control over these features. The easiest manual focus and exposure controls are ones that are manipulated by a ring around the lens body. Tiny little knobs or slider switches on the side of the camera are more difficult to use.

- **Storage media:** Make sure that tapes are affordable and widely available. MiniDV is now the most common recording format, and tapes are affordable and easy to find.

- **Zoom:** You'll see "400× ZOOM" splashed across the side of the camera. Such huge numbers usually express *digital* zoom, which is (in my opinion) virtually useless. Check the fine print next to the digital zoom figure and you should see a figure for *optical* zoom. Optical zoom is something you can actually use, and most mass-market digital camcorders offer around 10× to 25× optical zoom.

What is Bluetooth — and do I need it?

As you shop for camcorders, you'll notice that some newer models advertise that they incorporate a technology called *Bluetooth*. This is a new wireless networking technology that allows various types of electronic components — including camcorders and computers — to connect to each other using radio waves instead of cables. Unfortunately the maximum data rate of current Bluetooth technology is comparatively low (less than 1 megabit per second). In practical terms, that means Bluetooth won't be suitable for capturing digital video from your camcorder for the foreseeable future. A few camcorders incorporate Bluetooth technology anyway, and that may (or may not) come in handy if you still own the same camcorder a few years from now. But for now, Bluetooth isn't terribly useful in a camcorder, and I don't recommend spending extra money to get it.

When you start spending over $1,500 for a camcorder, some people begin to look at you differently. They don't think you're crazy; they think you're a "professional." Actually, true "professional" videographers are shooting the 11:00 news with cameras that start at $20,000. So there you are with your $2,000 Canon GL2 — not quite a professional, but not exactly a typical consumer either. While I hesitate to slap a label on anyone (I hardly know you!), industry people obsessed with categorizing customers would refer to you as a *prosumer* (a buyer in-between pro and consumer). Don't slap them; you will often see this term (affectionately) used to describe higher-quality gear in the video world.

Video decks

The first time I heard the term *video deck*, I thought it referred to the deck on a cruise ship where everyone goes to watch movies. Not so. *Video deck* is actually just a fancy term for a *videocassette recorder,* which you may know as a VCR. If you want to talk like a true video geek, however, *video deck* must become part of your lexicon.

Why do you need a video deck? A high-quality deck becomes really useful if you plan to distribute your movies on tape. With the proper electronic connections, you can output a movie directly from your computer to videotape. Also, if you have a deck that uses the same tape format as your camcorder, you can save wear and tear on the camcorder's tape mechanism when you capture video into your computer. Good video decks aren't cheap, however, and a typical VHS VCR doesn't offer much in the way of quality or editing capabilities. When looking for a video deck, consider the following:

✔ **Format:** S-VHS decks are good for outputting movies to VHS tape and provide decent quality. MiniDV decks and other formats are also available from a variety of sources. Some decks even offer both S-VHS and MiniDV in the same unit.

✔ **FireWire:** Some newer decks have FireWire connections. As with camcorders, this greatly simplifies the process of interfacing with your computer and Premiere Elements.

✔ **Device control:** You should be able to control a FireWire video deck (for example, fast-forwarding and rewinding) using controls in Adobe Premiere Elements.

If you're just starting to get involved with video editing, a video deck may seem like an extravagance. But the more time you spend capturing and outputting video, the more useful a good video deck can be. And like I said, using a video deck to capture and export video can save a lot of wear and tear on the tape drive in your expensive camcorder.

Audio recorders

All modern camcorders have built-in microphones, and most digital camcorders can record decent-quality audio. However, you may find that the built-in audio recording never exceeds "decent" on the quality scale. There are two simple solutions to recording better audio:

✔ Use a high-quality accessory microphone.

✔ Record audio separately.

If you want to connect a better microphone to your camcorder, the best place to start is with your camcorder's manufacturer (you'll need a *really* long cable — just kidding). Usually accessory microphones are available from the manufacturer. These accessory units make use of connections, accessory shoes, and other features on your camcorder.

Separate sound recorders give you more flexibility, especially if you just want to record audio (but not video) in a certain location. Many professionals use DAT (digital audiotape) recorders to record audio, but DAT recorders are usually quite expensive. Digital voice recorders are also available, but the amount of audio they can record is often limited by whatever storage is built into the unit. For a good balance of quality and affordability, I recommend a MiniDisc recorder. For more on MiniDisc recorders, see Chapter 21.

Capture hardware

A digital camcorder and a powerful computer equipped with Adobe Premiere Elements won't do you much good if you can't get video from the camcorder into the computer. For this you need *capture hardware*, so called because it captures audio and video into your computer.

FireWire (IEEE-1394) devices

FireWire is a high-speed interface developed by Apple Computer and first released in 1996. *FireWire* is actually Apple's trademark name for the technology officially known as IEEE-1394, named for the international standard to which it conforms. Sony and a few other companies call the interface i.Link. All DV-format camcorders have a FireWire interface. Although Apple originally developed FireWire with digital video in mind, the IEEE-1394 interface is also used by other devices including external hard drives, still cameras, and scanners.

A FireWire interface makes capturing digital video really easy. You just connect a cable between the FireWire port on your computer and the FireWire port on your camcorder, and then capture video using Premiere Elements. It's easy because all Premiere really has to do is copy digital video data from the camcorder onto your hard drive.

Why is the process of getting video from a camcorder tape onto your hard disk called *capturing* instead of just *copying*? Digital video is recorded onto a camcorder tape in an endless stream of data. The tape does not contain data files like those found on a computer hard drive. When you capture some of that video, you are basically taking a chunk of the video data and capturing it into a file that can be stored on your hard drive and used by your software programs (including Premiere Elements).

Many new Windows-based PCs come with FireWire ports, but some don't, so double-check your own PC. You should see a 6-pin FireWire port that resembles Figure 2-1. If you don't see one, you can purchase a FireWire expansion card from many electronics retailers. Installing a FireWire card in your PC has three indispensable prerequisites:

- ✔ Windows 98 Second Edition (SE) or higher (This shouldn't be a problem because you have to use Windows XP with Premiere Elements anyway.)

- ✔ A vacant expansion slot in your computer

- ✔ PC hardware expertise

To work with Premiere Elements, your FireWire card must be OHCI compliant. This specification shouldn't be a problem to achieve because virtually all FireWire cards sold since the late 1990s are OHCI compliant. If you're not sure whether your FireWire card is OHCI compliant, check it using the Windows XP Device Manager as described in Chapter 6.

If you aren't familiar with expansion slots and don't have experience with hardware upgrades, consult a professional PC technician. If your computer is still under warranty, don't even *look* at a screwdriver until you've reviewed the warranty terms to determine whether — and how — upgrades should be performed.

Figure 2-1:
The FireWire port on your computer should look something like this.

Analog video capture devices

Analog video is a bit trickier than digital video to get into your computer because it must first be digitized. Capture cards are available to help you do this bit of magic, but keep in mind that Adobe Premiere Elements cannot directly capture video from an analog capture card. Fortunately, analog capture cards almost always come with their own video capture programs. As I describe in Chapter 6, you can use the card's included software to capture analog video onto your hard drive in AVI or MPEG format, and then import the captured video into Premiere Elements for editing.

Whatever capture card you decide to use, review the specs carefully before you make a buying decision. Many FireWire cards are marketed as "video capture cards" even though they can only capture video from digital camcorders.

Another solution may be an external video converter which sits on your desktop and connects to your computer's FireWire port. The benefit of a video converter that connects to a FireWire port is that you can capture video directly into Premiere Elements, because as far as Premiere is concerned the video streaming in from the FireWire port is digital video. Video converters are described in more detail in Chapter 21.

Chapter 3

Revving Up Premiere Elements

Computer software designers work hard to make sure that their programs are easy to use. When you open a new program for the first time, you often see a tutorial or a wizard screen that helps you get started without having to adjust a lot of settings or learn a bunch of cryptic menu commands. Adobe Premiere Elements is much easier to use than its predecessors, but unlike many other programs you should spend some time configuring Premiere Elements before you start working.

Premiere Elements is an advanced program that accommodates a variety of editing styles, and you can configure Premiere Elements to use your preferred style. Premiere Elements also offers some options that you should review to ensure that your movie comes out right. This chapter helps you configure Premiere Elements for making movies your way, take charge of important program settings, and get familiar with some useful options.

Arranging the Premiere Elements Workspace

Look around at the workspace in your office, or wherever it is you plan to use Adobe Premiere Elements. You probably have the computer set up a certain way, the mouse in your favorite spot, and a ring on the desktop that reminds you where you normally place your coffee cup. You have everything just where you like it, and it works.

When you work in Adobe Premiere Elements, you have a brand-new virtual workspace on the screen. Just as you can rearrange the physical workspace around your desk, so you can customize Premiere Elements and set up its workspace just the way you like it. You can move windows around, close some items, and open others.

Premiere Elements also offers a couple of preset workspaces. To begin exploring them, launch Adobe Premiere Elements by choosing Start⇨All Programs⇨Adobe Premiere Elements. After you've launched the program a couple of times, it should appear in the list of frequently used programs in the Windows XP Start menu.

The left side of the Windows XP Start menu includes a list of recently used programs, giving you quick access to the programs that you have used most recently. However, if you don't use Premiere Elements for a couple of weeks you may find that it no longer appears in this list. You can add it to the list of permanent quick-access programs that appears at the top of the Start menu. Just click-and-drag the icon for Premiere Elements to the top section of the Start menu, near the Internet Explorer link, as shown in Figure 3-1.

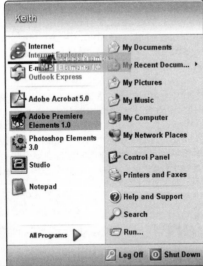

Figure 3-1: Drop a ghost image of the Premiere Elements shortcut on the top of your Start menu.

When you see the Premiere Elements welcome screen, click the New Project button. Don't worry about the other buttons in the welcome screen for now; I explain how to start real movie projects in Chapter 5. In the New Project dialog box that appears, give your new project a name (any old name will do) and then click OK. Premiere Elements opens.

Using preset workspaces

If you've used other Adobe programs such as Photoshop or Illustrator, you know that Adobe likes to organize program features into floating windows, toolbars, and palettes. These items can be moved around all over the screen, just as you might rearrange your desk several times through the course of a workday. Completed tasks get moved off to the side to make way for next tasks.

With all these windows and palettes and things floating around, the Premiere Elements workspace can start to look cluttered after a while. Fortunately you can quickly and easily reorganize screen elements using one of several pre-designed workspaces. To open a workspace, choose Window➪Workspace and then choose a workspace from the submenu that appears. The six standard workspaces are

- ✔ Capture
- ✔ Edit
- ✔ Effects
- ✔ Advanced Effects
- ✔ Titles
- ✔ DVD

Each workspace is designed to accommodate a certain kind of work. The next few sections describe each workspace in greater detail.

If you have used Adobe Premiere version 6 or earlier, you may be wondering what happened to the A/B Workspace. Simply put, Adobe gave it the axe. The Premiere Elements Editing workspace is similar to the Single-Track Editing workspace found in older versions of Premiere. The A/B Workspace was an alternative editing workspace, and after surveying a variety of users during the development process for Adobe Premiere Pro, Adobe decided that the A/B Workspace had fallen out of favor. Premiere Elements follows the example of Premiere Pro by not offering the A/B Workspace, but because you can now use transitions in any video track, the A/B Workspace is kind of moot anyway.

The Capture workspace

The Capture workspace is probably where you'll start most of your Adobe Premiere Elements movie projects. Before you can edit a great movie, you need some footage to edit; the Capture workspace is where you obtain that footage from your camcorder.

To open the Capture workspace, click the Capture button on the Premiere Elements toolbar, or choose Window➪Workspace➪Capture. The capture workspace appears, as shown in Figure 3-2. I show you how to capture video using the Capture workspace in Chapter 6.

Figure 3-2:
The Capture
workspace
features the
Capture
window.

The Edit workspace

The Edit workspace is where you'll probably spend most of your time when you work in Premiere Elements. It's the default workspace that appears when you start a new project, and if you've switched to another workspace, you can bring back the Edit workspace whenever you want by choosing Window⇨ Workspace⇨Edit, or just clicking the Edit button on the Premiere Elements toolbar. The Edit workspace looks a lot like Figure 3-3. Key features include

✔ **Media window:** This is the storage place for all of the media associated with your project. Whenever you capture video or create and import media files, they are stored here. I show you how to organize items in the Media window in Chapter 6.

✔ **Monitor window:** The Monitor window allows you to view and trim clips before you place them in the Timeline, and it allows you to view and edit the Timeline itself. I talk a lot about the Monitor in Chapters 7 and 8, among others.

✔ **Timeline:** This is the most important window in Premiere Elements because it is where you drop audio and video clips to assemble them into a movie.

✔ **How To window:** The sole purpose of this window is to provide timely assistance as you work. Like a little Big Brother, this window monitors your every action as you work in Premiere Elements, but it is meant to provide help and assistance, not to harass and oppress. If you ever find yourself stumped in the middle of a project, let your eyes wander over to the How To window. Some helpful tips may be just a mouse-click away.

The Effects workspace

Another preset workspace provided by Premiere Elements is the Effects workspace (Window⇨Workspace⇨Effects). This workspace is similar to the Edit workspace, but it adds the Effects window, as shown in Figure 3-4. The Effects window provides quick access to the available effects and transitions for both audio and video. See Chapter 9 for more on working with transitions, Chapter 12 to find out how to use video effects, and lucky Chapter 13 for information about creating audio effects.

Media window   Monitor window   How To window

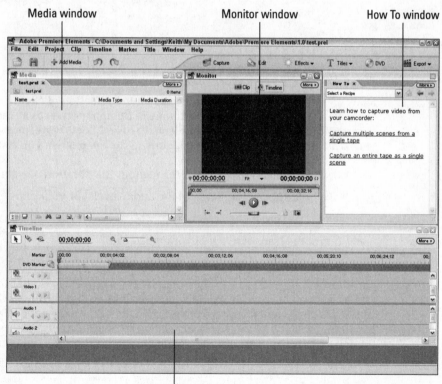

Figure 3-3: The Edit workspace is a good place to perform most edits.

Timeline

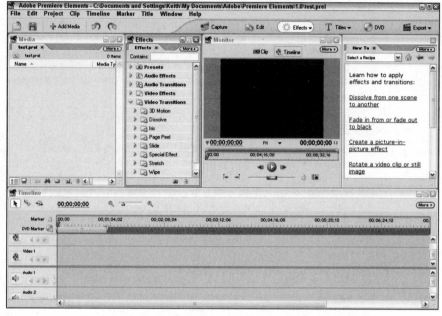

Figure 3-4:
The Effects
workspace
provides
quick
access to
effects and
transitions.

The Advanced Effects workspace

Many affordable video-editing programs offer a selection of effects that you can use in your movie projects. But none of them offer the advanced effects controls found in Adobe Premiere Elements. The Effects workspace allows you to fine-tune all effects and transitions to the *nth* degree; you can also

- ✔ Vary the application of effects throughout the duration of a single clip
- ✔ Make precision adjustments of the audio levels for your clips
- ✔ Move clips across the screen
- ✔ Control the transparency of your video clips

In other words, the Advanced Effects workspace is where you perform your advanced editing in Premiere Elements. This workspace is similar to the Effects workspace, but the Media window is hidden and the Effect Controls window is displayed. Figure 3-5 shows the Effect Controls window for a video clip in my "Hummingbirds" project. The array of buttons, indicators, and other controls may appear intimidating here, but I show you how to master all of them in Chapter 12.

The Titles workspace

The Titles workspace is similar to the Capture workspace in that it's really more of an independent window than an actual workspace. When you click Titles on the Premiere Elements toolbar or choose Window➪Workspace➪ Titles, the Adobe Title Designer appears, as shown in Figure 3-6.

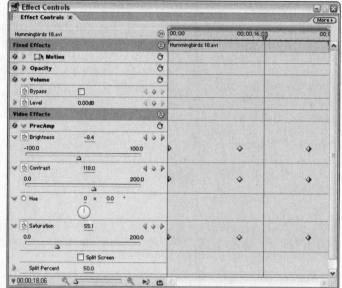

Figure 3-5:
Premiere
Elements
gives
you great
control over
your clips
and effects.

Not so long ago, most video-editing professionals created all of their titles using special title-making software. But then the designers at Adobe incorporated the advanced new Adobe Title Designer with the release of Premiere Pro. The Title Designer is now a part of Premiere Elements as well. The Adobe Title Designer gives you an incredible level of control over the appearance and positioning of titles used in your movies. I show how to create titles using the Adobe Title Designer in Chapter 14.

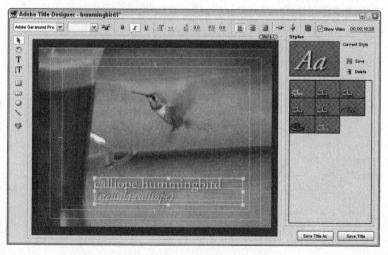

Figure 3-6:
Create
informative
and attrac-
tive titles
in the
Adobe Title
Designer.

The DVD workspace

Digital video has been around for a few years now, but the availability of affordable DVD burners has been a more recent development. It doesn't seem like very long ago that Apple's $5,000 G4 PowerMac with DVD-R "SuperDrive" was the most affordable DVD recording system available, but now the price of recordable DVD drives has dropped to under $100. Many new PCs come with DVD burners built in, and Premiere Elements makes recording your movies directly to DVD pretty darn simple.

Choose Window➪Workspace➪DVD to open the DVD workspace, or click the DVD button on the toolbar. The focus of the DVD workspace is the DVD Layout window, shown in Figure 3-7. I show you how to create and customize DVD menus in Chapter 17.

Restoring a workspace

If you're like me, you probably end up moving windows all over the Premiere Elements screen as you work, and you may even close some windows altogether. At some point you may realize that your Premiere Elements workspace is a jumbled mess. Don't worry; this mess is very easy to clean up. Just choose Window➪Restore Workspace and then choose the workspace that you want to restore, such as Edit or Advanced Effects. The default arrangement for your chosen workspace is instantly restored and the whole screen is generally de-cluttered. This process is so easy that I often find myself wishing for a Restore Workspace button on my real desk!

Figure 3-7:
Quickly
create DVD
menus in
the DVD
workspace.

Adjusting Premiere Preferences

Adobe Premiere Elements offers a plethora of settings, and you could easily spend a day or two trying to sort through them all. Some settings are immediately relevant to your work; some won't be used until you perform more advanced work. The next few sections show you some key settings that help you make more effective use of Premiere Elements on a daily basis.

Setting up your scratch disks

I hear some of you scratching your heads. "What in the Wide, Wide World of Sports is a scratch disk?" A *scratch disk* is the disk on which you store all your video stuff. When you capture video onto your computer, you capture it to the scratch disk. Likewise, many transitions, effects, and edits must be *rendered* — that is, they are actually applied to the clips — before those clips can be exported as part of a movie. The rendered clips are stored as *preview files* on the scratch disk. The scratch disk is your Premiere Elements storage place — your video data bucket, so to speak.

If your computer has just one big hard drive, you don't necessarily have a separate scratch disk. Your scratch disk may actually be a folder on your main hard drive. But if you can get a separate hard disk to use exclusively as a Premiere Elements scratch disk, I strongly recommend it. Because big and fast hard drives are so cheap these days, there is almost no reason to *not* have a separate hard drive dedicated to serving as your scratch disk.

A scratch disk must be both big and fast. Those digital video files can take up a lot of space, and if your disk isn't fast enough, you'll drop frames during rendering and when you try to output video to tape. I recommend a 7200 RPM IDE drive at the very least, or if you can afford it, a SCSI drive. See Chapter 2 for more on selecting hard drives.

You can choose different scratch disks and folders for different types of files. Premiere Elements always uses the location you specify. To set up your scratch disks, follow these steps:

1. **On the Premiere Elements menu bar, choose Edit⇨Preferences⇨ Scratch Disks.**

   The Scratch Disks section of the Preferences dialog box appears, as shown in Figure 3-8.

2. **Use the Captured Video and Captured Audio menus to adjust the scratch disk settings for the video and audio that you capture using Premiere Elements.**

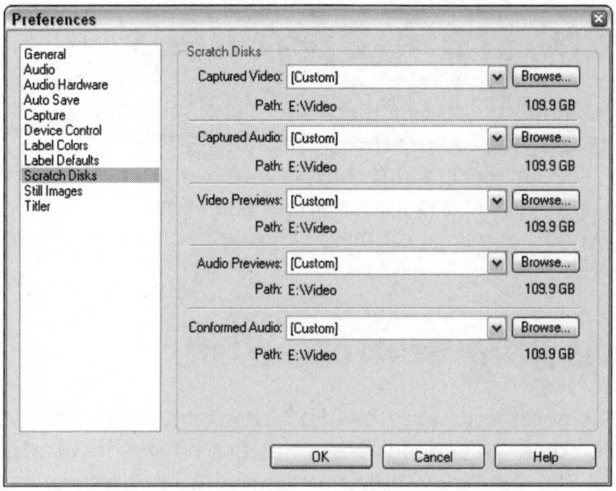

Figure 3-8:
Configure
your storage
space using
the Scratch
Disks
settings.

When you capture movies from a camera, video deck, or other source, the location specified in the Captured Video menu is where the video files are stored. The default location for all scratch disks is a setting called Same as Project — which means the same location where you save your project file when you create a new project. If you have a separate hard drive that you want to use just as a video scratch disk, choose Custom from the drop-down menu next to each item, and then click Browse to choose a specific drive and folder. In Figure 3-8, I have chosen the custom location E:\Video for all of my scratch disk locations.

3. **Choose a scratch disk for previews from the Video Previews and Audio Previews drop-down menus.**

When you want to preview or export part of your project or the whole thing, Premiere Elements usually must render several preview files. Just as with Captured Video and Captured Audio, the default location for these preview files is Same as Project, which as the name suggests is the folder where your Premiere Project (.PREL) file is saved. You can select a different folder if you want.

4. **Choose a scratch disk for conformed audio files from the Conformed Audio drop-down menu.**

Conformed audio files store track information and other audio changes made by Premiere Elements. (I recommend using the same setting here that you used for your audio and video previews.) Conformed audio is described in Chapter 13.

5. **Click OK when you're done adjusting your Scratch Disk settings.**

The Preferences dialog closes. From now on, whenever you capture audio or video it's stored in the locations that you specified in the Scratch Disk settings.

If your computer is part of a network, you can choose network drives on other computers when you set up your scratch disks. However, I strongly recommend against using network drives as scratch disks. Most networks are not fast enough or reliable enough to adequately handle large video files without dropping frames and causing other problems.

Reviewing other options

Premiere Elements has many options and preferences that you can fiddle with to make the program work the way *you* want it to. The new Preferences dialog box (shown in Figure 3-8) is a lot easier to use than in older editions of Premiere because you can quickly jump to different groups of settings by simply clicking a category in the list on the left side of the dialog box. To open the Preferences dialog box, choose Edit➪Preferences and then choose any item from the submenu that appears. Preferences are organized into the following groups:

- ✔ **General:** The most important General settings are the Default Duration settings for video and audio transitions — these determine how long a transition takes when you first apply it to an audio or video clip. Of course, you can always adjust the duration for any transition; you may find it useful to change the default settings. The duration for video transitions is expressed in *frames*, and the default duration for audio transitions is expressed in *seconds*. A slider control in General preferences also allows you to make the Premiere Elements program window brighter or darker.

- ✔ **Audio:** There's one and only one setting available here, and it's called "Play audio while scrubbing." Believe it or not this option has nothing to do with listening to music while washing dishes (sorry, dish washing advice is beyond the scope of this book). When you move slowly or frame-by-frame through a video clip in Premiere Elements, that process is called *scrubbing*. You'll scrub video a lot as you identify exact locations for edits. But because you're not playing at full speed you may find that audio sounds funny or even annoying while you scrub video. If so, remove the check mark next to the "Play audio while scrubbing" option.

- ✔ **Audio Hardware:** If you have multiple audio input/output sources on your computer, you can tell Premiere Elements which ones to use by setting the Audio Hardware preferences.

- ✔ **Auto Save:** Choose whether Premiere Elements automatically saves your projects, and control how often those auto-saves occur. I recommend that you keep the default settings, which automatically save your work every 20 minutes. This way, you won't lose hours of work simply because your dog tripped over the computer's power cord; at most you'll lose 20 minutes of work, and that's not so bad.

✔ **Capture:** Here you can tell Premiere Elements to simply abort video capture if any frames are dropped. (I strongly recommend that you leave the Report Dropped Frames option checked; if frames get dropped, you'll want to know.)

✔ **Device Control:** Set control options for your video-capture and output hardware here. (See Chapter 6 for more on working with device-control settings.)

✔ **Label Colors:** Do you like to color-code your work? Then you're in luck because Premiere Elements lets you apply color-coded labels to all kinds of program elements such as video clips, audio clips, titles, and other types of media. Use this preferences group to choose label colors.

✔ **Label Defaults:** Different types of media and elements are given different colored labels by default. Control those default colors here.

✔ **Scratch Disks:** Determine where the video files for your project are stored on your computer. (See the previous section for more on adjusting Scratch Disk settings.)

✔ **Still Images:** Control the default duration for still images here. Again, you can always change the duration of stills when you've included them in a project, but you may find it handy to change the default duration.

✔ **Titler:** The Adobe Designer includes a font browser that lets you preview the appearance of fonts. The preview usually just shows the letters AaegZz in the various font faces. If you don't like those letters, choose different letters in the Titler preferences.

Customizing the Windows in Premiere Elements

You are an individual (just like everyone else), so you probably want to personalize the software you use to make it better suit your needs. We don't all have the same work habits, and what works for me may not be ideal for you. The programmers at Adobe realized that your idea of the perfect working environment may not be the same as theirs — so they've given you quite a bit of control over some of Premiere Element's windows. You can even customize some keyboard commands.

Using the Media window

The Media window works kind of like Premiere Elements' filing cabinet. All files that you use in a project are listed in the Media window. By default, files are displayed in a basic list, displaying various details about each file. I usually find this display mode to be the most useful for Premiere Elements, but the Media window also provides an Icon view that can be useful too. Icon view (shown in Figure 3-9) displays files and items as thumbnail icons that help you better visualize the nature of each item. To use Icon view, click the Icon button in the lower-left corner of the Media window.

The Media window also contains a menu that lets you further customize the way the window looks. To access this menu, click the More button in the upper-right corner of the Media window. You can activate several useful options from this menu:

- ✔ Click View⇨Preview Area to turn the preview window at the top of the Media window on or off.

- ✔ Open the Thumbnails submenu and choose a different size for thumbnail images used in Icon view.

- ✔ Click Edit Columns in the Media window menu to open the Edit Columns dialog box. This dialog box controls which columns appear in list view. Place check marks next to columns that you want to use, or select a column title and click Move Up or Move Down to change the order in which columns appear. You can even create your own columns by clicking Add and giving your new column a name. Click OK to close the Edit Columns dialog box.

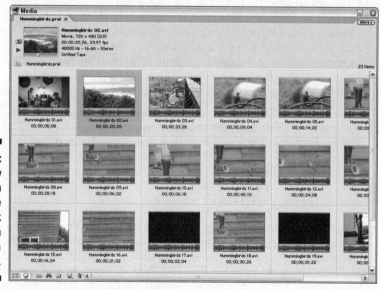

Figure 3-9:
Icon view
is an
alternative
way to look
at items in
the Media
window.

Modifying the Timeline

Throughout this book, I show the Timeline with default view settings. However, you can adjust some useful view options using a couple of different tools. These tools include:

✔ **The More button:** Click this button in the upper-right corner of the Timeline to open the Timeline window "More" menu. Here you can choose Track Size and select a new size for tracks from the submenu. Or you can choose Add Tracks to add audio or video tracks to the Timeline. A dialog box appears, enabling you to add tracks to the Timeline. I show you how to work with Timeline tracks in Chapter 8. Premiere Elements supports up to 99 video tracks and 99 audio tracks in a single Timeline.

The Timeline window "More" menu also includes an option called Snap. Snap is kind of handy sometimes because when you click-and-drag a clip or other item to the Timeline, the item automatically snaps into place on the edit point or next to an adjacent clip. If you find this behavior annoying, choose More⇨Snap to disable the Snap option.

✔ **The Set Display Style button for video tracks:** Click this button on the track header for a video track to toggle between display styles. The default setting for video tracks only shows the first frame of the clip as a thumbnail at the beginning of the clip. In Figure 3-10 I've chosen the display style that shows a visual progression of frames across the clip.

✔ **The Set Display Style button for audio tracks:** Click the Set Display Style button on the track header for an audio track to toggle between audio view options. When the line on audio tracks is yellow, a waveform of the audio clip appears in the background. A waveform is a visual line-graph representation of the audio levels in an audio clip. Moving the yellow line adjusts balance between left and right stereo audio channels. When the line is black, moving the black line adjusts audio volume, also called *gain*.

✔ **The Zoom slider:** Use this slider, located at the top of the Timeline window, to zoom in or out on the Timeline. The plus (+) and minus (–) keys on your keyboard also let you zoom quickly in or out.

Using the Monitor

The Monitor window is a pretty important part of the Premiere Elements workspace because it's where you view your video while you work. The Premiere Elements monitor has a single screen, which means you must toggle back and forth between Clip and Timeline modes. Use the Clip and Timeline buttons at the top of the Monitor window to switch modes.

Set display style   Zoom slider   More menu

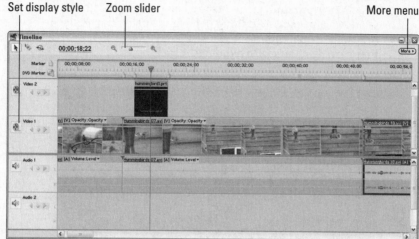

Figure 3-10:
Change the
way clips
appear in
the Timeline
window.

When the Monitor is in Clip mode, whatever clip you currently have selected
in the Media window appears. Use Clip mode to edit clips before you put
them in the Timeline. In Chapter 7, I show you how to edit clips in Clip mode.
When the Monitor is in Timeline mode, the current contents of the (surprise!)
Timeline are visible. The Monitor shows the current location of the edit line
in the Timeline. I describe Timeline editing in Chapter 8.

You can customize a couple of things in the Monitor window:

✔ **Safe Margins:** Click the More button in the upper-right corner of the
Monitor window and choose Safe Margins from the menu that appears.
Safe Margins appear around your video image, as shown in Figure 3-11.
The inner line is the *title safe margin*, and the outer line is the *action safe
margin*. If your program will be viewed on broadcast-style TV screens,
some action or titles might get cut off at the edge of the screen if they
fall outside the title-safe and action-safe margins. I recommend that you
keep the Safe Margins option enabled while editing.

✔ **Magnification:** Click the menu just below the Monitor window picture
and choose a magnification percentage to zoom in or out on the video
image. Most of the time you will probably just want to keep the default
Fit setting so that the video image automatically resizes to fill the
window if you decide to resize the Monitor window.

Customizing keyboard commands

Adobe Premiere Elements follows the same basic design paradigm as most
other modern software programs. The Premiere Elements workspace is
designed as a GUI (*graphical user interface*, often pronounced "gooey"), which

means that program elements are laid out graphically. You navigate program windows and execute editing commands using the mouse to click buttons, drag-and-drop items, and choose menu items. You can do almost anything in Premiere Elements with a mouse.

Figure 3-11:
View your
work in the
Monitor
window.

Still, don't throw away that keyboard just yet. Many Premiere users find that the mouse just doesn't have enough buttons to quickly perform some important actions. Thankfully, many common commands are accessible by using keys on the keyboard. In fact, Adobe worked hard to ensure that Premiere Elements uses some of the same industry-standard keyboard commands as other professional editing programs. An example is the use of J, K, and L to reverse, pause, and play video, similar to the shuttle controls used by many other professional video-editing programs.

To view some of the most common keyboard commands in Premiere Elements, choose Help⇨Keyboard (sorry, you'll have to use the mouse for this one). If you want to customize keyboard commands, choose Edit⇨Keyboard Customization. The Keyboard Customization window appears, as shown in Figure 3-12.

This window has two drop-down menus at the top. The first drop-down menu lets you choose a set of keyboard commands. The default set is the Adobe Premiere Elements Factory Defaults (which you can return to at any time by choosing it from the Set menu). The second menu displays different items for which you can set your own keyboard shortcuts. The choices in this menu are

- **Application:** The majority of keyboard commands can be found here. Virtually all Premiere Elements program commands can be found in the Application group.

- **Windows:** This group contains commands that are specific to the various windows in Premiere Elements.

Scroll down the lists to see the keyboard shortcuts assigned to each Premiere Elements command. To change a command, click the shortcut in the Shortcut column and type a new shortcut. If your new shortcut is already used by another command, that fact is noted at the bottom of the window.

If you make a lot of changes, I recommend you save your keyboard-command set. To do so, click Save As and give your command set a descriptive name like "Keyboard Commands." Afterward, your custom keyboard-command set is available as a choice in the Set menu.

You can find a quick-reference to standard keyboard shortcuts on the Cheat Sheet in the front of this book. Tear that bad boy out and keep it handy next to your computer for quick reference. If you find that the combination of your keyboard and mouse still don't provide as much video-editing control as you'd like, see the section about multimedia controllers in Chapter 21 for yet another option for taking control of Premiere Elements.

Figure 3-12:
Use the
Keyboard
Customiza-
tion window
to set
your own
keyboard
commands.

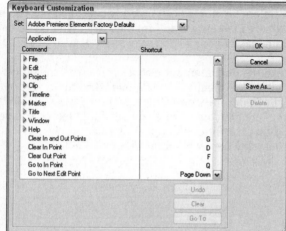

Installing Plug-Ins for Premiere Elements

One of the things I really like about Adobe software — from the ubiquitous Acrobat Reader all the way up to Premiere — is that the company designs its programs so that capabilities can be customized through the use of plug-ins. Some third-party software companies get pretty creative with the features they add. Plug-ins for Premiere Elements can add new special effects, video transitions, video export options, advanced title appearance options, and more. Adobe provides a list of select plug-ins for Premiere Elements online at

```
www.adobe.com/products/plugins/premiere/main.html
```

When you obtain a Premiere Elements plug-in, make sure that the plug-in is designed to work specifically with Premiere Elements. Installation instructions *should* be provided by the publisher. Ideally, the plug-in comes with a setup program or installer that takes care of everything for you. Keep in mind, how-ever, that many plug-in publishers assume that you know a thing or two about how Premiere Elements is installed and configured on your system. Therefore, you may not receive installation instructions, and you may need to do some manual installation procedures. Oh, joy!

Don't worry. The main thing to know is that all plug-ins for Adobe programs are stored in a program-specific "plug-ins" folder somewhere on your hard drive. When you obtain a new plug-in, often you're expected to copy the plug-in file to that specific folder manually. Of course, it helps to know where the folder *is*. No problem. On a PC running Windows XP, the folder should be right about here:

```
C:\Program Files\Adobe\Premiere Elements 1.0\Plug-ins
```

Make sure that Premiere Elements is completely closed *before* you install a new plug-in. If Premiere Elements is still running when you try to install a plug-in, the program may crash and you may lose unsaved work.

Again, carefully read the documentation that comes with the plug-in (there might be a Readme file) for specific installation instructions. After you place the plug-in file in the folder mentioned here, it should be available the next time you open Premiere Elements. For example, if the plug-in adds a new transition, look for that transition to appear as an option in the Transitions group on the Effects tab when you restart Premiere Elements.

Chapter 4

Introduction to Moviemaking

. . . .

. . . .

Digital video and computer-based movie editing is today's technological hot topic, but home movies aren't exactly a new concept. Portable hand-cranked 16mm film cameras first appeared in the 1920s, and in 1932 Kodak introduced the 8mm film format. By the 1950s 8mm film cameras had become downright affordable, and the milestones continued to tick by. Home movie cameras sprouted zoom lenses in the late 1950s; in 1964 Kodak introduced the Super 8 format, with its easier-to-handle film cartridges; in 1973 a magnetic audio recording system was added to Super 8 cartridges.

Despite many advances, film-based movie cameras still had a few disadvantages. The film had to be developed before it could be watched, and viewing movies required special movie projectors and a big blank wall or a projection screen. In 1976, JVC introduced the VHS videotape format, and by the 1980s most home movie enthusiasts had replaced their antiquated film cameras with video camcorders. Digital video camcorders appeared in the 1990s, and the rest, as they say, is history.

While movie camera technology has progressed steadily over the last 80 years or so, home movie editing is still a relatively new concept. Sure, you could always "edit" your old film movies by cutting-and-splicing the film with a razor blade and cellophane tape. And home videos can be edited by creatively juggling the pause and record buttons on your VCR and camcorder. But professional-style movie editing wasn't really practical for the low-budget enthusiast until about the year 2000, when personal computers that were powerful enough to edit video finally became semi-affordable.

If you're new to video, this chapter is for you. Here I introduce you to digital video technology, and I show you how digital video makes video editing easy. This chapter also introduces you to video technologies and concepts to help you make more effective use of Adobe Premiere Elements. (If this chapter whets your appetite for information on the basics of digital video and moviemaking, check out my other book, *Digital Video For Dummies,* 3rd Edition, also published by Wiley.)

What Is DV?

DV is an abbreviation for *digital video*. Next subject.

Oh, you want a more detailed explanation? No problem. Computers, as you probably know, aren't very intelligent. They don't understand the serene beauty of a rose garden, the mournful song of a cello, or the graceful motion of an eagle in flight. All computers really understand are ones and zeros. And yet, we force computers to show us pictures, play music, and display moving video. The infinitely variable sounds and pictures we perceive must be converted into the language of computers: ones and zeros. This conversion process is called *digitizing*. Digital video is (you guessed it) video that has been digitized.

To fully understand the difference between *analog data* — the rich audio and light waves that we humans perceive and sound and images — and digital data, suppose you want to draw the profile of a hill. An analog representation of the profile (see Figure 4-1) would follow the contour of the hill perfectly because analog values are infinitely variable. However, a digital contour of that same hill would not be able to follow every single detail of the hill because, as shown in Figure 4-2, digital values are made up of specifically defined individual bits of data.

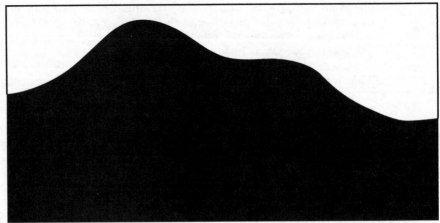

Figure 4-1:
Analog data
is infinitely
variable.

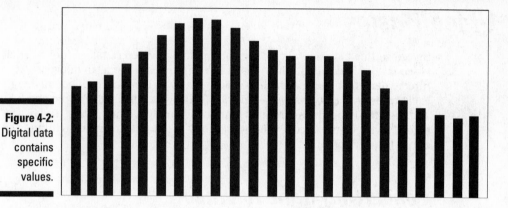

Figure 4-2:
Digital data
contains
specific
values.

Comparing Digital to Analog

It could be said that a digital recording will always be theoretically inferior to an analog recording because the analog recording can contain more values. But the truth is that major advances in digital technology mean that this "limitation" really doesn't matter. Yes, a digital recording must have specific values, but modern recordings have so many unique values packed so closely together that human eyes and ears can barely tell the difference. In fact, casual observation often reveals that digital recordings appear to be of higher quality than analog recordings. Why?

One of the problems with analog recordings is that they are highly susceptible to deterioration. Every time analog data is copied, some of the original data is lost. This phenomenon is called *generational loss* and can be observed in that dark, grainy copy of a copy of a copy of a wedding video that was first shot over ten years ago. But digital data doesn't have this problem. A one is always a one, no matter how many times it is copied, and a zero is always a zero. Likewise, analog recordings are more susceptible to deterioration after every playback, which explains why your vintage *Meet the Beatles* LP pops, hisses, and has lost many of its highs and lows over the years.

Even though digital video isn't susceptible to generational loss, I still recommend that you work from copies and always keep the unedited master tape in a safe place. You never know when you may need to recover original footage some time in the future.

When you consider the implications of generational loss on video editing, you begin to see what a blessing digital video really is. You will constantly be copying, editing, and recopying content as you edit your movie projects — and with digital video, you can edit to your heart's content, confident that the quality won't diminish with each new copy you make.

Video Basics

Before getting into a detailed description of what video *is,* take a look at what video *is not.* Video is not film. What's the difference? In film, an image is captured when chemicals on the film react with light. In modern video, an image is captured by a *charged-coupled device* (CCD) — a sort of electronic eye — and then the image is recorded magnetically on tape. Many "films" today are actually shot using video, even though they are output to and distributed to movie theaters on film.

Converting light to video

Little Jenny picks a dandelion on a sunny afternoon. She brings the fluffy flower to her lips, and with a puff, the seeds flutter gently away on the breeze (they land in the neighbor's immaculate yard and spawn dozens more of the unappreciated yellow flowers). As this scene unfolds, light photons bounce off Jenny, the dandelion stem, the seeds, and anything else in the shot. Some of those photons pass through the lens of your camcorder. The lens focuses the photons on transistors in the CCD. The transistors get excited, and the CCD converts this excitement into data, which is then magnetically recorded on tape. This process, shown in Figure 4-3, is repeated approximately 30 times per second.

Most mass-market, consumer-oriented DV camcorders have a single CCD, but higher-quality cameras have three CCDs. In such cameras, each CCD is dedicated to capturing a specific light color (red, green, or blue). Multi-CCD cameras are expensive (most price out on the far side of $1,500), but the image produced is near-broadcast quality.

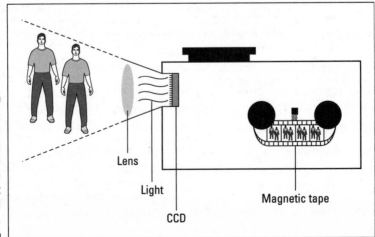

Figure 4-3:
The CCD converts light into the video image that is recorded on tape.

Lens

Light

CCD

Magnetic tape

The prehistoric ancestors of camcorders (those portable video cameras of about 20 years ago) used video-pickup tubes instead of CCDs. Tubes were inferior to CCDs in many ways, particularly in the way they handled extremes of light. With video-pickup tubes, points of bright light (such as a light bulb or reflection of the sun) bled and streaked across the picture, and low-light situations were simply too dark to shoot.

Reviewing video standards

Several new terms have entered the videophile's lexicon in recent years: NTSC, PAL, HDTV. These terms identify a variety of broadcast television standards. It's important to know these terms if you plan to edit video. Your cameras, TVs, and tape decks probably conform to only *one* broadcast standard. Which standard is for you? That depends upon where you live:

- ✔ **NTSC:** *National Television Standards Committee*. Used primarily in North America, Japan, and the Philippines.

- ✔ **PAL:** *Phase-Alternating Line*. Used primarily in Western Europe, Australia, Southeast Asia, and South America.

- ✔ **SECAM:** *Sequential Couleur Avec Mémoire*. This category actually covers several similar standards used primarily in France, Russia, Eastern Europe, Central Asia, and most of Africa. From a practical standpoint, the SECAM video standard is virtually identical to PAL.

Adobe Premiere Elements supports all three major broadcast formats. When you begin a project, you should always adjust the project settings to the correct format. (See Chapter 5 for more on setting up a new project.) If you are working with SECAM video, simply use Premiere Elements' settings for PAL video.

Mastering broadcast compatibility issues

The most important thing to know about these three broadcast standards is that they are *not* compatible. In other words, if you try to play an NTSC-format videotape in a PAL video deck, the tape won't work, even if both decks use VHS tapes. This is because VHS is merely a physical *tape* format, not a video format.

With DVD (digital versatile disc) players it's a little trickier. Some DVD players — especially those sold in PAL countries — can play both NTSC and PAL DVDs. In many cases, however, the video signal output by the DVD player matches the disc format, so if you play a PAL disc it will probably only play on a PAL TV, and if you play an NTSC disc it will probably only play on an NTSC

TV. A few special DVD players can actually convert the video format for output, and your player's documentation should provide information about this. Ideally, try to burn DVDs only in the video format used in your country.

In other words, you can't count on your videos to be viewable all over the world. If you're editing a video for distribution all over the world, you will need to output different versions of the movie in both PAL and NTSC format. Chapter 17 shows how to control the export format when you burn DVDs, but if you want to export to videotape in a different broadcast format, you will need to use a different program such as Adobe Premiere Pro.

The reason for all this incompatibility is that video standards differ in two primary ways:

- ✓ **Different frame rates.** A video image is made up of a series of still images that flash by so quickly that they produce the optical illusion of motion. Each of these still images is called a *frame*. The frame rate of video is the rate at which individual frames flash by. Frame rate is usually abbreviated *fps* (frames per second).

- ✓ **Different resolutions.** A video picture is usually drawn as a series of horizontal lines. An electron gun at the back of the picture tube draws lines of the video picture, much like the way the printer head on your printer moves back and forth as it prints words on a page. The resolution of a video image is usually expressed in the number of these horizontal lines that make up the image.

Table 4-1 details the differences.

Table 4-1	Video Standards	
Standard	*Frame Rate*	*Resolution*
NTSC	29.97 fps	525 lines
PAL	25 fps	625 lines
SECAM	25 fps	625 lines

All three video standards listed in Table 4-1 are *interlaced*. This means that the horizontal lines are drawn in two passes rather than one. Every other line is drawn on each consecutive pass, and each of these passes is called a *field*. On a PAL display, which shows 25 fps, there are actually 50 fields per second.

Noninterlaced displays are also common. Modern computer monitors, for example, are all *noninterlaced,* meaning that all the lines are drawn in a single pass. Some HDTV (High-Definition Television) formats are noninterlaced, whereas others are interlaced. Noninterlaced displays are also sometimes called *progressive scan* displays.

What was that about HDTV?

A full accounting of all the High-Definition Television (a.k.a. HDTV) formats would practically fill a book by itself. Resolution in HDTV is measured in pixels (like a computer monitor) rather than horizontal lines (like NTSC and PAL). Resolutions for HDTV formats range from as low as 640 x 480 pixels up to 1920 x 1080. Although 640 x 480 may sound low if you have been around computers for a while, it's still pretty good compared to traditional television displays. Frame rates for HDTV range from 24 fps

noninterlaced, and up to 60 fps (interlaced or progressive scan).

Because of all the uncertainly surrounding HDTV, I recommend against developing video for specific HDTV formats until a single format emerges as a standard in your geographic area. Instead, develop video for your local broadcast format (NTSC, PAL, or SECAM) and assume (hope?) that your audience members have converters on their high-definition TVs.

The many aspects of aspect ratios

Different moving-picture displays have different shapes. The screens in movie theaters, for example, look like long rectangles, whereas most TV and computer screens are almost square. The shape of a video display is called the *aspect ratio*. The following two sections look at how aspect ratios affect editing in Adobe Premiere Elements.

Image aspect ratios

The aspect ratio of a typical television screen is 4:3. This means that for any given size, the display is four units wide and three units high. To put this in real numbers, measure the width and height of a TV or computer monitor that you have nearby. If the display is 40 cm wide, for example, you should notice that it's also 30 cm high. If a picture completely fills this display, the picture is also said to have an aspect ratio of 4:3.

Different numbers are sometimes used to describe the same aspect ratio. The 4:3 aspect ratio is sometimes expressed as 1.33:1. Likewise, the 16:9 aspect ratio is sometimes expressed as 1.78:1. But do the math and you'll see that these different numbers still equal the same basic shape.

Many movies are distributed on tape and DVD today in a *widescreen* format. The aspect ratio of a widescreen picture is usually (but not always) 16:9. If you watch a widescreen movie on a 4:3 TV screen, you will see black bars — sometimes called *letterbox* format — at the top and bottom of the screen. Widescreen movies are popular because they more closely match the aspect ratio of the movie-theater screens for which the movies were originally shot. Figure 4-4 illustrates the difference between the 4:3 and 16:9 aspect ratios.

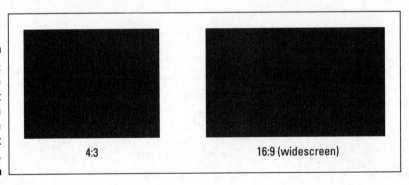

Figure 4-4:
The two
most
common
image
aspect
ratios.

4:3   16:9 (widescreen)

A common misconception is that 16:9 is the aspect ratio of all big-screen movies. In fact, various aspect ratios for film have been used over the years. Many movies have an aspect ratio of over 2:1 — the image is more than twice as wide as it is high! But for most films, 16:9 is considered close enough. More to the point, it's just right for you because if your digital camcorder has a widescreen mode, its aspect ratio is probably 16:9. Adobe Premiere Elements fully supports 16:9 media, and in Chapter 5, I show you how to set up a project for widescreen video.

Whatever aspect ratio you shoot video in — 4:3 or 16:9 — you will need to be aware of your video's aspect ratio as you edit your movies. This becomes important when preparing still images for use in movies, or when choosing settings for a new movie project.

Pixel aspect ratios

You may already be familiar with image aspect rations, but did you know that *pixels* can have various aspect ratios too? If you've worked with a drawing or graphics program on a computer, you're probably familiar with pixels. A pixel is the smallest piece of a digital image. Thousands — even millions — of uniquely colored pixels combine in a grid to form an image on a television or computer screen. On computer displays, pixels are square. But in standard video, pixels are *rectangular*. In NTSC video, pixels are taller than they are wide — and in PAL or SECAM, pixels are wider than they are tall.

Pixel aspect ratios become an issue when you start using still computer graphics in projects that also contain standard video. If you don't prepare the still graphics carefully, they could appear distorted when viewed on a TV. You'll notice the same problem when you export video frames as still images. For more on preparing still graphics for use in movie projects, see Chapter 6. See Chapter 15 for more on exporting still frames from your video.

Understanding timecode

A video image is actually a series of still frames that flash rapidly on the screen. Every frame is uniquely identified with a number called a *timecode*. The location and duration of all edits that you perform on a movie project use timecodes for reference points, so a basic understanding of timecode is critical. You'll see and use timecode almost every time you work in Adobe Premiere Elements. Timecode is usually expressed like this:

```
hours:minutes:seconds:frames
```

Thus the fourteenth frame of the third second of the twenty-eighth minute of the first hour of video is identified like this:

```
01:28:03:13
```

You already know what hours, minutes, and seconds are. Frames are the individual still images that make up video. The frame portion of a timecode starts with zero and counts up from there. In PAL or SECAM video, frames are counted from 00 to 24 because the frame rate of PAL and SECAM is 25 fps. In NTSC, frames are counted from 00 to 29. The frame count starts at 00, which is why the fourteenth frame mentioned above has the timecode 13.

"Wait!" you exclaim. "Zero to 29 adds up to 30 fps, but Table 4-1 says that the frame rate is 29.97."

You're an observant one, aren't you? As mentioned earlier, the frame rate of NTSC video is 29.97 fps (refer to Table 4-1). NTSC timecode actually skips frame codes 00 and 01 in the first second of every minute — except for every tenth minute. Work it out (let's hear it for calculators!), and you see that this system of reverse leap-frames adds up to 29.97 fps. This is called *drop-frame* timecode. In Premiere Elements and most other video-editing systems, drop-frame timecode is expressed with semicolons (;) instead of colons (:) between the numbers.

Why does NTSC video use drop-frame timecode? Well, back when everything was broadcast in black and white, NTSC video was an even 30 fps. For the conversion to color, more bandwidth was needed in the signal to broadcast color information. Dropping a couple of frames every minute left enough room in the signal to broadcast color information, while at the same time keeping the video signals compatible with older black-and-white TVs. (Clever, those earthlings . . .)

Comparing Camcorder Formats

You can find a variety of camcorder formats today for almost any budget. If you're buying a new camcorder you should only choose a digital camcorder because digital camcorders offer better quality and are easier to use with Premiere Elements.

By far the most common digital format today is MiniDV, but MiniDV isn't quite the only game in town. Some alternatives are very expensive and oriented toward video professionals, while others are different just for the sake of being different. I describe the most common camcorder formats in the following sections.

Always check the price and availability of blank media before you buy any camcorder. If blanks are unavailable or too expensive, your camcorder could become virtually useless.

MiniDV

MiniDV has become the most popular standard format for digital videotapes. Virtually all consumer digital camcorders sold today use MiniDV, which means that blank tapes are now easy to find and reasonably affordable. If you're still shopping for a camcorder and are wondering which format is best for all-around use, let me cut to the chase: MiniDV is it.

MiniDV tapes are small and more compact than even audiocassette tapes. Small is good because smaller tape-drive mechanisms mean smaller, lighter camcorders. Tapes come in a variety of lengths, but the most common length is 60 minutes.

All MiniDV devices use the IEEE-1394 FireWire interface to connect to computers, and the DV codec is used to compress and capture video. (*Codecs* are compression schemes — codec is a shortened form of *c*ompression/ *dec*ompression.) Codecs are described later in this chapter in the "Decoding Codecs" section. The DV codec is supported by virtually all FireWire hardware and video-editing software, including Adobe Premiere Elements.

Digital8

A few years ago, MiniDV tapes were expensive and difficult to find. Several manufacturers began to offer alternative formats for digital camcorders, and many of those alternatives are still available. Perhaps the most common alternative to MiniDV is Digital8, created by Sony. Digital8 cameras record DV video on Hi-8 videotapes, which are about the size of audiocassette tapes. Digital8 camcorders are available from both Sony and Hitachi. A 120-minute Hi-8 tape can store 60 minutes of Digital8 video.

Because Hi-8 is a popular format for analog camcorders, Hi-8 tapes have been affordable and widely available for several years. But more recently, the price of MiniDV tapes has come down enough to make Digital8 camcorders less advantageous. Nothing is wrong with Digital8 camcorders; I have an older one (a Sony DCR-TRV103), and it works great. In fact, they are very handy: like MiniDV camcorders, Digital8 camcorders use the DV codec. Plug a Digital8 camcorder into your FireWire port and Premiere Elements won't know the difference. It's just that the future of DV recording is MiniDV, not Digital8.

In theory, MiniDV camcorders can record slightly higher resolution than Digital8 camcorders, but in practice the resolution recorded by similarly priced Digital8 and MiniDV camcorders is about the same. The video recorded by a $500 Digital8 camcorder is going to look just like the video recorded by a $500 MiniDV camcorder.

My advice: If you have a Digital8 camera already and you're happy with it, keep it around and keep your eye on the MiniDV market. If you're in the market for a new camcorder, though, definitely look at the previous section about MiniDV.

Other consumer-grade options

Various other recording formats have appeared on the mass market. Some camcorders use a built-in DVD (digital versatile disc) recorder for storage, but DVD-based camcorders have a few drawbacks. They tend to

- Be bulky
- Drain batteries quickly
- Provide inferior video quality compared to most MiniDV camcorders
- Be incompatible with Premiere Elements, because they record video in MPEG2 format rather than the standard DV format

A few other, more obscure digital camcorder formats have come and gone as well. Sony, for example, briefly offered some very small digital camcorders that used a proprietary format called MicroMV. MicroMV camcorders can be used with Premiere Elements, so if you already have one you should be fine. But if you're looking to buy a new camcorder and stumble upon a MicroMV unit, keep in mind that blank tapes and other parts may become very hard to find in the near future.

Professional-grade formats

Do you have $20,000 burning a hole in your pocket? You could spend that sum very quickly on professional-grade video equipment. Wonderful though MiniDV may be for general-purpose use, it does present some shortcomings when used in a professional environment. If you're thinking of making an upgrade, professional-grade (or *prosumer*) formats offer several advantages over MiniDV:

- ✔ Pro-grade tapes are usually more *robust* than MiniDV, which means that they can withstand more shuttling (fast-forwarding and rewinding) and other editing operations.

- ✔ Professional formats usually include outputs that aren't included on many MiniDV camcorders. In addition to the standard FireWire, S-Video, and composite outputs usually found on MiniDV, pro-equipment often includes component video and Serial Digital Interface (SDI) outputs.

- ✔ Some newer pro-grade digital cameras can shoot at 24 fps, the same frame rate that's used for film. This format is called 24P. Professional-grade camcorders can also sometimes record in the HD (high definition) format. Keep in mind, however, that the 24P and HD video formats are not supported by Premiere Elements.

- ✔ Audio-video synchronization is often more precise on professional formats.

Many professional-grade formats are actually derivations of MiniDV. The DVCPro format from Panasonic and the DVCAM format from Sony are both based on the MiniDV format, but they offer more robust assemblies and tracks that are better suited to heavy-duty editing. Sony also offers the Digital Betacam format, which is based on the vaunted Betacam SP analog format. Older pro-digital formats included D1, D2, D3, and D5. These formats also offered robust design, but the video resolutions were lower than the newer MiniDV-based formats.

The bottom line: If you're a video hobbyist, amateur videographer, or corporate video producer on a fixed budget, MiniDV remains a perfectly adequate format, especially if you aren't operating on a professional-grade budget.

Analog formats

Analog video formats have a lot of history, but they're fading quickly from the scene. A major portent of the death of analog came in late 2001, when Sony announced that it would discontinue its beloved Betacam SP format. Betacam SP was long preferred among video professionals, but Sony opted to drop the format because digital equivalents offer virtually the same quality for far less money.

Because analog video has been around for so long, countless formats exist. Common analog formats found in consumer video camcorders include VHS, VHS-C, 8mm, and Hi-8. You've probably seen these formats around, and you may have even owned (or still own) a camcorder that uses one. Besides the generational-loss problems of analog video, analog formats usually provide fewer horizontal lines of resolution. Even the highest-quality analog formats can't approach the video quality of modestly priced digital camcorders.

Of course, the biggest problem with analog video is that you can't capture it directly into Premiere Elements. If you want to capture analog video onto your computer you'll need to use a third-party solution, as I describe in Chapter 6. Once the analog video is captured onto your computer in a common digital format such as MPEG, it can then be imported into Premiere Elements for editing.

Decoding Codecs

A digital video signal contains a lot of data. If you were to copy uncompressed digital video onto your hard drive, it would consume 20MB (megabytes) *for every second of video*. Ouch! Simple arithmetic tells us that one minute of uncompressed video would use over 1GB (gigabyte). Even with an 80GB hard drive, you would have room for only about an hour of uncompressed video — assuming that big drive was empty to begin with. Dire though these numbers may seem, storage isn't even the biggest problem with uncompressed video. Typical hard-drives (and other components in your computer) usually can't handle a transfer rate of 20MB per second; some frames will be dropped from the video during the transfer process.

To deal with the massive bandwidth requirements of video, digital video is compressed using compression schemes called *codecs*. The term codec is short for *compressor/decompressor*. The DV codec, used by most digital camcorders, compresses video down to 3.6MB per second. This data rate is far more manageable, and most modern computer hardware can handle it. When you capture digital video from a camcorder using a FireWire interface, a minute of video consumes just over 200MB of hard-drive space. Again, most modern computers can manage that.

Why do codecs matter to you? Adobe Premiere Elements enables you to choose from a variety of codecs when you output movies for the Internet (see Chapter 16 for more on preparing movies for online use). If you capture analog video from a capture card, you'll have to choose a codec for the captured video. Logically enough, the more you compress your video, the more quality you lose. So consider the following issues when you choose a codec:

✔ **Is the movie intended for Internet playback?** A majority of Internet users still have pretty limited bandwidth. Users with high-speed broadband access still account for well fewer than half of all Internet users.

The rest still use dial-up connections with speeds slower than 50 Kbps (kilobits per second). This means that if you're outputting for the Internet and you want your movie to be usable for as many people as possible, you should use higher compression. Alternatively, you may choose to provide several levels of compression for various bandwidths. Provide a bigger, higher-quality version for broadband users, and a smaller, more compressed version for dial-up users.

✔ **Is the movie intended for CD-ROM or DVD playback?** Most CD-ROM drives also have serious bandwidth limitations, so you need to use a codec that uses a high compression ratio. If you are outputting for DVD, you need to use the MPEG-2 codec because that's the compression scheme DVD players use.

✔ **Are you outputting back to tape?** If so, your own output hardware is your primary concern.

See Chapter 15 for recommendations on specific codecs to use when you're outputting video for various formats.

The Nonlinear Editing Method

My grandfather is a tinkerer. Over the years, he has tinkered with wood, old lawn mowers, and even 8mm film. He wasn't content to simply shoot home movies with his old 8mm film camera and then watch them as developed, so Grandpa actually edited his source footage into interesting films. He performed edits by cutting the 8mm film with a razor blade and then splicing scenes together in a different order, using cellophane tape (Scotch tape) to hold the splices together.

The process described above is what professional video editors call *linear editing,* and all motion pictures were edited this way many years ago. Video, too, was once edited linearly, and until recently, linear editing was the only option available for home video users. Consider the process of dubbing video from a camcorder onto a tape in a VCR. If there is a scene on the camcorder tape that you want to leave off the VHS tape, you might pause recording on the VCR until that scene has passed. This process is another form of linear editing because you perform all of your edits in order from beginning to end. Linear editing is terribly inefficient. If you dub a program and then decide to perform an additional edit, subsequent video usually has to be redubbed.

What is the alternative? *Nonlinear editing,* of course! As the name implies, nonlinear edits can be performed in any order; you don't have to edit material in a specific, one-step-follows-another order. Nonlinear editing is made possible by the miracle of the computer and programs like Adobe Premiere Elements. Suppose (for example) that you have a program in which Scene 1 is followed by Scene 2, but you decide that you want to squeeze in another scene — we'll call it Scene 1.5 — between Scenes 1 and 2. In Premiere Elements, you simply place Scene 1.5 in the Timeline between Scenes 1 and 2 (as shown in Figure 4-5), and Premiere automatically moves Scene 2 over to make room for Scene 1.5 (see Figure 4-6). Imagine trying to perform this kind of edit by shuttling tapes in a pair of video decks — take a moment to wince — and you realize what a blessing a nonlinear editor (NLE) like Premiere Elements really is.

Figure 4-5: To insert a scene between two existing scenes, just drop the new scene in the appropriate place on the Timeline.

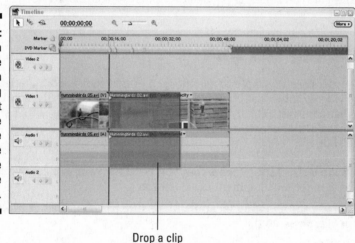

Drop a clip

Figure 4-6: When you perform an insert edit, Premiere automatically shifts subsequent material in the Timeline.

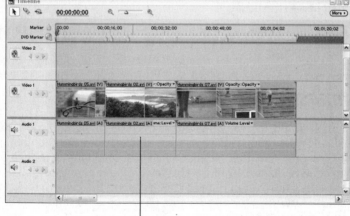

Inserted clip

Shooting Better Video

Throughout the years, editors have been called upon to create movies that are worth watching. But ultimately, a video editor can wield only so much magic. If you want to make a great movie, you need to start with great video footage because there is only so much improvement that an editing program like Premiere Elements can make. And if you don't think "great" video footage is possible (yet) given your equipment and talents, you *can* still improve your techniques enough to make your results a lot more watchable. The following sections give you some simple tips that can help you shoot video like the pros.

Planning the shot

Camcorders are so simple to use these days that they encourage seat-of-the-pants videography. Just grabbing your camcorder and hastily shooting the UFO that happens to be flying overhead is fine, but for most other situations, some careful planning will provide better quality. You can plan many aspects of the shot:

- ✔ **Make a checklist of shots that you need for your project.** While you're at it, make an equipment checklist too.

- ✔ **Survey the shooting location.** Make sure passersby won't trip over your cables or bump the camera.

- ✔ **Talk to property owners or other responsible parties.** Make sure you have permission to shoot; identify potential disruptions (wandering livestock, air traffic if you're near an airport, scheduled mud-wrestling matches — the usual).

- ✔ **Bring more blank tapes and charged batteries than you think you'll need.**

Composing the shot

Like a photograph, a great video image must be thoughtfully composed. Start by evaluating the type of shot you plan to take. Does the shot include people, landscapes, or some other subject? Consider what kind of tone or feel you want to achieve. Figure 4-7 illustrates how different compositions of the same shot can affect the overall tone. In the first shot, the camera looks down on the subject. Children are shot like this much too often, and it makes them look smaller and inferior. The second shot is level with the subject and portrays him more favorably. The third shot looks up at the subject and makes him seem important, almost larger than life.

Dressing your cast for video success

My guess is that most of your video "shoots" will actually be pretty informal affairs, where you basically record an event that was scheduled to happen whether you brought your camcorder or not. Thus, you may have a hard time convincing everyone who is attending that they should dress appropriately for video. But there definitely are some types of clothes that work better in video than others — and if you have any control at all over what the people in your video wear, try making these suggestions:

✔ **Avoid clothes with lots of thin parallel lines or stripes:** Thin parallel lines (like those you'd find on coarse corduroy or pinstripe

suits) don't get along well with TV screens; they create a crawling or wavy visual effect called a *moiré pattern*.

✔ **Limit the use of very bright shades of red and blue.** Red is especially problematic because it tends to bleed into neighboring portions of the video image. This doesn't mean everyone in your movie should wear dark, drab colors, however. In the best of all possible shoots, your subjects' clothing is bright enough to lend some interest, but contrasts with the background somewhat so they don't get lost in the video image.

Figure 4-7:
Composition greatly affects how your subject is perceived.

Panning effectively

Another important aspect of composition is *panning,* or moving the camera. A common shooting technique that snapshot enthusiasts use with home camcorders is to pan the camera back-and-forth, up-and-down, either to follow a moving subject or to show a lot of things that don't fit in a single shot. This technique is called *firehosing* and is usually not a good idea. Practice these rules when panning:

✔ **Pan only once per shot.**

✔ **Start panning slowly, *gradually* speed up, and slow down again before stopping.**

✔ **Slow down!** Panning too quickly — say, over a landscape — is a common mistake.

✔ **If you have a cheap tripod, you may find it difficult to pan smoothly.** Try lubricating the tripod's swivel head. If that doesn't work, limit tripod use to stationary shots. Ideally you should use a higher-quality tripod with a fluid head for smooth panning.

✔ **Keep the camera level with the horizon.** A tilting horizon is very disorienting.

✔ **If you're shooting a moving subject, try moving the camera with the subject, rather than panning across a scene.** This reduces out-of-focus issues with the camera lens, and it also helps to keep the subject in frame.

Using (not abusing) the zoom lens

Most camcorders have a handy zoom feature. A *zoom lens* is basically a lens with an adjustable focal length. A longer lens — also called a *telephoto lens* — makes faraway subjects appear closer. A shorter lens — also called a *wide-angle* lens — allows more of a scene to fit in the shot. Zoom lenses allow you to adjust between wide-angle and telephoto views.

Because the zoom feature is easy to use and fun to play with, amateur videographers tend to zoom in and out a lot. I recommend that you avoid zooming during a shot as much as possible. Overuse of the zoom lens disorients the viewer, and it creates focal and light problems whether you're focusing the camera manually or using the auto-focus option. Some zoom-lens tips include the following:

✔ **Avoid zooming whenever possible.** Consider your purpose before you touch that dial.

✔ **If you must zoom while recording, zoom slowly.** You may need to practice a bit to get a feel for your camera's zoom control.

✔ **Consider repositioning the camera instead of using the zoom lens to compose the shot.** Wide-angle lenses have greater *depth of field*. This means that more of the shot is in focus if you're zoomed out. If you shoot subjects by zooming in on them from across a room, they may move in and out of focus. But if you move the camera in and zoom the lens out, focus will be less of a problem.

Lighting the shot

Light can be subdivided into two basic categories: good light and bad light. Good light allows you to see your subject, and it flatters your subject by exposing details that you want shown. Shadows aren't completely eliminated, but the shadows don't dominate large portions of the subject either. Bad light, on the other hand, washes out color and creates lens flares — the reflections and bright spots that show up when the sun shines across the lens — and other undesired effects. Consider Figure 4-8. The right side of the subject's face is a featureless white glow because it's washed out by intense sunlight. Meanwhile, the left side of the face is obscured in shadow. Not good.

Figure 4-8: Improper lighting spoils this shot.

How do you light your shots effectively? Remain ever aware of both the good light and the bad. If you don't have control over lighting in a location, try to compose the shot to best take advantage of the lighting that is available. Here are some more lighting tips that may come in handy:

- **Bounce intense lights off a reflective surface.** Light reflecting from a surface, such as a white sheet or foil screen, is more diffused, providing more flattering lighting than shining bright light directly on the subject.

- **Use multiple light sources of varying intensity.** Light on the front of the subject brings out facial details, while light from above and behind highlights the subject relative to the background.

- **Watch for backlight situations like the one shown in Figure 4-9.** Try to put extra light on the foreground subject, avoid bright backgrounds, or increase the camera's exposure control. Some cameras have an automatic backlight compensation feature, though as you can see on the right side of Figure 4-9, sometimes the just creates more problems.

- **Shield your lens from bright light sources, particularly the sun.** Intense light can reflect on the lens glass and cause flares that only show up later on video. If your camera lens doesn't have a black hood, you can use your hand or black tape to make a temporary shield (check the viewfinder to ensure that your shield doesn't appear in the shot).

- **Check your camera's documentation.** Your camcorder might include built-in features to help you deal with special lighting situations, such as sporting events or a sun-washed beach.

- **Use lens filters.** A neutral-density filter, for example, reduces light in bright outdoor settings and makes colors appear more vivid. A polarizing filter controls how reflective surfaces (like water or glass) appear.

Figure 4-9:
Egad, who
is that
shadowy
figure on the
left? Oh,
there he
is, horribly
over-
exposed on
the right.

Shooting the shot

Perhaps the most important tip I can give you before you shoot your video is this: *Know your camera.* Even the least-expensive digital camcorders available today are packed with some pretty advanced features. For example, most digital camcorders include image stabilization, in-camera effects, and the ability to record 16-bit stereo audio. But these advanced features won't do you much good if they aren't turned on or are on but configured improperly. Spend a few hours reviewing the manual that came with your camcorder and practice using every feature and setting.

Keep the camcorder manual in your gear bag when you hit the road. It may prove an invaluable reference when you're shooting on location. Also, review the manual from time to time; no doubt some useful or cool features are lurking that you forgot all about or never saw the first time you reviewed the manual. If you've lost your manual, check the manufacturer's Web site. You might be able to download a replacement manual.

Virtually all modern camcorders include automatic exposure and focus control. But no matter how advanced this automation may seem it's not perfect. Get friendly with the manual exposure and focus controls on your camera (if it has them) and practice using them. If you always rely on auto focus, inevitably your video will show the queasy effects of the lens "hunting" for the right setting during some shots — especially if you shoot moving subjects or in poor light. If your camera has a manual focus mode, you can avoid focus hunting by turning off auto focus. Also, getting handy with the manual exposure control (also called the *iris*) will ultimately give you more control over light exposure in your video.

Part II
Basic Editing in Adobe Premiere Elements

The 5th Wave   By Rich Tennant

"Do you think the 'Hidden Rhino' clip should come before or after the 'Waving Hello' video clip?"

In this part . . .

*V*ideo editing can be broken down into three basic steps: Capture, edit, and export. The chapters in this part of *Adobe Premiere Elements For Dummies* cover the first two steps. First, you start by creating new movie projects. Then you find out how to capture video from your digital camcorder and how to import other kinds of media.

When you have some media to work with, I show you how to perform basic editing to turn your media into a basic movie. I also cover adding transitions between video clips, a common (and often essential) editing task.

Chapter 5

Starting Movie Projects

· ·

· ·

*S*oftware companies like to create names for program functions, controls, and windows that are meant to be analogous to something in "real" life. For example, if you want to delete a file on a Windows PC, you put it in the *Recycle Bin*. When you want to check your e-mail, you look in your *Inbox*. Sometimes the analogies work, and sometimes they don't. I used to have an Internet service that had pages named *Runway* and *Boardwalk*. One of them was a page of search engines, and the other a Web directory. Which was which? I forgot all the time.

The people at Adobe probably could have gotten more creative with the names given to parts of Premiere Elements. Thankfully, they picked a few words that worked and stuck with them. When you work on a movie project, for instance, that project is called a (drum roll, please) *project*. It doesn't get much simpler than that, folks. This chapter is all about projects in Adobe Premiere Elements. I show you how to create new projects, open existing projects, review and adjust the settings for your projects, and how to open projects from other versions of Adobe Premiere.

Starting New Projects

When you first launch Adobe Premiere Elements, you probably see a welcome screen similar to Figure 5-1. The screen gives you quick access to several important commands:

> ✔ **New Project:** No big surprises here! If you're starting a new project, click the New Project button.

> ✔ **Open Project:** Have to open an older project that doesn't appear in your list of recent projects? Click the Open Project button and browse to the desired project file.

✔ **Capture Video:** This button is almost exactly like the New Project button — when you click it you're prompted to create a new project. The difference is, when your new project is created the video capture window instantly appears. Adobe added this button to the Premiere Elements welcome screen because it (rightly) figured that capturing video is the first step that most people take when making a new movie. I show how to capture video in Chapter 6.

✔ **Recent Projects:** A list of projects that you have recently worked on appears next to Recent Projects. Click the name of a project to open it. If you've never worked on a project in Premiere Elements, your list of recent projects is probably empty.

✔ **Tutorial:** The tutorial button is for people who just bought Premiere Elements and feel completely lost. Fortunately, you have this book to guide you through the many exciting facets of Premiere Elements.

If you're new to Premiere Elements you may want to try out Adobe's tutorial. For another great Premiere Elements tutorial, check out "Making Your First Movie" in Chapter 1 of this book.

✔ **Setup:** Click this button to change the default project settings for your project. I show you how to choose settings later in this chapter.

✔ **Adobe:** Click the Adobe button in the lower-right corner of the welcome screen to visit Adobe's Web site for Premiere Elements. Adobe's Web site is a good place to check for updates or download plug-ins and other extras.

✔ **Exit:** Oops! If you opened Premiere Elements by mistake (don't feel bad, it happens to the best of us) or you changed your mind about working on a movie project right now, just click the Exit button in the lower-left corner to close the program. No harm, no foul.

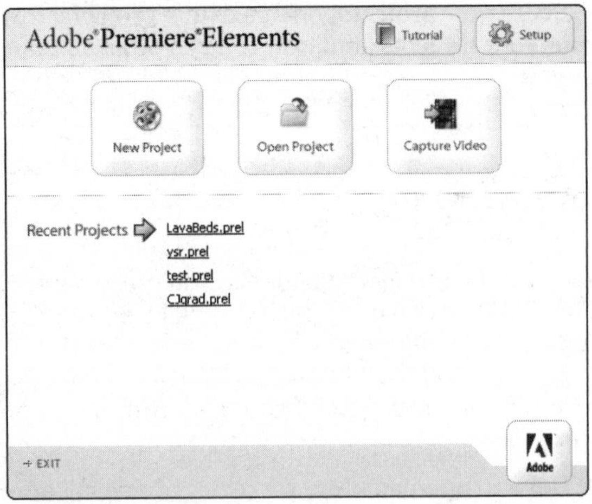

Adobe®Premiere®Elements   [Tutorial]   [⚙ Setup]

New Project   Open Project   Capture Video

Figure 5-1:
This friendly
welcome
screen
appears
whenever
you launch
Premiere
Elements.

Recent Projects ⇨ LavaBeds.prel
ysr.prel
test.prel
CJgrad.prel

← EXIT   Adobe

The easiest way to create a new project is to simply click the New Project button. The New Project dialog box appears, as shown in Figure 5-2. Give your project a name, and choose a location in which to save the project file. The default location for project files is a special Premiere Elements subfolder of your My Documents folder. Click OK to create the project.

Figure 5-2:
Give your
new project
a filename.

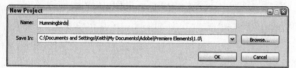

You probably know that video files can eat up a lot of hard drive space. In Chapter 2 I even recommend that you install a separate hard drive in your computer just for storing video. However, the project files for your movies don't have to be on that separate hard drive. You can keep project files in the My Documents folder if you wish, even if your C: drive doesn't have much free space. Project files are very small because they don't contain any actual audio or video; instead, project files contain pointers to the large audio and video files used by your projects.

Changing project settings

When you click the New Project button, a project is created using default settings. In some cases you may want to change the default settings. Two circumstances in which you should change the settings include

- ✔ **Widescreen:** Some camcorders can record video in widescreen format, which means that the image's aspect ratio is 16:9, giving it a more rectangular appearance (see Chapter 4 for more on aspect ratios). If you recorded widescreen video and want to produce your movie in widescreen format, you must choose a widescreen preset in Premiere Elements. Otherwise, your widescreen video images will be squished up into a 4:3 aspect ratio by the default project settings in Premiere Elements.

- ✔ **PAL or NTSC:** When you first install Premiere Elements, the setup program asks where you live and decides what your default video standard should be. As I describe in Chapter 4, if you live in North America your default video standard should be NTSC. But if you need to edit PAL footage from a PAL camcorder, you need to choose a PAL preset for your project.

The video standard and screen aspect ratio settings for a Premiere Elements project cannot be changed after the project has been created. Thus, it is important that if you need to work with widescreen video or a foreign video format, you must use a preset to start your project.

To create a custom project, follow these steps:

1. **In the Premiere Elements welcome screen, click Setup.**

   The Setup dialog box appears, as shown in Figure 5-3.

2. **Click a preset in the Available Presets list on the left side of the dialog box.**

   A description of the preset appears to the right. You'll notice that Standard presets each say "4:3 interlaced" under their respective descriptions. This means that the video images have a 4:3 aspect ratio and have interlaced video fields. Widescreen presets each say "16:9 interlaced" because they offer a 16:9 aspect ratio. Preset descriptions also list the geographical regions where the NTSC and PAL video standards are generally used.

3. **Select the preset that you want to use and click Save as Default.**

   The Setup dialog box closes and the Premiere Elements welcome screen appears.

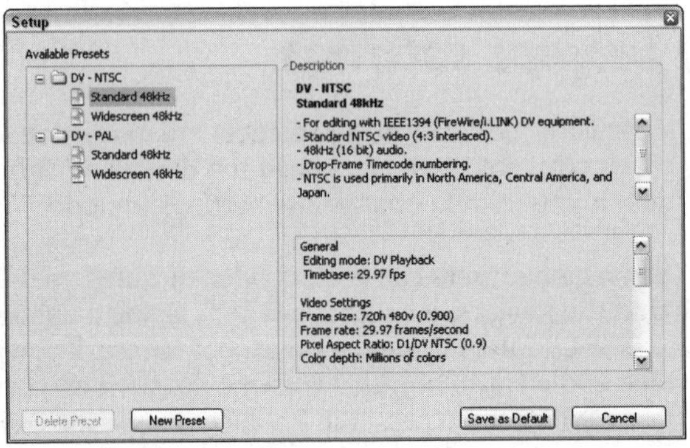

Figure 5-3: You can choose custom project settings here.

When you click New Project in the Premiere Elements welcome screen, a new project is created using the preset you chose as the new default.

Creating your own presets

Do you find that the default settings in Premiere Elements' presets don't quite suit your exact needs? For example, do you find that you always have to add a couple of video tracks to each project? If so, you can create a new preset with some custom settings:

1. **In the Setup dialog box, click New Preset.**

   The Custom Presets dialog box appears.

2. **Click a settings category on the left, and adjust settings for your new preset on the right.**

   The Custom Presets dialog box is almost identical to the Project Settings dialog box. I describe the settings available in the Project Settings dialog box later in this chapter.

3. **Click Save.**

   The Name Preset dialog box appears.

4. **Enter a name and description for your preset and then click OK.**

   Your custom preset now appears in the Setup dialog box under a folder named "Custom." You can set this preset as your default preset just as you would any other preset.

Opening an existing project

Premiere Elements gives you a lot of ways to open a project that you've been working on. Premiere Elements works like most other Windows programs, which means that you can use any of the following standard methods to open a project:

✔ Launch Premiere Elements and choose a project from the Recent Projects list in the Premiere Elements welcome screen (see Figure 5-1).

✔ In Premiere Elements, choose File⇨Open Recent Project⇨and choose a project from the submenu that appears.

✔ In Premiere Elements, choose File⇨Open Project and browse to the project file.

✔ Click the Open Project button (it looks like a folder) on the Premiere Elements toolbar.

✔ In Windows, choose Start⇨My Recent Documents and select a Premiere Elements project from the list (if the one you want appears in the list).

Reviewing and Changing Project Settings

When you click the New Project button to create a new project in Premiere Elements, default settings are automatically applied to your project. These settings describe the format of your movie project, specifying such things as the size of the video picture, the number of frames per second, and the default appearance of some of the Premiere Elements program windows when your project opens. Some of these settings can be changed, and some cannot.

To review project settings for a project that is open, choose Project⇨Project Settings⇨General. The Project Settings dialog box appears, as shown in Figure 5-4. The Project Settings dialog box includes four categories of options. Click a category in the list on the left to review options on the right. The options in each category are described in the following sections.

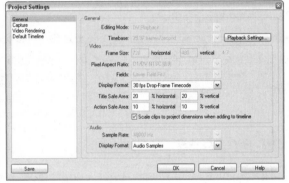

Figure 5-4:
Adjust
project
settings
here.

General settings

General project settings in the Project Settings dialog box determine the basic audio and video format for your project and other settings of a, well, *general* nature. Important General settings include

✔ **Playback Settings:** Click this button to open the DV Playback Settings dialog box, as shown in Figure 5-5. The settings in this dialog box control how your media plays on a DV device connected to your computer, such as a DV camcorder. Playback settings are divided into four basic categories:

• **Video Playback:** As you edit your video you will constantly be playing it back to see how your edits look. If you enable the Play Video on DV Hardware option, video from your project will play both in the Premiere Elements window and on your DV device, if the DV device happens to be connected to your computer and turned on. In Chapter 15, I explain the benefits of previewing video on an external monitor.

- **Audio Playback:** Just as you can play video, you also can play audio through your external DV device. If your external DV device is a simple camcorder, however, you are likely to find that playback from the camcorder's built-in speaker is pretty pathetic. I usually choose the Play Audio on Audio Hardware option, which means the audio plays through my computer's sound card and speakers.

- **Real-Time Playback:** Unlike many older editing programs, Adobe Premiere Elements allows you to preview special effects and other advanced edits in real time. You no longer have to wait seconds, minutes, or even hours while render files are created. Real-time previews require a very powerful computer, however, and you may find that your computer isn't able to play those effects on your computer screen and on an external DV device simultaneously. If you encounter jerky playback or other problems with real-time previews, choose the Playback on Desktop Only option.

- **Desktop Display Mode:** If you find that video playback quality on your computer is very poor, check your computer's documentation to see if the video display adapter supports Direct3D. If it doesn't, or you're not sure, choose the Use GDI option here. Does that improve video playback? If not, the problem is probably something else. See Chapter 2 for more on choosing a computer that works great with Adobe Premiere Elements.

Figure 5-5:
This dialog box controls how your project is played back on external hardware.

✔ **Display Format (under Video):** This menu controls how timecode is displayed while you work in your project. (See Chapter 4 for a detailed explanation of timecode.) If you're working with NTSC digital video, I strongly recommend that you keep the 30 fps Drop-Frame Timecode settings.

✔ **Title Safe Area:** As I describe in Chapter 14, most TVs cut off portions of a video image at the edges of the screen. This problem is called *overscan*. To make sure that titles don't get cut off by overscan, this setting enables Premiere Elements to temporarily display Title Safe margins in the Monitor window. The margins are just lines that appear over the video image to show which parts of the image may get cut off by TV overscan. Don't worry, the lines aren't permanent and won't show up when you export your video; they're just there to help you while you work. You can adjust the size of the Title Safe Area if you wish.

✔ **Action Safe Area:** This setting is similar to the Title Safe Area and is designed to ensure that important action on the screen isn't cut off by overscan. The Action Safe Area is usually a little closer to the edges of the screen than the Title Safe Area.

✔ **Scale clips to project dimensions when adding to timeline:** When this option is checked, clips that have a different size or shape are automatically scaled up or down to match the project settings. If the clip has a different aspect ratio — for example, you place a 16:9 widescreen clip in a 4:3 fullscreen sequence — the inserted clip is resized without affecting the aspect ratio. This creates a letterbox effect for the inserted clip.

✔ **Display Format (under Audio):** Control how audio is expressed on-screen by using this menu. I find that the Display Audio Samples option is easiest to work with.

A bunch of other settings are shown but unavailable in the General Project Settings. These settings include the Editing Mode, Frame Size, Timebase, Audio Sample Rate, and more. Adobe Premiere Pro allows you to change those settings, but in Premiere Elements the fields are provided merely for informational purposes.

Capture settings

Capture settings control the default source from which you will capture video. The choices available here depend on what hardware is installed on your system. DV/IEEE 1394 Capture is the only option available in the Capture Format menu because it is the only type of capture that Premiere Elements supports. If you want to capture video from another source, such as an analog capture card, you will need to capture it using other software. See Chapter 6 for more on capturing analog video.

If your camcorder (or other DV source) is currently connected to your FireWire port and is turned on, you will also see a DV Settings button in the Capture settings screen. Click this button to reveal the DV Capture Options dialog box (see Figure 5-6). With this dialog box, you can control whether audio or video plays on your computer during capture.

If you have a computer that is on the low end of the system requirements scale for Adobe Premiere Elements (see Chapter 2), you may want to remove the check marks next to both of the options under During Capture. This can prevent dropped frames (where some frames of video don't get captured, resulting in flawed playback quality) during video capture on slower computers.

Figure 5-6:
Uncheck
the bottom
two options
if you have a
slower
computer.

Video Rendering settings

As you edit a project and add transitions and effects to your video, Premiere Elements must apply your edits using a process called *rendering* (building preview files for video). When Premiere Elements renders your work, it creates temporary files on your hard drive that allow your edits to play properly. Video Rendering settings control the format of these *render files*. Premiere Elements doesn't allow you to change the format of render files, but that's not exactly a huge tragedy in my opinion because render files are only temporary files anyway.

The Video Rendering options also contain a check box called Optimize Stills. If your project has a lot of still images, choose this option to reduce rendering time. Optimizing stills could cause some playback problems, however. If you encounter glitches or other problems when the stills play, disable optimization.

Default Timeline settings

The Default Timeline settings control how Premiere Elements sets up your workspace when your project first opens. The Video Tracks option allows you to specify the default number of tracks in the Timeline when you first open the program (you'll find out how to use tracks in Chapter 8). The Default Timeline settings dialog box also lets you specify the default number of audio tracks.

Don't worry too much about the number of audio or video tracks you specify in the Default Timeline options. All these settings do is set how many tracks you start out with; you can easily add more tracks later if you want.

Saving a Project

Saving a project in Adobe Premiere Elements is pretty straightforward. Just choose File ⇨Save from the menu bar and you're done. As with most Windows programs, pressing Ctrl+S on your keyboard quickly saves your project. Or better yet, just click the toolbar button that looks like a floppy disk. That's the Save Project button. If you want to save the project with a different name, choose File⇨Save As, and if you want to save a backup copy of your project file, choose File⇨Save a Copy.

You probably could have figured out how to save a project on your own, so why this section? One of the interesting things about Premiere Elements is that although video files tend to be very large, project files are actually quite small. Indeed, the project file for a 30-minute movie may be smaller than 50 kilobytes (KB). This is because the project file doesn't contain any actual audio or video. But the project file *does* contain

- ✔ Edit points that you create
- ✔ Pointers to the original source clips
- ✔ Information about effects that are applied to the project
- ✔ The layout of Premiere Elements windows and palettes from the last time you worked on the project

Because Premiere Elements project files are so small, it's a good idea to frequently save backup copies of a project. This way, you can easily go back to an earlier version of your project if you don't like some of the changes that you've made. You can tell Premiere Elements to save a new version of your project automatically, while archiving old versions, every few minutes or so. I show you how to adjust auto-save settings in Chapter 3.

So where *are* all the big files? Not only do the source files for your audio and video take up a lot of disk space, but the process of rendering work for playback or output creates huge render files as well. All these big files live on your *scratch disk*. Your scratch disk might simply be your main hard drive, or you may have a hard drive dedicated solely to video storage. (See Chapter 3 for more information about scratch disks.) On a Windows XP system, the default scratch disk for audio and video that you capture is

```
C:\Documents and Settings\YourUserName\My Documents\Adobe\
              Premiere Elements\1.0\
```

Before you start deleting files from the scratch-disk folder, make sure you don't need those files anymore. If, for example, you delete a video file from the scratch disk, any projects that use that file become incomplete. And if you delete preview files, you have to spend long minutes (or hours) re-rendering those previews if you ever need them again.

Chapter 6

Capturing and Organizing Your Media

In This Chapter

▶ Capturing video to edit

▶ Importing video, audio and other media

▶ Using media-management tools to keep your multimedia organized

*I*f you have a word processing program like Microsoft Word, you can simply open the program and start typing to create a brand new file. Likewise, if you have a graphics program you can open the program and start drawing a new picture. But Adobe Premiere Elements is a little different, because you can't just open the program and create a movie from nothing. Before you can really put Premiere Elements to use, you must capture some video from your camcorder and import other kinds of media like still pictures or audio files.

This chapter guides you through the process of capturing audio and video using Premiere Elements, whether you're capturing video from your digital camcorder or importing it from another source. This chapter also shows you how to organize your media. Organization becomes increasingly important as you build a collection of dozens or even hundreds of video clips, audio clips, still images, and more.

Capturing Video

Most of my movies begin life as concepts floating around in the gray matter of my brain. A cartoonish light bulb appears overhead, and before I know it I'm shooting video, editing it in Premiere Elements, and sharing my grand production with anyone fortunate enough to be in the room at that moment. That "editing it in Premiere Elements" step can be broken down into three basic phases:

✔ Importing or capturing clips to Premiere Elements

✔ Editing clips together into a movie

✔ Exporting the finished movie for viewing on a computer or on television

Obviously, before you can edit your project, you need something to edit. You can get source material into Premiere Elements by importing existing files or by capturing media from an external source (usually a digital camcorder). The following sections show you how to capture audio and video in Premiere Elements. (I cover importing video files, still graphics, music, and other media later in the chapter.)

Getting your hardware set up

This is the part of the book where I'm supposed to show you a simple diagram of a camcorder connected to a computer by a cable. If only it were that easy! Preparing your computer for video capture can actually be complicated, and you must approach the process carefully if you want to capture video that looks great and is free of glitches.

The next couple of sections describe several ways to make your computer behave itself during capture. You can use these same techniques to increase performance during editing, rendering, and output too!

Priming your PC for editing in Premiere Elements

Most computers made in the last few years offer astounding memory and power capabilities at incredibly low prices. But digital video capture puts very high demands on computers, so high that even the latest-and-greatest PC powerhouse can be strained if it isn't set up properly. The processor, RAM, and hard drive must all be able to work fast to capture video without *dropping frames* (not capturing some frames of video because the computer can't keep up with the video stream) or causing other problems. As you prepare to capture video, follow these basic guidelines:

✔ **Close other applications.** Make sure that e-mail programs, MP3 players, Web browsers, and other programs are turned off. These programs use valuable resources that should be dedicated to video editing.

✔ **Defragment your hard drive.** Although some computer experts don't believe it's necessary anymore to regularly defragment hard drives on PCs running Windows XP, claiming that the need to constantly defrag is a relic of older, inferior versions of Windows, the experts who make these claims probably don't do much video editing. Almost nothing strains a hard drive like video editing, so it's critically important that your hard drive be optimized for best possible performance. To defragment your hard drive using Windows XP, choose Start➪All Programs➪ Accessories➪System Tools➪Disk Defragmenter.

✔ **Disable screen savers and fancy desktop appearance schemes.**

✔ **Adjust your power-management settings.** Use the Power Options icon in your Windows Control Panel to adjust power-management settings so that your monitor and hard disks won't shut down in the middle of a long capture job. I recommend that you use the "Always On" power scheme when capturing, editing, or exporting video.

✔ **Temporarily disable unneeded memory-resident items that are not directly related to video capture or vital operating system functions.** Unneeded items include antivirus programs, Internet programs, and system monitors. In Windows, memory-resident programs can often be disabled using System Tray icons, as shown in Figure 6-1. Right-click each icon and choose Close or Disable for as many of them as possible.

✔ **Take control of virtual memory.** If you do all of the things recommended in this list and still have capture problems, you may need to manually configure virtual memory in Windows XP. Virtual memory is hard drive space that Windows XP uses like system memory in the event that physical RAM runs short. The initial size of virtual memory should be twice the size of physical RAM or 1024 MB, whichever is less. Set the maximum size of virtual memory at four times the size of physical RAM.

Configuring virtual memory can be complicated, so before you adjust memory settings you should pick up a book that provides memory-management procedures for Windows XP. I recommend *50 Fast Windows XP Techniques* by Yours Truly (Wiley), which covers memory management, among other things.

Figure 6-1: Close as many System Tray icons as possible.

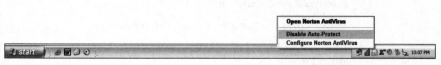

If your computer matches the system requirements I outline in Chapter 2, chances are you won't have any trouble capturing video. Controlling the way Windows manages memory is an advanced topic that I can't fully cover here. I strongly urge you to pick up a book that covers your operating system in detail, such as the aforementioned *50 Fast Windows XP Techniques*, *Windows XP For Dummies,* by Andy Rathbone, or *Windows XP Bible*, by Alan Simpson and Brian Underdahl (all published by Wiley).

Configuring DV capture hardware

Configuring your computer for video capture may not be easy, but at least configuring DV (digital video) hardware is. Along with high video quality, simplicity is one of the main strengths of DV. The most common way to capture video from a DV camcorder or video deck — and the only method directly supported by Premiere Elements — is to use a FireWire (IEEE-1394) port on your computer. You need to tell Premiere Elements what specific piece of DV hardware you're using, though. Follow these steps:

1. **Connect your DV camcorder or deck to your FireWire port using an appropriate cable.**

2. **Turn on the device.**

   If you're capturing video from a camcorder, turn it on to VTR (video tape recorder) mode, not camera mode. If Windows displays a message saying that a DV device was detected, choose Take No Action and click OK.

3. **Launch Premiere Elements.**

   If Premiere Elements is already open when you plug in the camcorder or other device, you may be forced to quit the program and restart it. This is a weird glitch, but it's sometimes the only way to ensure that Premiere Elements recognizes your DV hardware.

4. **Create a new project, as described in Chapter 5, or open an existing project.**

5. **In Premiere Elements, choose Edit⇨Preferences⇨Device Control.**

   The Preferences dialog box appears, displaying Device Control options.

6. **Click Options.**

   The DV Device Controls Options dialog box appears, as shown in Figure 6-2.

7. **Choose the appropriate video standard (NTSC or PAL) from the Video Standard drop-down list.**

   See Chapter 4 for more on video standards.

8. **Choose the brand of your camcorder or DV device from the Device Brand menu.**

9. **Choose a type or model number from the Device Type menu.**

   If your DV device doesn't seem to be listed, click Go Online for Device Info. Premiere Elements checks Adobe's online hardware database and updates as necessary.

10. **Choose a format from the Timecode Format menu.**

    The Timecode Format you use depends on the video standard you chose in Step 7. Generally speaking, NTSC-format video (used primarily in North America and Japan) uses Drop-Frame timecode, and everything else uses Non Drop-Frame timecode.

11. **If you see the word "Offline" next to the Check Status button, click Check Status to see if Premiere Elements can detect your camera.**

    If the program remains in Offline mode, make sure that the camera is turned on to VTR mode, the battery is charged, and your FireWire cable is properly connected.

12. **Click OK twice to close the dialog boxes when you're done.**

Figure 6-2:
Tell
Premiere
Elements
what kind of
camcorder
you have.

Troubleshooting DV configuration mishaps

If you got hung up on Step 11 in the previous section, there is probably something wrong with your DV device, your computer, or both. A big hint is whether you were able to locate the brand (Step 8) and model (Step 9) of your device.

If your device wasn't specifically listed, it simply may not be supported by Premiere Elements. Check the documentation that came with the device (or the manufacturer's Web site), and find out what the recommended procedure is for capturing video.

Adobe Premiere Elements is designed to work only with devices that use the DV format. This usually means a digital camcorder that uses the MiniDV or Digital8 tape format. Analog camcorders aren't compatible, and most DVD-based camcorders won't work with Premiere Elements either. If you want to use Premiere Elements to edit video from an unsupported camcorder, you'll need to use different software as described in the section "Capturing analog video" later in this chapter.

If your device was listed and still registers as offline, follow these troubleshooting tips:

  ✔ **Close and restart Adobe Premiere Elements.** While you're at it, go ahead and restart your computer, too. Make sure that the camcorder's power is turned on to VTR or Player mode *before* you restart Premiere Elements.

  ✔ **Double-check the physical connection to your computer.** Is the FireWire cable properly installed and secure? The small ends of FireWire cables, which connect to camcorders, are prone to slipping out; I have accidentally knocked mine loose while shifting things around on my desk.

✔ **Check to see whether any device drivers need to be installed.** The device manufacturer's documentation may provide information about this. Open the System icon in the Windows XP Control Panel, click the Hardware tab, and then click Device Manager. (DV devices are most often listed under Imaging Devices, as shown in Figure 6-3.) If the power is on, the device is connected, and you can't find a listing for the device in the Device Manager, then the software device driver may not be properly installed. Another possibility is that there is a physical problem with a component.

While you're in the Device Manager, make sure that your IEEE-1394 Bus Host Controller (your FireWire port) is OHCI-compliant and configured properly. A yellow exclamation mark means the item is *not* configured properly on your system. To correct this problem, consult the documentation for the digital device or access the technical support that for the FireWire controller card or your computer. If you're not sure whether your 1394 Bus Controller is OHCI-compliant, check the controller's documentation. Usually the Device Manager listing for your 1394 Bus Controller will say something about being OHCI-compliant, like the one shown in Figure 6-3. If you don't see "OHCI-compliant" in the name of the 1394 Bus Controller, it may not be compatible with Premiere Elements.

✔ **Be sure that the DV device recognizes the FireWire connection.** The display or viewfinder on your camcorder may show an indication such as "DV IN" if the connection is detected.

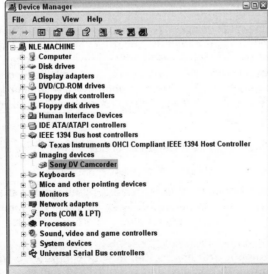

Figure 6-3:
Use the Device Manager to make sure your hardware is functioning properly with your computer.

Understanding device control

Remember that movie *Back to the Future*, where Christopher Lloyd's character controlled a toaster, a coffeepot, a dog-food dispenser, and various other appliances with his computer? Yes, it really has been two decades since that movie came out, and no, we still don't control our coffee machines or feed our pets with computers. However, thanks to a technology called *device control*, we can control camcorders and video decks with our computers. (It's a start.)

Device control is one of the most accurately named technologies to come along in quite some time. It allows you to control your devices using a computer. For example, if your DV camcorder is connected to your FireWire port, you can start playing the tape in that camcorder by clicking the Play button in the Adobe Premiere

Elements program screen. When you click Play in Premiere Elements, the program sends a "Play" command through the FireWire cable and the tape drive in your digital camcorder starts to play. Cool, huh?

Not only is device control cool, but it's also very useful. When you capture video, synchronization between the computer and the videotape player is crucial — Premiere Elements has to access and use the timecode recorded on the tape so that problems such as dropped frames can be instantly identified.

Okay, McFly, now that you understand device control, maybe you can explain how that DeLorean traveled through space and time.

Capturing digital video

Preparing to capture video (as explained in the previous sections in this chapter) is the most challenging part of the process. Actually capturing video is a snap.

If you have jumped ahead and plan to just plug in your camcorder and start capturing without much preparation, you may experience troubles — particularly dropped frames (the loss of essential video content). If you experience trouble during capture, check out the preceding pages of this chapter.

After your hardware is configured and ready for capture, follow these steps to identify video that you want to capture and then capture it:

1. **Connect all the necessary cables, turn on your hardware, launch Premiere Elements, start a new project, and perform all the other preparatory steps described earlier in this chapter.**

   If you want your captured video to be stored in a particular folder or hard drive, choose Edit⇨Preferences⇨Scratch Disks and adjust scratch disk settings as described in Chapter 3.

2. **In Premiere Elements, click the Capture button on the toolbar or choose File⇨Capture.**

   The Capture window appears.

3. **Click the Play button.**

   If your camcorder supports device control (see the sidebar nearby), the tape in the camera plays. If not, you will need to use the controls on the camcorder itself to control playback.

4. **Use the controls located beneath the viewer section of the Capture window to review the tape.**

   To identify the exact frame at which you want to start capturing, use the left and right arrow keys on your keyboard. Figure 6-4 details the various playback controls.

   The Step Back and Step Forward buttons in the Capture window enable you to move back or forward a single frame at a time.

   One of the handiest features in Adobe Premiere Elements is *scene detection*. As the name implies, scene detection detects each time the scene changes, which usually occurs when you pause the camcorder between shots. If you know that you want to capture an entire scene on the tape, click the Previous Scene button in the preview window. Premiere Elements automatically rewinds the tape to the beginning of the scene and automatically pauses the tape at the first frame of that scene. To detect the end of the scene, click Next Scene. Premiere plays the tape forward to the end of the scene and stops the tape on the first frame of the next scene.

5. **Type a name for your video clips in the Clip Name field.**

   The Clip Name field is located in the upper-left corner of the Capture window. Try to give a name that is somewhat descriptive so that you'll be able to identify the clip when you clean your hard drive a couple of years from now and you stumble upon the folder containing your old clips.

6. **Click the More button in the upper-right corner of the Capture window and make sure that the Scene Detect option is checked (refer to Figure 6-4).**

   With this option checked, Premiere Elements detects the breaks between scenes as you capture video and automatically creates separate video clips for each scene. Having separate clips for each scene can be very helpful later on, especially if you're editing a long video project.

   The More menu also includes options to capture just video or just audio. In most cases you will want to capture both, but if you only want to capture one or the other you can choose a different option here.

7. **When you find the spot where you want to start capturing, rewind the tape at least five seconds.**

   When you start to capture video, the camcorder's tape drive takes a moment to get up to full playback speed. This means that you may not capture the first couple of seconds of a video clip if you don't rewind just a bit. Rewinding the tape a few seconds ensures that this won't be a problem. Video pros call this *pre-rolling*, and you can measure five seconds by watching the timecode indicator in the lower-left corner of the capture window, as shown in Figure 6-4. The display format for timecode is `hours;minutes;seconds;frames`.

8. Click Capture.

Premiere Elements starts to capture video. The Capture window provides some useful information during capture. For example, if you have Scene Detect enabled, the Clip Name automatically changes incrementally as each new scene is detected. In Figure 6-5 you can see that I am currently capturing a clip named "Hummingbirds 11.avi." The number 11 was automatically inserted into the name by Premiere Elements because it is the eleventh scene that has been detected so far.

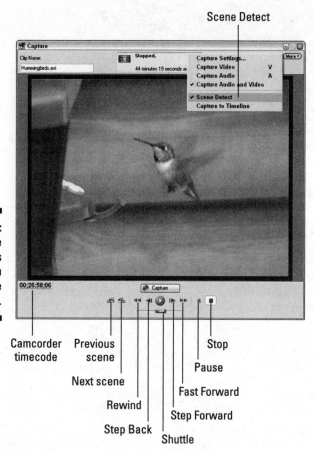

Figure 6-4:
Use these controls when you capture video.

The indicator at the top of the Capture window provides the current status of the capture. It also shows how much video can be captured in the remaining free space on your hard drive. In Figure 6-5 Premiere Elements estimates that my hard drive has enough free space to capture another eight hours, 14 minutes, and 38 seconds of video.

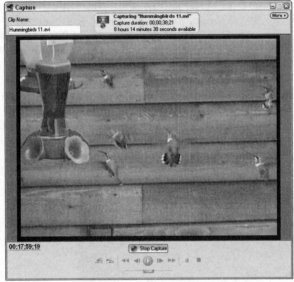

Figure 6-5:
Premiere
Elements
captures
video
from my
camcorder.

9. **When you've captured enough, click Stop Capture.**

   Premiere Elements stops capturing video and stops playback on your camcorder, if Device Control is supported. If playback doesn't stop automatically, press Stop on your playback device.

When the capture job is done, click Edit on the Premiere Elements toolbar (or choose Window⇨Workspace⇨Edit). The editing workspace loads, and you can locate your video clips in the Media window, as shown in Figure 6-6.

Scene detection works by using the clock that is built into your camcorder. Virtually any modern camcorder has a built-in clock and calendar; the date and time of each recording is recorded onto the videotape along with audio, video, and timecode. There is always a time gap between scenes (that gap may be seconds, minutes, hours, or even days). Premiere Elements can use those gaps to identify the beginning of each new scene.

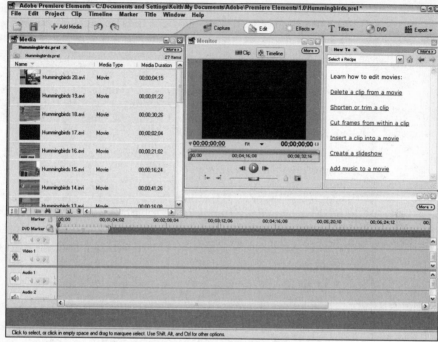

Figure 6-6:
Captured
clips are
organized in
the Media
window.

Dealing with dropped frames

Of all the capture problems you may encounter, by far the most common —
as well as the hardest to troubleshoot — is the infamous *dropped frame*. If
you're capturing NTSC video from a DV camcorder, for example, Premiere
Elements captures 29.97 frames per second (fps). If something in the computer gets choked up, it may miss, or *drop,* one or more frames during capture. Dropped frames create unacceptable quality problems for captured
clips in Premiere Elements because essential digital data is gone — poof.

But how do you know whether a frame has been dropped? Glad you asked. If
you finish capturing a clip and a Properties dialog box appears, that is a bad
sign. Review the statistics in this dialog box. If you see a line that says, `This
movie appears to have DROPPED FRAMES,` you almost certainly dropped
frames during capture — and that usually means you have to redo the capture.

Determining the cause of dropped frames can be challenging, but there are a
few possible causes:

  ✔ **A timecode break:** A timecode break on the tape can confuse Premiere
     Elements into thinking it dropped frames when it really didn't. Timecode
     breaks often occur when you reuse tapes by recording new footage
     over old footage you no longer want. When you reach the end of the

new recorded footage, the timecode may change and thus confuse Premiere Elements. If you have been reusing tapes — not something I recommend — you might want to consider this as a possible cause of dropped-frame reports.

✔ **A hard disk error:** The most common cause of dropped frames is that the hard disk can't maintain the required data rate during capture. Usually this isn't a problem on computers that match even the minimum system requirements for Adobe Premiere Elements, but it is not beyond the realm of possibility either.

If you have captured a clip that has dropped frames, right-click that clip in the Media window and choose Properties. For DV-format video, the Average Data Rate *should* read about 3.6MB per second. If the Average Data Rate is lower, or if the Date Rate/Sec graph is not a perfectly straight line (like the one in Figure 6-7), your hard drive couldn't keep up with the data stream. Common causes include

- Programs other than Adobe Premiere Elements were open during capture.

- The hard drive has not been defragmented recently.

- Another computer was trying to access the hard drive over your network (if you have one) during capture.

If your hard disk does appear to be the culprit, you can try to correct the problem by methodically re-preparing your computer for capture as described earlier in this chapter. Close unneeded programs, defragment your hard drive, buy more RAM, or consider upgrading your drives. If your capture card came with its own capture software, you may want to try using that software to capture, and then import the captured clips into Premiere Elements for editing.

✔ **A problem with the DV device:** If your Date Rate/Sec graph is a straight line but you still dropped frames, the cause is more likely your DV device or the tape.

 If you have a separate hard drive used primarily for video capture, and you have a network, make sure that the hard drive is not shared with your network. To check, right-click the drive in My Computer and choose the Sharing and Security option from the menu that appears. In the dialog box that appears, disable sharing if the drive is shared and click OK.

Capturing analog video

I don't think there's much question that Adobe Premiere Elements offers a far, far greater selection of features and movie creation capabilities than any other program in its price range. But this program is built down to a price, and one of the features that didn't make the transition from Premiere Pro down to Premiere Elements is the ability to capture analog video directly into the program.

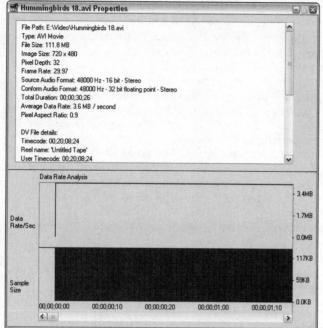

File Path: E:\Video\Hummingbirds 18.avi
Type: AVI Movie
File Size: 111.8 MB
Image Size: 720 x 480
Pixel Depth: 32
Frame Rate: 29.97
Source Audio Format: 48000 Hz - 16 bit - Stereo
Conform Audio Format: 48000 Hz - 32 bit floating point - Stereo
Total Duration: 00;00;30;26
Average Data Rate: 3.6 MB / second
Pixel Aspect Ratio: 0.9

DV File details:
Timecode: 00;20;08;24
Reel name: 'Untitled Tape'
User Timecode: 00;20;08;24

Figure 6-7:
This dialog
box helps
identify the
cause of
dropped
frames.

You may have analog video that's stored on an old VHS video tape, or video recorded using a Hi8 or VHS-C camcorder. Chances are you have more than a few analog video tapes lying around, and if you want to use any of that video in your Premiere Elements projects, you have two options:

✔ **Use a FireWire video converter.** A video converter is an external device that connects to your computer's FireWire or USB port. The converter has analog video connections so that you can connect it to any VCR or analog camcorder. As you play video from the analog device the video converter converts the video to digital video. Many mass-market video converters today only work with USB ports, but if you can get your hands on a converter that connects to your computer's FireWire port (such as the Canopus ADVC-55), you will find that it is much easier to use with Adobe Premiere Elements. Premiere Elements can capture video directly from a FireWire video converter, but not from a USB converter. FireWire video converters typically cost about $200. One of the nice things about an external video converter is that you don't have to crack open your computer's case and install fragile hardware. Just plug in a couple of cables and you're ready to go!

✔ **Use a third-party analog capture system.** Many companies offer affordable analog video capture cards. An analog capture card captures video from analog sources such as a VHS VCR or Hi8 camcorder. You cannot capture video directly from an analog capture card into Premiere Elements, so you should choose an analog capture card or USB video converter that comes with its own capture software. A good, affordable system — especially if you have many analog tapes you'd like to edit — is Pinnacle Studio AV/DV. For about $150 this package gives you a capture card that is both a FireWire card and an analog capture card. You can use the FireWire function of the card with Premiere Elements, but to capture analog video you must use the included Pinnacle Studio software, as shown in Figure 6-8. Studio doesn't offer nearly as much video-editing power as Premiere Elements, but you can use it to capture analog video and then export that video as an MPEG file, which can then be imported into Premiere Elements. For more on using Pinnacle Studio, see my book *Digital Video For Dummies,* 3rd Edition (Wiley).

The best solution for capturing analog video is to use a FireWire video converter. To capture video with a FireWire video converter

1. **Connect the converter to your computer's FireWire port.**

2. **Connect your VCR or analog camcorder to the converter.**

3. **Capture video using the procedure described earlier in this chapter for capturing digital video in Premiere Elements.**

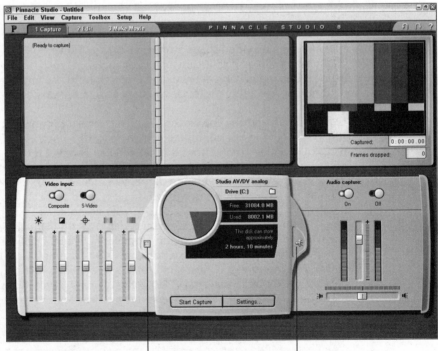

Figure 6-8:
Use third-party software such as Pinnacle Studio to capture analog video.

Open Video Input control panel   Open Audio Capture control panel

One problem with capturing analog footage, of course, is that you won't be able to take advantage of device control. That means you'll have to juggle your hands as you press the Play button on your VCR and click Capture in the Premiere Elements Capture window. Also, scene detection won't work when capturing from a video converter. For more information on specific video converters, check out Chapter 21.

Importing Audio, Video, and other Media

There is no doubt in my mind that all the video you record with your camcorder is indescribably perfect just the way it is. But, if I may be so bold, wouldn't it be *even better* if you enhanced it a bit with some music, or perhaps some illustrative stills? Good, I'm glad you agree. Premiere Elements can import all kinds of media, even video produced by other applications. Supported formats include

- AI: Adobe Illustrator graphic
- AIFF: Audio Interchange File Format
- AVI: Audio/Video Interleave, also called Video for Windows; Premiere Elements saves captured video in this format
- BMP: Bitmap still graphic
- DV: Digital video format
- EPS: Encapsulated PostScript file
- FLM: FilmStrip
- GIF: Graphics Interchange Format image
- ICO: Windows icon file
- JPEG: Joint Photographic Experts Group image
- MPEG: Motion Picture Experts Group movie
- MP3: MPEG Layer-3 audio
- MOV: QuickTime movie
- PICT: Macintosh image format
- PCX: PC Paintbrush image
- PNG: Portable Network Graphics
- PRTL: Adobe Title Designer file
- PSD: Adobe Photoshop document
- TGA: Targa bitmap graphic
- TIFF: Tagged Image File Format

    ✔ WAV: Windows sound format

    ✔ WMA: Windows Media Audio

    ✔ WMV: Windows Media Video

Any of the formats in this list can be imported into Premiere Elements and used in your projects. Of all these formats, you may find that still graphics and audio files are among the most common. In the following sections, I show you how to import audio from an audio CD or another source and how to prepare still graphics for use in Premiere Elements. After you've done that, you can move to the last section, which describes how to actually import files (stills or not).

Importing files of any kind (whether they're still, video, or audio files) that don't belong to you can get you in hot water if you don't have express permission from the originator or owner of the files. I'm no copyright expert, so the best I can do is advise you that if you have any questions about whether you're using files inappropriately, err on the side of caution. For general information about copyright and the Internet, check out www.whatiscopyright. org. For more specific information about technology law in the U.S., check out www.bitlaw.com.

Capturing audio clips

With Premiere Elements you can capture audio all by itself if you want — whether it's just the audio recorded on your videotape, or music from an audio CD in your CD-ROM drive.

If you want to use audio from an audio CD, first record the track(s) you want onto your hard drive, using third-party recording software. Adobe Premiere Elements can import MP3 files, as well as Windows Media Audio (WMA) files. Being able to import WMA files is handy because you can record audio from almost any CD to your hard disk in WMA format using Windows Media Player. To copy music using Windows Media Player, follow these steps:

1. **Place an Audio CD in your CD-ROM drive and launch Windows Media Player by choosing Start⇨All Programs⇨Windows Media Player.**

2. **In Windows Media Player, click Copy from CD.**

    After a few moments, a list of tracks on the current audio CD appears. Usually Windows Media Player automatically identifies the album, songs, and artist using an online music database, but if your musical selections are more obscure Media Player displays the songs as Unknown. You can manually enter song names, the name of the artist, and other information about the song if you wish.

3. **To manually enter a song or artist name, click the field, wait for a second, and then click again. Type a name.**

   Entering a descriptive name and artist name for the song helps you find it later.

4. **Use the playback controls to play the tracks and identify songs that you want to copy.**

5. **Place check marks next to each song that you want to copy.**

6. **Click Copy Music at the top of the Windows Media Player window.**

   Windows Media Player shows the copying in progress. When the desired files are copied to your hard disk (Windows Media Player displays the message, `Copied to Library`), go ahead and close Windows Media Player.

7. **In Premiere Elements, choose File➪Import.**

8. **Browse to the folder containing the song that you copied.**

   Unless you've changed Windows Media Player's default settings, the copied songs appear in the My Music folder of your My Documents folder. Folders are automatically created to organize music by artist and album.

9. **Choose the song you want to import and click Open.**

   The imported song now appears in your Media window.

Preparing still images for your movie

You're probably pretty accustomed to seeing images that have a 4:3 aspect ratio. Your computer's monitor most likely has a 4:3 aspect ratio. Most still photos that you take have a 4:3 aspect ratio. And of course, most TVs have a 4:3 aspect ratio. So dropping a 4:3 digital photo into a DV-based video project should be easy, right? Not really. That's because the smallest element of any digital image, the *pixel,* is shaped like a tiny rectangle in NTSC or PAL video images, whereas pixels in still images are usually square.

If you don't know much about aspect ratios and pixels, I suggest that you spend some time in Chapter 4. There you can find some important fundamentals about working with video, including the important differences between screen and pixel aspect ratios.

Determining the correct size for still images

Before you insert a still image into a video project, you must consider pixel aspect ratio. Digital graphics like JPEG and TIFF files usually have square pixels; video usually has rectangular pixels. The frame size of NTSC video is usually 720 x 480 pixels. Do the math and you'll find that this does *not* work out to 4:3 (it's actually 3:2). However, it still *appears* to have a 4:3 aspect ratio because NTSC video pixels are slightly taller than they are wide.

To account for this difference, you have to adjust the image size of your still photos before you import them into Premiere Elements. Otherwise, the still graphics that you insert may appear squished or stretched. Here are some numbers you should jot down if you plan to insert still images into your movies:

- ✔ For output to NTSC video (in North America, Japan, and the Philippines), your images should be 720 x 534 pixels *before* importing them into Premiere Elements.

- ✔ For PAL video (in Western Europe, Australia, Southeast Asia, and South America), the images should be 768 x 576 pixels *before* you import.

Adjusting the size of still images

When you determine the proper size for still images, you must resize the images in a graphics program before importing them into Premiere Elements. To adjust the size of an image using Adobe Photoshop Elements, follow these steps:

1. **Open the image and save it as a Photoshop document (PSD) before performing any edits.**

   Photoshop documents can be imported directly into Premiere Elements.

2. **In Photoshop, choose Image⇨Resize⇨Image Size.**

   The Image Size dialog box appears.

3. **In the Image Size dialog box, remove the check mark next to Constrain Proportions, as shown in Figure 6-9.**

4. **In the Pixel Dimensions section of the Image Size dialog box, choose Pixels from the drop-down menus and then enter the appropriate dimensions:**

   - 720 (NTSC) or 768 (PAL) in the Width field
   - 534 (NTSC) or 576 (PAL) in the Height field

   Don't concern yourself with the Document Size section. You only use that when printing still graphics out on paper.

5. **Click OK, and then save and close the image.**

   After you click OK in the Image Size dialog box, your still image probably looks somewhat distorted. Don't worry; after the image is imported into an NTSC or PAL video program, it will look right. Trust me.

Figure 6-9:
Adjust
the size of
your still in
Photoshop
before
importing
it into a
video project.

Importing stills and other media

Importing still graphics, audio files, and other neat things into Premiere Elements is really easy. If you're importing a still image into a project that is based on NTSC or PAL video, first adjust the image size as described in the previous section. Then follow these steps:

1. **In Premiere Elements, choose File⇨Add Media.**

   You can also import an entire folder if you wish, or a Premiere Elements project.

2. **Browse to the file that you want to import.**

   Note that All Supported Media is selected in the Files of Type menu by default. If you want to search for files of only a certain type, choose the desired type from this menu.

3. **Click Open.**

   The imported file appears in your Media window.

If the file you want to import doesn't show up in the Add Media window — and you're certain that you're looking in the correct folder — the file may be of a type that isn't supported by Premiere Elements. (To double-check, see my list of supported file types earlier in this chapter.)

Keeping Your Media Organized

When most people think of Adobe Premiere Elements, they think mainly of video, but this is truly a multimedia-rich program. You'll no doubt work with many different kinds of media in Premiere Elements — audio, video, still graphics, and even text. You'll wind up using files from all over your computer, and possibly even your network. Keeping track of all this media stuff can be a challenge, but Premiere Elements can help. This section shows you how to manage your media.

Managing scratch disk space

Premiere Elements does its best to make efficient use of your disk space. For example, suppose you import a video clip into three different projects. Does this mean you have three separate copies of that clip on your hard drive? No, in all three projects Premiere Elements points to the same source file. Although this is an efficient way to do business, it also means you must be careful about moving, deleting, or renaming source files. If you move, delete, or rename a source file, any projects that point to that source file can't access it. Inaccessible files are also called *offline* files in Premiere Elements.

Where does Premiere Elements store all your source files? They are stored on your scratch disk, which can be a separate hard drive or a specific folder on your main hard drive. To determine the location of your scratch disk, choose Edit➪Preferences➪Scratch Disks. The Scratch Disks section of the Preferences dialog box appears as shown in Figure 6-10. Paths are given for your scratch disks for captures and previews for both audio and video, as well as conformed audio.

Conformed audio files are basically copies of audio files that have been conformed to your project, incorporating your various edits. (For more on working with audio, see Chapter 13.)

Using Scratch Disk information in the Preferences dialog box, you can browse your hard drive (using Windows Explorer or My Computer) and identify large source files that are taking up a lot of disk space. In particular, check for the following:

✔ **Adobe Premiere Elements Auto-Save folder:** This folder is usually located in the My Documents folder, and not necessarily in the same place as your scratch disks. The folder contains archived back-up copies of project files (.PREL). These usually don't take up much space, but you can safely delete archives for older projects you're done with. Before deleting archives, make sure that the original project files are backed up on a CD-R or other safe place, of course.

✔ **Adobe Premiere Elements Preview Files folder:** This folder is located in your scratch disk folder for Video Previews. Rendered preview files are stored here, subdivided into folders labeled by project as shown in Figure 6-11. If you see a folder for an old project that you're not working on anymore, you can probably save a lot of disk space by deleting that folder. Just keep in mind that if you ever want to work on that project again, you may have to sit through the rendering process all over again while the preview files are recreated.

✔ **Capture files:** Captured media ends up as files on your scratch disk. Some of those files, particularly video files, take up a lot of space, as shown in Figure 6-12. You can save a lot of that space by deleting old video files, but make absolutely certain that none of the files you delete are needed by current projects. Projects always link back to the original source file, so if you delete a source file, any projects that used it now have offline media. Make sure that you still have the original source tapes for those media in a safe place. If in doubt, burn copies of the files to a CD or DVD before you delete them.

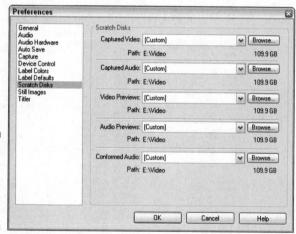

Figure 6-10:
Check your scratch disk locations here.

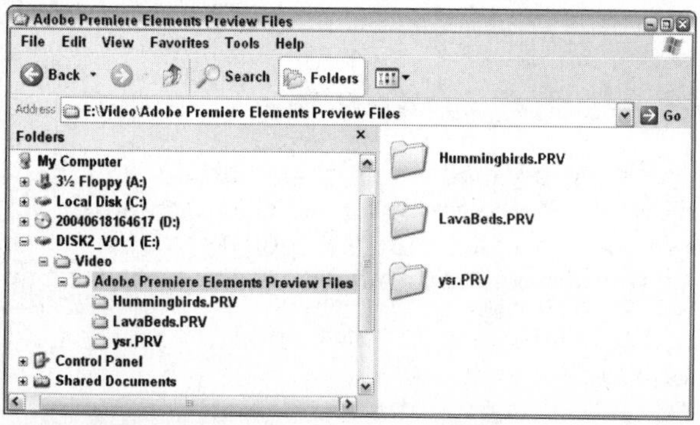

Figure 6-11:
You can safely delete preview file folders for older, completed projects.

When viewing the contents of a folder in Windows Explorer or My Computer, click View➪Details. Details view provides a more informative view of your files, as shown in Figure 6-12. In Details view you can easily see the size of each file.

✔ **Conformed Audio Files folder:** Some of the conformed audio files in this folder get surprisingly big. If you see any files in here that you know are for old projects, you can delete them. Deleting conformed audio doesn't have any affect on the original source file for the audio. Conformed audio files are discussed in Chapter 13.

✔ **Project files:** These files don't use up much space, and I generally recommend against deleting them. The default location for Project files is in the `Adobe\Premiere Elements\1.0` subfolder of your My Documents folder.

For more on using and configuring scratch disks, see Chapter 3.

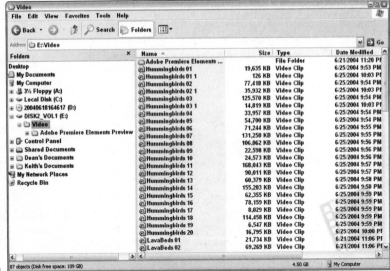

Figure 6-12: Video source files can take up a lot of hard drive space.

Using the Media window

As you work in a project, any media that you import or capture is added to your Media window. The Media window is usually pretty small, but if you expand the window, as shown in Figure 6-13, you'll see a lot more information about your clips. (You can expand the Media window by clicking-and-dragging on the lower-right corner of the window.) Key functions you can perform in the Media window include:

- ✔ **Use folders to organize material.** Folders in the Media window work just like folders on your hard drive. You can create your own folders by clicking the Folder button at the bottom of the Media window. Click-and-drag items to move them into bins.

- ✔ **Customize the view of the Media window.** Click More⇨View⇨Preview Area to expose the Preview area as shown in Figure 6-13. Choose either List or Icon view from the View menu to change the way items are shown in the Media window. Figure 6-14 shows Icon view, which I sometimes use to better identify the contents of each clip.

- ✔ **Click New Item to quickly create a title, black video, bars and tone, color matte, or counting leader.**

  These are elements that you often add to the beginning of end of a video for technical purposes. I explain how to use black video, bars and tone, color mattes, and counting leaders in Chapter 15.

- ✔ **Add comments to your video clips.** In Figure 6-13 you can see that I've added comments to a couple of my video clips. For example, next to the clip `Hummingbirds 14.avi` I've added the comment, `Cole watching birds`. I may find this information useful later.

- ✔ **In List view, click a column head to sort clips by that heading.**

The Preview area is, in my opinion, one of the most useful features of the Media window, but it isn't displayed by default. As describe above, click More⇨View⇨Preview Area to reveal it. In the Preview area you can click Play to preview a clip, as well as view other details about the clip.

Setting a new poster frame

Figure 6-14 shows the Media window in Icon view. Icon view can help you better visualize the contents of each clip. To change the size of the icon for each clip, click More⇨Thumbnails and choose Small, Medium, or Large from the submenu that appears.

The picture shown on the icon for each video clip is called the *poster* frame, and usually the poster frame is simply the first frame of the clip. Sometimes, however, you may want to use a poster frame from later in the clip. To set a new poster frame for a clip:

1. **Click a clip once in the Media window.**

   The clip becomes active in the Preview area in the upper left corner of the Media window.

2. **Click Play next to the preview area to start playing the clip.**

   The Play button turns into the Stop button when the clip starts to play.

Set Poster Frame

Preview area

More menu

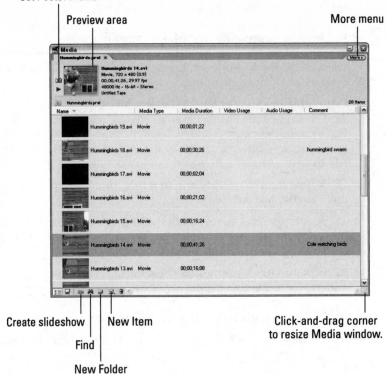

Create slideshow | New Item

Click-and-drag corner
to resize Media window.

Find

New Folder

3. **Click Stop when you see the frame that you want to use as the new poster frame.**

You need to be nimble with the mouse button because the Media window's little Preview area doesn't let you move back and forth through a clip frame by frame.

4. **When the desired frame appears in the Preview area, click the Poster Frame button.**

The Poster Frame button is located just above the Play button. The new poster frame now appears on the clip when you view it in Icon view.

Creating a slideshow

The Premiere Elements Media window includes a new button called the Create Slideshow button. When you select a bunch of items in the Media window and click Create Slideshow, all of the selected items are automatically placed in the Premiere Elements Timeline. You may find this useful for two reasons:

✔ If you just want to quickly place a bunch of clips in the Timeline without spending a lot of time setting *in points* and *out points* (see Chapter 7) or choosing *unique transitions* (see Chapter 9), just select the clips you want to use in the Media window and click Create Slideshow. The selected clips are automatically placed in the Timeline. If you've ever used Adobe Premiere Pro, you might recognize the Create Slideshow button as just a renamed "Automate to Timeline" button.

✔ If you have a bunch of still images that you want to set to music, select the stills in the Media window and click Create Slideshow. The name of this button suggests that still-image slideshows are primarily what Adobe had in mind for this feature. In Chapter 15 I show you how to use this feature in conjunction with Adobe Photoshop Elements to create a slideshow DVD.

To create a slideshow, follow these steps:

1. **Ctrl+click each item in the Media window that you want to use in the slideshow.**

   To save time, you can select the items in the order in which you want them to appear in the slideshow.

2. **When all of the items are selected, click the Create Slideshow button at the bottom of the Media window.**

Figure 6-14:
Icon view
can help
you better
visualize the
contents of
each clip.

The Create Slideshow dialog box appears. Settings to review include

- **Ordering:** Choose Selection Order from this menu if you followed the tip in Step 1 so that items are placed in the Timeline in the order in which you selected them in the Media window. Otherwise just choose Sort Order to use clips in the order in which they appear in the Media window.

- **Media:** If you selected video clips choose the Take Video Only option if you plan to set the slideshow to music and you don't want to use the audio from those video clips.

- **Image Duration:** Specify how long you want each still image to appear.

- **Apply Default Transition:** If you want to use the default transition (usually a nice cross-dissolve) between each clip, place a check mark next to this option. See Chapter 9 for more on working with transitions and setting a default transition.

- **Transition Duration:** If you are using a default transition between each image, specify the duration for each transition here. Because NTSC video has 29.97 frames per second, a duration of 30 frames means that the transition will take approximately one second from start to finish. You'll have to experiment with transition durations a bit to get a result that you like.

3. **Click OK when you are done reviewing slideshow settings.**

Premiere Elements automatically places the selected items in the Timeline, thus creating your slideshow.

Chapter 7

Trimming and Editing Video Clips

• •

• •

*L*ike plays, movies are made up of scenes that are put together in a certain order so that the show makes sense and is enjoyable to watch. Before you can turn scenes into a movie in Premiere Elements, you need to identify just what those scenes will be. Each scene — called a *clip* in video-editing parlance — must be previewed both for video and audio content. Then you decide which portions of a clip you want to use, and in some cases you may want to leave virtual sticky-notes on some scenes to remind yourself later of an important spot in the scene.

After you've captured some video as described in Chapter 6, this chapter leads you through the next steps — previewing your video clips, selecting portions of clips to use in projects, and performing other tasks to make your clips ready for use in a movie project.

Reviewing Your Clips

Clips that you capture or import into Premiere Elements all wind up in the Media window (see Chapter 6 for more on capturing and importing clips). Clips come in many flavors, from video to audio, still graphics, titles, color mattes, and black video. And that's just the tip of the iceberg.

You can generate any of the last five items in this list by clicking the New Item button at the bottom of the Media window. (For more on working with titles, see Chapter 14. See Chapter 15 for information on when and how to use bars and tone, black video, and counting leaders.)

Getting the details on your clips

You can learn a lot about a clip in the Media window. To view a brief summary, click a clip. The clip is loaded into the preview area in the upper-left corner of the Media window, as shown in Figure 7-1. You'll also see a summary of the clip's length, frame size, and audio quality as appropriate. This summary appears just to the right of the preview window.

If the preview area doesn't appear at the top of your Media window, click the More button in the upper-right corner of the Media window and choose View⇨ Preview Area. The Preview area appears as shown in Figure 7-1.

When you review the details of a clip, there are several things you should look at:

- **Frame size:** Does the frame size of the video clip or still image match your project? Clips that you imported into Premiere Elements may not have the same frame size as clips that you captured from your digital camcorder. For example, if you imported a clip with the frame size 320 x 240, the image quality of that clip may appear blocky and pixilated when it's inserted into a project that consists mainly of DV-format video.

- **Pixel aspect ratio:** Next to the frame size is a number in parentheses. This number is the pixel aspect ratio. (I explain pixel aspect ratios in Chapter 4.) A pixel aspect ratio of 1.0 means that the pixels are square. A number above or below 1.0 indicates rectangular pixels. NTSC video usually has a pixel aspect ratio of 0.9, and PAL footage usually has a pixel aspect ratio of 1.067.

  If the pixel aspect ratios for your still images and video don't match up, the still images might appear slightly squished when you export your movie. To avoid this hazard, resize still images before you import them into your project. See Chapter 6 for the exact steps and sizes to use when preparing still images for use in a video project. Resized stills will still show a 1.0 pixel aspect ratio in the Premiere Elements Media window, but if you resize the images as described in Chapter 6, these stills will appear properly in the movie.

- **Frame rate:** Does the frame rate for all of your video clips match? If you mix frame rates in a single project, jerky video may be the sad result.

  If you have a clip with a frame rate that doesn't match the rest of your video, import that clip into a new Premiere Elements project. Place the clip in the Timeline and export it as an MPEG or AVI file with a frame rate that matches your original project. Then import the new clip into your original project.

- **Audio quality:** The audio sample rate is listed, as well as whether the clip is stereo or mono. I show you how to work with audio in Chapter 13.

Frame size and pixel aspect ratio

Play

Clip length and frame rate

Set Poster Frame

Audio quality

Figure 7-1:
The Media
window can
tell you a
lot about
your clips.

If you require even more information about a clip, right-click it in the Media window and choose Properties from the menu that appears. A Properties dialog box opens, containing more detailed information than you likely need to know about the clip. These details can help you troubleshoot problems that you may be experiencing with that clip.

Playing clips in the Monitor window

When you select a clip in the Media window, a preview of it appears in the tiny preview window in the upper-left corner. If the clip is audio or video, you can play it by clicking the Play button just to the left of the preview window. You can move to specific parts of the clip using the slider underneath the preview window.

As you can see, the clip previews provided in the Media window are pretty small. If you get tired of squinting, you may want to load the clip into the Monitor window to preview it. Besides giving you a bigger window in which to preview the clip, the Monitor is also where you will pare the clip down to just the portion you want to use in your movie. Follow these steps to play your clip in the Monitor window:

1. **Switch to the Editing workspace mode by choosing Window⇨ Workspace⇨Editing.**

   Or you can click the Edit button on the Premiere Elements toolbar.

   The Monitor window appears, if it wasn't already open.

2. **Click-and-drag a clip from the Media window and drop it in the Monitor window.**

   The clip appears in the Monitor window, as shown in Figure 7-2.

3. **Use the playback controls at the bottom of the Monitor window (as in Figure 7-3) to preview the clip.**

Figure 7-2:
A clip from the Media window has been loaded into the Monitor.

The Monitor window offers buttons and tools for controlling playback and various other editing actions. Some of the controls shown in Figure 7-3 are described throughout this chapter and in Chapter 8.

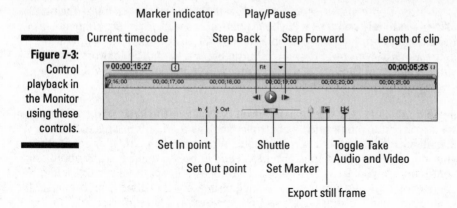

Figure 7-3:
Control
playback in
the Monitor
using these
controls.

Take a close look at the playback controls right now by loading a clip into the Monitor and clicking the Play button. Somewhere in the middle of the clip, click the Pause button (the Play button turns into the Pause button after you click Play). Now you can play with some controls that help you identify specific frames in a clip:

✔ **Click the Step Forward button.** The clip moves forward by one frame. You can also press the right-arrow key on your keyboard to move forward one frame at a time.

✔ **Click the Step Back button.** The clip moves back a frame. You can also control the Step Back function by pressing the left-arrow key.

✔ **If you want to remember a certain spot in the clip, move to the spot and click the Set Marker button.** This places a marker at the current location in the clip. A marker is kind of like a virtual sticky-note. I show you more about using markers later in this chapter.

✔ **Place the mouse pointer directly on the Shuttle control.** Click-and-drag the control to the right. Notice that as you drag the Shuttle farther to the right, the clip advances forward at an increasing rate. Drag the Shuttle left to play the clip backward. Let go of the Shuttle by releasing the mouse button. The Shuttle snaps back to the middle and the clip stops playing. Shuttle controls have been common on professional video equipment for years because they provide quick yet precise control over playback.

✔ **As a clip plays, notice that a pointed indicator moves to show you your current location in a clip.** This pointed indicator is often called the CTI, short for *current time indicator*. Another common name for the CTI is *playhead*.

In addition to the visible Monitor window controls, Adobe Premiere Elements allows you to rely heavily on keyboard buttons as well. Premiere Elements uses the industry-standard key combination of J-K-L to control shuttle operation in the Monitor window. Press **J** to shuttle back, **L** to shuttle forward, and **K** to stop. Notice that the J, K, and L keys are conveniently located right next to each other on your keyboard.

If you don't like using the mouse-button controls *or* the keyboard, you may want to invest in a multimedia controller such as the Contour SpaceShuttle A/V, manufactured by Contour A/V Solutions. A multimedia controller connects to your computer and has special buttons and knobs to make moving about and controlling playback easier. The SpaceShuttle A/V's ergonomic design and dial control for shuttling and frame advance ultimately save time, frustration, and wrist movement. I discuss controls from Contour A/V Solutions in Chapter 21.

Working with Clip Markers

In a perfect universe, there would be peace on Earth, we'd all be drinking free Bubble-Up and eating rainbow stew, and every clip of video would start and end at exactly the right time. Alas, this world is not quite perfect just yet. But at least with video you can provide the illusion of perfection by using *In points* and *Out points*. In and Out points are critical in video editing because they let you control which portions of a clip appear in the video program and which portions don't appear. The following sections serve up steps for perfecting your clips by using In points, Out points, and other markers.

Setting In and Out points

Setting In points and Out points on a clip is pretty easy, and Premiere Elements gives you a couple of different methods to choose from. I strongly recommend that you set In and Out points on a clip *before* you insert it into your project's Timeline. For this process, I recommend using the Editing workspace (Window⇨Workspace⇨Editing).

The In point is the spot where the clip begins playing in the project. In general, you should not set the In point at the very beginning of the clip if you can avoid it. The main reason for not doing so is to facilitate transitions between clips. *Transitions* — described in Chapter 9 — are ways to smooth our or dress up the changes between scenes in a movie. Suppose (for example) you want to apply a Cross Dissolve transition to the beginning of a clip, and you set it to last for one second — during this one-second period, the previous clip fades out and the new clip fades in. By default, Premiere Elements facilitates such a transition by using the "extra" material just beyond the In and Out points of the adjacent clips.

An Out point is, of course, the spot where you want to stop using the clip. As with In points, Out points should not be set at the very end of a clip if you can possibly avoid it.

Keep in mind that transitions need leeway, so try not to set In points and Out points too close to the beginning or end of a clip.

After you have used the Monitor controls to position the CTI where you want to set an In point or Out point, Premiere Elements provides a couple of methods for setting these points (refer to Figure 7-3 for control locations):

 ✔ In the Monitor, click the Set In Point or Set Out Point buttons.

 ✔ Press **I** (In point) or **O** (Out point) on your keyboard.

After you've marked In and Out points on a clip, the duration of your marked clip portion appears to the upper-right of the Monitor window controls. As you can see in Figure 7-4, I have set In and Out points to select exactly five seconds of this clip.

Figure 7-4:
Mark In and Out points before editing clips into the Timeline.

CTI   Duration of marked clip

Using clip markers

In points and Out points usually get all the attention in books like this, but you can use other markers in your clips as well. Markers come in handy because they can serve as virtual sticky-notes, marking specific events or spots in a clip. To set a marker at the current position in the clip, right-click the CTI (refer to Figure 7-4) and choose Set Clip Marker from the menu that appears. A sub-menu offering several different kinds of markers appears. Different kinds of markers include

- ✓ **In, Out:** These are your basic In points and Out points, as described in the previous section.

- ✓ **Video In/Out, Audio In/Out:** Use these if you want audio and video to go in or out at separate points. Figure 7-5 shows that I edited a clip into the Timeline so that the Audio In point starts well before the Video In point. The Audio Out point also extends well past the Video Out point. You might use this technique to insert an audio track (or narration that explains the scene), while several different video images appear on-screen.

- ✓ **Unnumbered:** If you want to mark only a single spot in the clip, add an unnumbered marker. I like to use these to mark the location of visual events, which I later match with an audio soundtrack.

- ✓ **Next Available Numbered, Other Numbered:** Use numbered markers if you want to set more than one marker in the same clip. Choose Next Available Numbered if you just want Premiere Elements to select a number automatically. For example, if you've already set markers named `Marker 1` and `Marker 2`, Premiere Elements uses the name `Marker 3` when you choose Next Available Numbered. Choose Other Numbered if you want to set a specific number yourself.

Video In point   Video Out point

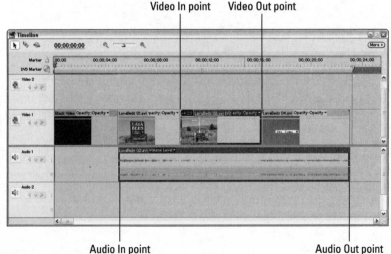

Figure 7-5: You can set separate In and Out points for audio and video.

Audio In point   Audio Out point

When you right-click the CTI, you see two other options in addition to the Set Clip Marker. You can choose Go to Clip Marker or Clear Clip Marker. Choose Go to Clip Marker to open a submenu of markers that you have already set. Click one of the markers to jump directly to that location.

If you want to delete a marker, right-click the CTI and choose Clear Clip Marker. Select an option from the submenu that appears. As you can see, you can clear the current marker, all markers, In points and Out points, or specific numbered markers.

Changing the Speed and Duration of Clips

What *is* a clip, really? When you see a list of clips in the Media window, you're looking at references to actual files on your hard disk. When you set markers on clips or perform edits, you're actually editing the references in Premiere Elements, and not the original source file. This is important because it leaves the original source file undisturbed for future use. It also saves storage space because you don't have multiple copies of the same material all over your hard drive.

You can even duplicate clips without eating up extra disk space. Duplicate clips come in handy when you have a really long clip containing a lot of material, some of which you might use in different parts of your project.

To duplicate a clip, right-click it in the Media window and choose Duplicate. A copy of the clip appears in the Media window. If you want to give the copy a more useful name, right-click it and choose Rename.

You can also change the speed or duration of a clip without affecting the original source file. The next couple of sections show you how to change the duration and speed of clips in Premiere Elements.

Changing the duration of still clips

The duration of a clip is determined by the length of time between the In and Out points for the clip. For audio or video clips, I usually recommend that you only adjust the duration of the clip by setting In and Out points (as I describe in this chapter). However, when you are working with still images or titles (I show how to create titles in Chapter 14) you may want to change the duration of the clip. You can safely change the duration of a title or still image and not worry about playback speed because the clip isn't moving to begin with. (If you want to change the speed of audio or video clips, see the next section in this chapter.)

Avoiding repetitive stress injuries with the Preferences dialog box

Do you ever feel like you keep repeating yourself? Do you find yourself performing the same redundant tasks? Do you ever get the feeling that you do the same thing over and over? And again and again? Before you form any habits that might lead to a repetitive stress injury, you may want to see if you can adjust the default settings in Adobe Premiere Elements to save yourself a lot of repeated effort.

Take still graphics, for example. If you use a lot of stills in your movie projects, you may find that you adjust the duration repeatedly for each still —

by the same amount almost every single time. Premiere Elements has a default duration for still graphics, and you can adjust that default if you want. To do so, choose Edit⇨Preferences⇨Still Image. The default duration for a still image is 150 frames, which works out to about five seconds in NTSC video, or six seconds in PAL video. If that doesn't work for you, simply enter a new number in the Default Duration box, using the frame rate of the video that you work with as a guide. To find out what other Adobe Premiere Elements preferences can be adjusted, check out Chapter 3.

You can set the duration of a still clip by entering a numeric duration value. The duration of a still clip determines how long the picture plays when it's inserted in a movie. To adjust the duration of a clip, follow these steps:

1. **Select a clip in the Media window.**

2. **Choose Clip⇨Time Stretch.**

   The Time Stretch dialog box appears. As you can see in Figure 7-6, when you adjust the duration of a still clip some options that only pertain to audio and video clips (Speed, Reverse, and Audio Pitch) are unavailable.

3. **Enter a new duration for the clip in the Duration field.**

   Clip duration is expressed in the same format as timecode, so it looks like this:

   ```
   hours:minutes:seconds:frames
   ```

   To enter a new duration, either type a new number or click-and-drag left or right on the timecode number. As you drag the mouse pointer left, the duration decreases. As you drag the mouse pointer right, the duration increases.

4. **Click OK when you're done.**

   The clip in Figure 7-6 is set to play for exactly five seconds.

   If you don't like the effect, you can reverse it. Just check out "Undoing Mistakes," later in this chapter.

You can also adjust a clip's duration in the Timeline. See Chapter 8 for more on changing the duration of clips in the Timeline.

Changing the playback speed of your clips

Besides adjusting the duration of a clip, you can also adjust the speed at which it plays. Speed adjustments can give you a fast motion or slo-mo effect. Before you dismiss speed adjustment as gimmicky, consider some useful applications of this feature:

✔ **Fix holes:** You can adjust the length of the clip without reshooting it. If you have a specific period of time in your project that a clip must fill, but the clip is shorter than the gap, slow the clip down slightly.

✔ **Fix bad pans:** You can use speed adjustments to correct shots that are too slow or too fast. For example, if you're not happy with the speed at which the camera pans across a scene — say, across a landscape — adjust the speed of the clip to speed up or slow down the pan as desired.

✔ **Set the tone:** You can use speed adjustments to change the mood or feel of a shot. If an action scene doesn't seem quite as exciting as you would like, speed it up just a bit. Conversely, if two lovers are bounding across a grassy meadow toward each other's embrace, slow the speed down a bit to increase the drama.

✔ **Create an audio effect:** You can create interesting voice effects by adjusting playback speed of audio clips. A faster speed makes the voice sound small and wacky (like Alvin and the Chipmunks), and a slower speed makes the voice sound large and ominous (like Darth Vader).

Just be aware of the potential negative effects of speed adjustment. While moderate speed adjustments to video may be imperceptible to the eyes of most viewers, even slight speed adjustments to audio tracks are almost always immediately obvious.

Also, you may find that your video doesn't seem to play smoothly when you slow it down or speed it up. When you slow down a clip, Premiere Elements must duplicate some frames so the clip still fills the required duration. When you speed up a clip, some frames are removed. Choose your speed-change percentage carefully to ensure that frames are added or removed evenly. Table 7-1 lists percentages that will give reasonably smooth speed changes in Premiere Elements. If you plan to change the speed of a clip, use one of these percentages for the smoothest possible playback.

Table 7-1	Safe Speed-Change Percentages for Video Clips
Safe Slow-Motion Speeds	*Safe Fast-Motion Speeds*
50%	100%
33.33%	200%
25%	300%
20%	400%
16.67%	500%

If you do a little math, you can see a pattern in the speed-change percentages in Table 7-1. If you turn all of the Safe Slow Motion percentages into ratios, you would see that they all start with the number one. The 50% speed gives a ratio of 1:2, which means that every single frame turns into *two* frames when Premiere Elements adjusts the speed. With a speed change of 25% (1:4), each frame becomes four frames. Likewise, all of the Safe Fast-Motion percentages end with 1 when converted to ratios. The 200% speed gives a ratio of 2:1, and the 300% speed gives a ratio of 3:1.

Adjusting the speed of a clip in Premiere Elements is pretty easy:

1. **Select a clip on which you want to adjust the speed.**

   You can choose a clip in the Media window, or one that has already been edited into the Monitor.

   I recommend that you work with a duplicate of the original.

2. **Choose Clip⇨Time Stretch.**

   The Time Stretch dialog box appears, as shown in Figure 7-7.

3. **Enter a new percentage number in the Speed field.**

   To make the clip play at double its original speed, enter **200**. To make the clip play at half its original speed, enter **50**. The duration of the clip is adjusted automatically, based on your percentage change. Again, I strongly recommend that you use a percentage from Table 7-1.

4. **If you want the clip to play in reverse, place a check mark next to the Reverse Speed option.**

   This option can be handy if you're going for a "fast rewind" look for the clip.

5. **Place a check mark next to Maintain Audio Pitch to, er, maintain the audio pitch of the clip.**

   This is another one of those really cool new features of Adobe Premiere Elements. If you maintain the audio pitch, you can make speed adjustments to video without making the accompanying audio sound like Alvin and the Chipmunks or Darth Vader (see my earlier comment on this subject). This feature is especially handy if you want to maintain ambient sounds such as crashing waves or chirping birds with a clip. Experiment with this setting, trying the clip with and without the Maintain Audio Pitch setting enabled. Play the clip each way and see how this option affects the audio.

6. **Click OK to close the Clip Speed/Duration dialog box.**

7. **Play the clip to preview your speed changes.**

   See "'Undoing Mistakes" if you're not sure you like what you've done to your clip.

Figure 7-7:
Changing
the playback
speed of
your clips
is easy.

Undoing Mistakes

Don't feel bad; everyone makes a mistake once in a while. For some of us, making mistakes is a way of life! Adobe programmers understand that you might make a goof occasionally — so they built Premiere Elements to be forgiving. Premiere Elements incorporates the Undo feature beloved by computer users the world over. If you make a mistake, you can quickly undo it by choosing Edit⇨Undo. The Edit menu lists the last action that was performed next to Undo so you know exactly what it is you're undoing. If you don't like using the Edit menu, you can also quickly undo an action using the keyboard shortcut Ctrl+Z.

Did you change your mind again? Perhaps that "mistake" wasn't such a bad thing after all. If you want to redo the mistake that you just undid, choose Edit⇨Redo (or press Ctrl+Shift+Z).

One of the more useful features in Premiere Elements is the History palette, shown in Figure 7-8. The History palette is hidden by default, but you can display it at any time by choosing Window⇨History.

The Premiere Elements History palette is even more forgiving than the Undo/Redo features that come with most other computer programs. It shows you a list of the last 100 edits you've made, in order, with the most recent edit at the bottom of the list. To move back in history, simply click an item in the list and then click the Trash bin icon at the bottom of the palette. When you click OK to confirm the action, you undo the selected item — *and all actions following it*. If you want to clear the history, click the right-facing arrow in the upper-right corner of the History palette and then choose Clear History.

Figure 7-8:
The History palette keeps a running record of your last 100 edits.

Chapter 8

Making Movies with the Timeline

Consider all of the tools of the trade for a painter. These tools include brushes, scrapers, a palette, containers of paint, and cleaning supplies. All of these tools are necessary, but ultimately all of the painter's work centers around the canvas. The painter's canvas is where all of the tools are put to use to create a work of art.

The Timeline window is the canvas in Premiere Elements. The other parts of Premiere Elements — the Media window, the Monitor, the Capture window, the History palette, and others — all serve crucial purposes, and that purpose is to put together movies in the Timeline. This chapter shows you how to turn your clips into movies worth watching using the Premiere Elements Timeline. Here I show you how to insert clips in the Timeline, move clips around and modify them, and how to insert DVD chapter references and other markers in the Timeline.

Making Sense of the Timeline

As I mention in Chapter 3, video is considered a *linear* medium because when you watch video, one scene follows another from start to finish. You can think of a movie as being laid out along a line through time. When you create a movie in Adobe Premiere Elements, the Timeline is the tool you use to assemble the various elements of your movie. Here you lay out all the different scenes and portions of the movie in order from start to finish (as shown in Figure 8-1).

Video tracks

Current timecode   Zoom slider   Timeline ruler

                                         CTI   Work Area bar

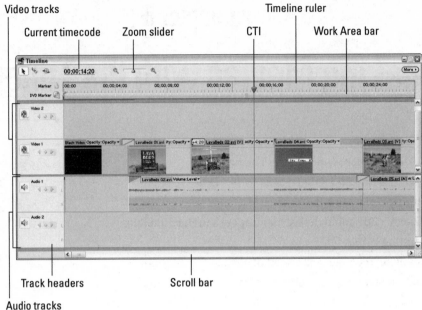

Figure 8-1:
The Timeline
is where you
assemble
your movies.

Track headers   Scroll bar

Audio tracks

As you can see in Figure 8-1, the Timeline shows a lot of useful information and is easy to navigate. Key features of the Premiere Elements Timeline include

- ✔ **Track headers:** Video tracks appear on the upper half of the Timeline, and audio tracks appear on the lower half. Scroll bars on the right side of the Timeline allow you to scroll sequentially through the various tracks. Each video and audio track has a header on the left side of the Timeline. The track headers remain visible even as you scroll the Timeline. Track headers contain important controls (described in the following section). The Premiere Elements Timeline can have up to 99 separate video tracks, as well as 99 unique audio tracks. I show how to add tracks to the Timeline later in this chapter.

- ✔ **Ruler, timecode, and CTI:** Your current location in the Timeline is indicated by the timecode (shown in the upper-left corner), ruler, and CTI (Current Timecode Indicator). When you play the Timeline, the CTI moves to show your exact location.

- ✔ **Work Area bar:** The yellowish bar just below the Timeline ruler is the Work Area bar. This bar covers your entire project by default, but you can resize the Work Area bar so that it only covers part of your project. I show how to do this — and give some examples for why you might do this — later in this chapter.

- ✔ **Zoom and scroll controls:** Use the zoom slider near the top of the Timeline to zoom the view in or out. You can also use the plus (+) and minus (–) keys on your keyboard to zoom in or out. Use the scroll bar at the bottom of the Timeline to scroll left or right.

Adding and renaming Timeline tracks

Tracks are perhaps the most important feature of the Premiere Elements Timeline because they allow tremendous versatility and control over the sound and pictures in your project. For example, one audio track might contain the sound that goes with a certain video clip, a second audio track may contain background music, and a third may contain voice-over narration. With multiple video tracks, you can perform special compositing effects, picture-in-picture effects, overlay titles, and more.

Adobe Premiere Elements allows you to have up to 99 separate video tracks, as well as 99 audio tracks. Although it is difficult to imagine what you might do with that many, I think it's definitely better to have too many tracks than not enough. Compare this number to many other affordable video-editing programs, which often only give you one or two tracks to work with, severely limiting your creative control over movie projects.

If you need more tracks in your Timeline than those already present, you can add them by following these steps:

1. **Choose Timeline⇨Add Tracks.**

   The Add Tracks dialog box opens as shown in Figure 8-2.

2. **Enter the number of tracks you want to add under Video Tracks or Audio Tracks (as appropriate).**

3. **Choose an option from the Placement menu.**

   In most cases you'll want to just stick with After Last Track.

4. **Click OK to close the dialog box and add your tracks.**

You can also add, delete, or rename tracks by right-clicking a blank area of any track header in the Timeline. You may find it handy to give some tracks more descriptive names, to better reflect what you put in that track. Track names won't appear in the final movie, so you can choose any name that you find useful as you edit.

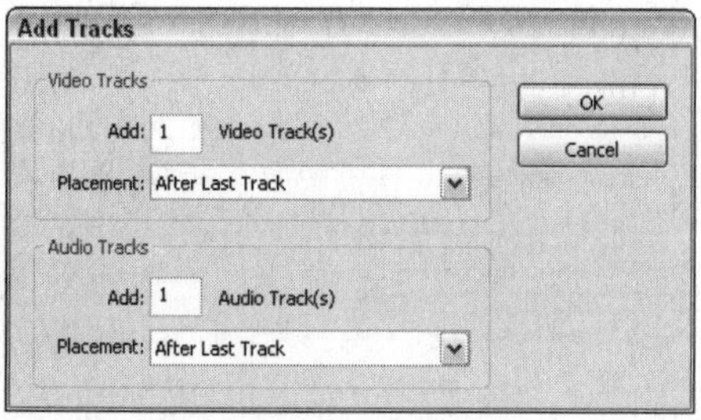

Figure 8-2:
You can add up to 99 video and audio tracks to the Premiere Elements Timeline.

Add Tracks	
Video Tracks	
Add: 1 Video Track(s)	OK
Placement: After Last Track	Cancel
Audio Tracks	
Add: 1 Audio Track(s)	
Placement: After Last Track	

Do you have some empty, unused tracks in your Timeline that are just taking up space? If so, right-click a track header and choose Delete Empty Tracks from the menu that appears. Only empty tracks can be deleted. If a track won't delete itself, scroll back and forth through the project to check the entire length of that stubborn track. Chances are there's a clip hiding somewhere on that track.

Working with the Work Area bar

As you look at the Timeline you'll notice a yellowish bar near the top of the Timeline, just underneath the Timeline ruler. This bar is called the Work Area bar, and by default it spans the entire length of your movie project. However, you can shrink the Work Area bar so that it only covers part of your project, as shown in Figure 8-3.

When you resize the Work Area bar so that it only covers part of your project, Premiere Elements only renders effects, transitions, and other edits that are covered by the Work Area bar. You may want to shrink the Work Area bar if you only want to export a portion of your movie project, for example. As I describe in Chapters 15 through 18, when you export your movie project you can choose to export the entire project or just the area spanned by the Work Area bar. The Work Area bar is just one more little feature that helps make Premiere Elements such a powerful yet easy-to-use program.

To change the size of the Work Area bar, simply click-and-drag on either end of the Work Area bar.

Click-and-drag   Work area bar   Click-and-drag

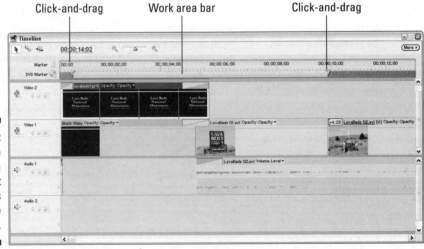

Figure 8-3:
Use the
Work Area
bar to select
portions
of a movie
project.

Using Timeline tools

Somewhere in a garage, closet, basement, or shed, you probably have a tool-box full of tools. Toolboxes are great for organizing screwdrivers, hammers, wrenches, and various other implements of destruction. Software programs typically have many different tools as well, and those tools are usually organized on toolbars.

Adobe Premiere Elements provides several important editing tools on a tool-bar in the upper-left corner of the Timeline, as shown in Figure 8-4. To use a tool, simply click it in the toolbar or press its keyboard shortcut. When you move the mouse pointer over the Timeline, the pointer image looks like the selected tool. Table 8-1 lists the tools, along with the keyboard shortcut and function for each.

Figure 8-4:
Use these
tools when
you work in
the Timeline.

Selection tool   Time-Stretch tool

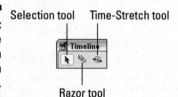

Razor tool

When you perform edits in the Timeline, the mouse cursor changes to show the tool that is currently active. Sometimes you may see a red slash across the mouse pointer when you try to perform some edits. If you see a red slash on the mouse pointer, this means you cannot use the currently selected tool on whichever clip happens to be under the pointer.

Table 8-1		Premiere Elements Timeline Tools
Tool	*Keyboard Shortcut*	*Function*
Selection Tool	V	Select clips for click-and-drag edits, as well as Ripple edits (described later in this chapter) to lengthen or shorten clips. This is the most commonly used tool in Premiere Elements.
Time Stretch Tool	X	Change the playback speed of a clip. See the section on changing clip speed later in this chapter.
Razor Tool	C	Split clips when you click them. Oddly enough, the tool works just like a razor blade.

Adding Clips to the Timeline

Before you start assembling stuff into the Timeline to make your movie, make sure you've used the Monitor window to edit clips and mark In points and Out points (Chapter 7 explains how). After you've completed that process, you can start editing your marked clips into the Timeline where your project is actually assembled. The following sections show you how to edit clips into the Timeline. Then I help you figure out what to do with those clips after you've placed them in the Timeline.

Editing clips into the Timeline is easiest when you work in the Editing workspace. To open this workspace, choose Window⇨Workspace⇨Editing. I cover workspaces in more detail in Chapter 3.

Inserting clips

A lot of the work you do in Adobe Premiere Elements requires you to simply drag and drop items onto new locations. And so it won't surprise you that editing clips into the Timeline requires the same technique. After you have set In and Out points for a clip in the Monitor window, the easiest way to add that clip to the Timeline is to simply drag and drop it from the Monitor directly to the Timeline. You can drag clips from the Monitor window or the Media window directly into the Timeline. As you can see in Figure 8-5, I am dragging a clip to the Timeline after marking In and Out points in the Monitor.

Why did slip, slide, and roll edits slip, slide, and roll away?

If you have used Adobe Premiere Pro or an earlier version of Premiere such as Premiere 6, you may be familiar with several other editing methods in addition to ripple edits. Other editing methods include roll edits, slip edits, and slide edits. Unfortunately, as part of Adobe's efforts to simplify Premiere Elements, these editing methods didn't make the transition from Premiere Pro to Premiere Elements.

Three-point edits and four-point edits didn't make the cut either. These editing methods are favored by many video-editing professionals who edit video on a daily basis and need advanced editing tools and features to work efficiently. I've always been a big fan of three-point edits myself, but I have to admit that they can be a little complicated to do at first. If you're a video editing professional and you absolutely need to be able to do three-point edits, roll edits, and other such techniques, you'll need to step up to Premiere Pro.

Set In points and Out points here.

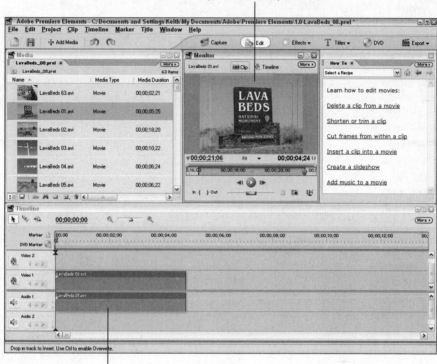

Figure 8-5:
Drag-and-
drop clips
from the
Monitor to
the Timeline.

Drag-and-drop clips from the Monitor to the Timeline.

Premiere Elements provides two other methods for placing a clip in the
Timeline as well. These editing methods — called *insert* and *overlay* — are
usually more precise and efficient ways to place clips in the Timeline at
exactly the desired location. Each type of edit is a little different:

✔ **Insert Edit:** The incoming clip is inserted at the current location of the
CTI (Current Time Indicator). Clips that fall after the CTI are moved over
to make room. Figure 8-6 shows an insert edit. I inserted a clip of black
video before the "Lava Beds" clip.

✔ **Overlay Edit:** The incoming clip is inserted at the current location of
the CTI, but instead of moving subsequent material over the incoming
clip the new clip simply replaces the old material. Figure 8-7 shows an
overlay edit. My clip of black video has replaced a portion of the "Lava
Beds" clip.

Figure 8-6: Insert edits insert clips between existing clips, shifting subsequent material to make room.

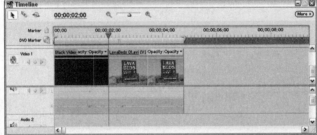

Figure 8-7: Overlay edits insert clips and replace subsequent material.

An important thing to keep in mind about insert and overlay edits is that in Premiere Elements they can only insert clips into the Video 1 track. To perform an insert or overlay edit, follow these steps:

1. **Use the Monitor window to set In and Out points for a clip (as described in Chapter 7).**

2. **Place the Timeline CTI at the exact location where you want the incoming clip to start.**

   Use the left- and right-arrow keys to fine-tune the location of the CTI, one frame at a time.

3. **In the Monitor window, click Clip to ensure that the incoming clip is active in the Monitor instead of the Timeline.**

4. **Choose Clip⇨Insert or Clip⇨Overlay to perform an insert or overlay edit.**

   The clip is inserted into track Video 1 of the Timeline.

You can also quickly perform insert or overlay edits using keyboard shortcuts. To do an insert edit, press the comma (,) key. To perform an overlay edit, press the period (.) key.

The clip now appears in the Timeline. Using this method of placing clips in the Timeline is usually more precise than dragging and dropping because you can pick an exact location for the edit using the CTI. Dragging and dropping clips can seem downright clumsy by comparison.

Overlay edits are especially useful when adding brief cut-ins to your video. For example, a long clip might show a figure skater gliding across an ice rink while the short overlaid clip briefly provides a close-up of the skater's face.

Moving clips in the Timeline

After you have some clips in the Timeline, it's time to move them around. Moving a clip is so easy that you've probably already figured out how: You simply click-and-drag clips to new locations. You can drag clips back and forth in a track, or drag them to a different track altogether.

If you're trying to move a clip at very small increments, you may get frustrated by the tendency of clips to snap to the nearest adjacent clip edge or to the CTI whenever the clip is close to their edges. To disable this snapping, click the More button in the upper-right corner of the Timeline and click Snap to remove the check mark next to it. This disables the snap-to-edges feature. Click the More⇨Snap again to enable snap-to-edges.

Performing ripple edits

No hip waders required. Honest. One of the changes you can make to clips in the Timeline is to make them longer or shorter. This kind of edit is called a *ripple edit* and basically just changes the In point or Out point for the clip. Consider the diagram in Figure 8-8. I want to trim some material off the end of Clip B, so I perform a ripple edit on the Out point for Clip B.

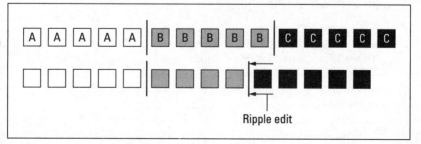

Figure 8-8: A ripple edit changes the duration of a clip.

Ripple edit

You can trim a clip down to a smaller size using a ripple edit, or you can extend the length of the clip. However, if you want to make the clip longer there must be sufficient material in the original source clip. For example, suppose you started out with a clip that was five seconds long. In the Monitor window you cut one second off the end of the clip before editing it into the Timeline. Using a ripple edit you can add some or all of that second you trimmed off, but nothing more. To perform a ripple edit, follow these steps:

1. **Choose the Selection tool in the Timeline.**

2. **Hover the mouse pointer over the edit point of the clip you want to ripple.**

   The mouse pointer changes to a bracket facing toward the affected clip.

3. **Click-and-drag the edit point.**

   As you drag the edit point, a ToolTip appears next to the mouse pointer showing how much material you are adding or removing.

Deleting blank space with Ripple Delete

It's virtually inevitable that you'll wind up deleting a clip from the Timeline. When you do so, a gaping hole is left in the Timeline where that clip used to be. You could fill in the space by dragging each subsequent item in the Timeline over, but this can be time-consuming, and if you've done a lot of advanced edits, you could make a mistake. Another solution might be to find an alternate clip that can be used to fill the vacancy left in the Timeline. If all else fails, you could insert a black matte with the word "Intermission" splashed across it. Then your audience thinks you meant to leave the space blank. (Yeah, it's so crazy it might just work. . . .)

The only problem with an "Intermission" placard is that really good intermission music can be difficult to choose. Better yet, use a ripple edit to automatically delete the blank space left over in the Timeline — and automatically shift all subsequent material over.

Ahh, genius! The great thing about doing a ripple delete is that all clips in *all* tracks automatically shift over. If you've done a lot of editing later in the Timeline that involves titles, compositing, or other effects that involve multiple Timeline tracks, doing a ripple delete means you won't have to go back and readjust all those edits because they'll automatically shift over the appropriate amount.

To perform a ripple delete, simply right-click the undesired void in the Timeline and choose Ripple Delete from the little menu that appears, as shown in Figure 8-9. If you don't like right-clicking, just click the void once with your left mouse button and then choose Edit⇨Ripple Delete.

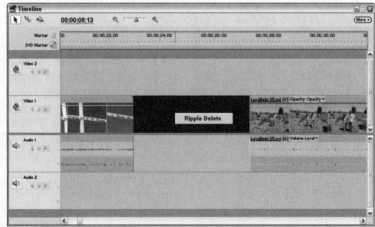

Figure 8-9:
Ripple
deletes
quickly get
rid of empty
space in the
Timeline.

Selecting clips in the Timeline

Most of the time as you edit your video you probably just work with one clip at a time. You can also select and work with multiple clips in the Timeline, a feature that often comes in handy. For example, if you want to select a portion of your movie and move it to a new part of the project, you can select all of the clips in that section and then click-and-drag them all to the new location at once. Premiere Elements gives you two methods for selecting multiple clips:

✔ Hold down the Shift key on your keyboard and click individual clips to select them. This method works best when selecting non-contiguous clips.

✔ Click-and-drag a box around the clips you want to select, as shown in Figure 8-10. This method works best when selecting contiguous clips.

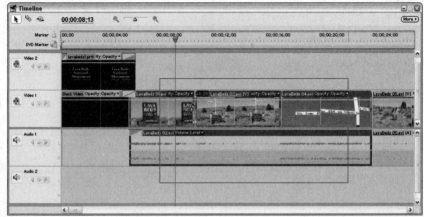

Figure 8-10:
Click-and-
drag around
a group of
clips to
select them.

Freezing video frames

At the risk of getting an old J. Geils Band song stuck in your head, consider the freeze frame. You can actually "freeze" video so that the video stops and a single frame appears on-screen. Adobe Premiere Elements allows you to freeze frames of video and keep them on screen. Here's how:

1. **Move the CTI in the Timeline to the exact frame you want to freeze.**

   You may need to use Step Forward and Step Back buttons at the bottom of the Monitor window to find the exact frame that you want to freeze.

   An even easier way to move forward or back one frame at a time is to use the left- and right-arrow keys on your keyboard. Press the left arrow to move one frame back and press the right arrow to move forward a frame.

2. **Click the clip to make sure it is selected and choose Marker⇨Set Clip Marker⇨Other Numbered.**

   The Set Numbered Marker dialog box appears.

3. **Enter 0 (zero) in the Set Numbered Marker field and click OK.**

   A small clip marker icon should now appear on the clip in the Timeline.

   When you view a list of video clips in the Media window, the preview image shown on each one is called the *poster frame*. In Chapter 6 I show how to set poster frames for clips in the Media window. As far as Premiere Elements is concerned, the poster frame and clip marker 0 are the same thing, so when you set clip marker 0 as described here you are essentially giving the clip a new poster frame.

4. **Choose Clip⇨Video Options⇨Frame Hold.**

   The Frame Hold Options dialog box appears as shown in Figure 8-11.

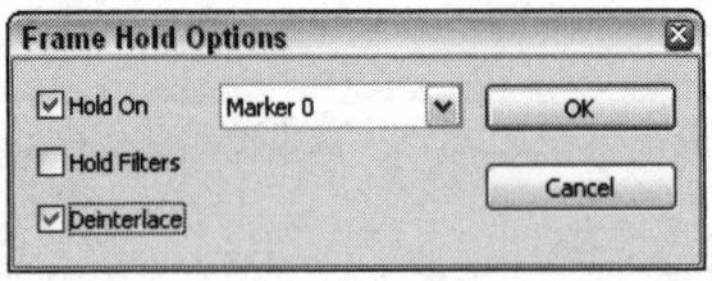

Figure 8-11:
You can freeze video clips in a single frame.

Frame Hold Options	☒
☑ Hold On Marker 0 ▼	OK
☐ Hold Filters	Cancel
☑ Deinterlace	

5. **Place a check mark next to Hold On and choose "Marker 0" from the menu as shown in Figure 8-11.**

   Note that you can freeze a clip on the In point or Out point as well.

6. **If the frame comes from interlaced video (NTSC or PAL DV video *is* interlaced) place a check mark next to the Deinterlace option.**

   This action prevents flickering when the frame appears on-screen and is most useful if the frame comes from a portion of the clip that contains fast motion or action.

7. **Click OK to close the dialog box.**

The entire clip now consists of a single frame, held static on-screen. Play your Timeline to see what it looks like. If you would rather that the clip plays normally until it gets to Marker 0 and then holds momentarily, you will need to split the clip into multiple parts using the Razor tool, as described in the following section.

Slicing clips in half with the Razor tool

A clip is the basic unit of measure in Adobe Premiere Elements. Something you often need to do with currency is change it into smaller denominations, just as you would if you're using money. For example, if you want to buy a soft drink from a vending machine, a $20 bill is probably too large a denomination. Likewise, you'll sometimes find that you need to make change (so to speak) with clips in Premiere Elements. Premiere Elements gives you a simple little tool that lets you quickly turn one large clip in the Timeline into many smaller ones. This tool is called the Razor and is located in the upper-left corner of the Timeline. Fittingly, the Razor button looks like a razor blade.

The Razor tool comes in handy more often than you might think. For example, suppose you want a clip to freeze in the middle of playback. You can set a poster frame and then choose Clip⇨Video Options⇨Frame Hold to freeze the clip, but this freezes the entire clip (see the previous section in this chapter). What if you want the clip to play normally until it reaches the desired frame? The solution is to slice the clip in two at the point where you want to freeze playback. Follow these steps:

1. **Place the CTI on the exact frame where you want to freeze the frame.**

   If you have already set the clip to Marker 0 on the spot where you want to freeze, select the clip and choose Marker⇨Go to Clip Marker⇨Numbered. Choose Marker 0 in the Go to Numbered Marker dialog box, and click OK. The CTI automatically moves to Marker 0.

2. **Click the Razor tool to select it.**

   When you hover the mouse pointer over a clip, the pointer turns into a razor blade.

3. **Hover the mouse pointer directly over the CTI so that the vertical line in the Razor tool icon matches up perfectly with the CTI.**

4. **Click the mouse button to razor the clip in two at this spot.**

    What was a single clip just a moment ago is now two clips, as shown in Figure 8-12.

    If you find that trying to hold the mouse pointer directly on the CTI is too imprecise, simply choose Timeline⇨Razor at Current Time Indicator. The clip is automatically razored at the exact location of the CTI.

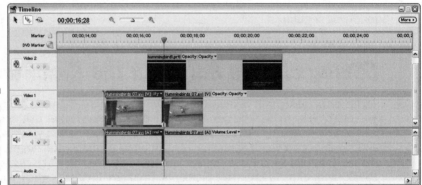

Figure 8-12: Razor the clip at the desired location.

Leave the first clip — the one before the CTI — alone so that it plays normally. On the second clip — the one that comes after the CTI — adjust the Frame Hold settings so that the clip holds on the In point. Now your video plays normally until it gets to that frame, at which time it freezes. If you want to see how to make your freeze-frame effect even cooler, check out the techniques I describe in Chapter 19.

When you're done using the Razor tool, don't forget to switch back to the Selection tool. Otherwise, you'll accidentally slice more clips apart the next time you try to click them. I've inadvertently razored a clip or two in my days. Of course, if you *do* accidentally razor a clip apart, casually look over your shoulder to make sure no one saw your goof. When the coast is clear, press Ctrl+Z or choose Edit⇨Undo to undo the mistake.

Changing playback speed

If you watched much TV in the 1970s, you probably remember a series called *The Six Million Dollar Man*. The show revolved around a former test pilot named Steve Austin (played by Lee Majors) who, after a horrific plane crash, was rebuilt using cybernetic enhancements (we assume that those enhancements cost about $6 million, including installation). The cybernetics gave Steve super strength and speed, abilities he used to fight crime and battle the forces of evil. Several times each episode, Steve Austin would run somewhere. In order to show that Steve was actually running inhumanly fast, we would see the hero running . . . in slow motion. (I guess it made sense to someone.)

Video technology has progressed a great deal since the '70s, but few computer-generated special effects would provide the same dramatic effect as slo-mo video and some well-chosen music. Changing the speed of your own clips in Adobe Premiere Elements is an effective (yet often overlooked) visual effect you can apply to video. You can adjust the speed of clips in the Timeline to create your own fast- or slow-motion effects.

Premiere Elements gives you two different methods for changing the speed of clips in the Timeline. The old-fashioned way involves entering numbers in a dialog box, like this:

1. **Select a clip in the Timeline for which you want to adjust the playback speed.**

2. **Choose Clip⇨Time Stretch.**

   The Time Stretch dialog box appears, as shown in Figure 8-13.

Figure 8-13:
Use the
Time Stretch
dialog box
to change a
clip's play-
back speed.

3. **Enter a new percentage in the Speed field.**

   If you want to slow the clip down, enter a rate that is below 100%. If you want to speed it up, enter a rate above 100%. Leave the Duration field alone for now.

4. **Click OK.**

The other method for changing playback speed is to use the Time Stretch tool in the Timeline. This tool is located in the upper-left corner of the Timeline, next to the Razor tool. Click this tool and then click-and-drag on the edges of clips in the Timeline. As you stretch and squeeze clips using the Time Stretch tool you change their playback speed. This method doesn't give you precise control over the rate of the time change, but it does come in handy if you have a specific block of time to fill. Just click-and-drag the clip until it fills the desired time.

If you ever decide to restore the clip to its original playback speed, simply open the Time Stretch dialog box as described earlier in this section and reset the Speed to 100%.

You may need to experiment a bit with the rate that you choose. In Figure 8-13, I cut the speed of the clip in half to 50%. You may find that some speed changes result in rough or jerky playback. (See Chapter 7 for specific recommendations on speed changes that should provide smoother playback.)

Using Timeline Markers

Markers can be extremely helpful as you work in the Timeline. You can use markers as reference points for key events, visual indicators as you edit, or cues for items such as Web links or DVD scene references. Any markers that were added to a source clip before it was added to the Timeline also appear in the Timeline (see Chapter 7 for more on working with clip markers). Markers that are added only to the Timeline, however, are not added to the source clips. Timeline markers appear on the Timeline ruler, as shown in Figure 8-14. DVD markers are green and appear on the Work Area bar.

Timeline marker   DVD marker

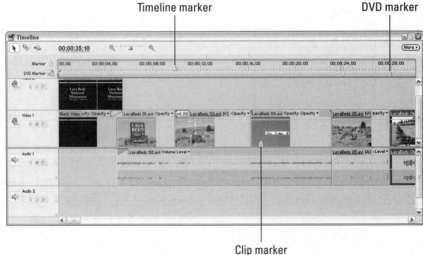

Figure 8-14: Timeline markers reside on the Timeline ruler.

Clip marker

Marking your place in the Timeline

Markers can serve various purposes. In Figure 8-14, I have added markers to indicate where specific visual events occur. You can use markers as references when you edit the project later. For example, if you decide to add some audio and you need to time the audio to match certain visual events, you can use

Timeline markers to line up the audio and video. To add a marker to the Timeline, follow these steps:

1. **Move the CTI to the exact location where you want to place a marker.**

   If necessary, use the left- and right-arrow keys on your keyboard to move frame by frame to the correct location.

2. **Choose Marker➪Set Timeline Marker➪and choose a marker from the submenu that appears.**

   You can choose to set an unnumbered marker, the next available numbered marker, or choose Other Numbered and create a marker with a specific number.

   The only real difference between numbered and unnumbered markers is the way they appear on the Timeline ruler, so it's really a matter of personal preference whether you use numbered markers, unnumbered markers, or a combination of both.

The marker now appears on the Timeline ruler. Pretty easy, huh? If you ever want to get rid of a marker, simply choose Marker➪Clear Timeline Marker and choose an option from the submenu to sentence a marker to the electronic ether.

Using DVD markers

Premiere Elements includes a special kind of marker called a DVD marker, and as the name implies these markers are designed to be used in movies that will be recorded to DVD. If you plan to record your movie to DVD, you'll probably want to create some DVD markers to serve as scene references. DVD markers come in handy for several reasons:

- ✔ When you create a DVD layout in Premiere Elements, the Scene Selection portion of the DVD menu uses the scene references that you create.

- ✔ When you watch the DVD in almost any DVD player, you can quickly jump from scene to scene by pressing the Next Scene and Previous Scene buttons on the DVD player's controls.

- ✔ You can use DVD markers to automatically stop playback or return the viewer to the DVD menu.

Creating DVD markers

You can create DVD markers manually. I recommend creating DVD markers at the beginning of major events or sections of your movie. To create a DVD marker, simply place the CTI where you want to place a DVD marker and choose Marker➪Set DVD Marker. A DVD Marker dialog box will appear as shown in Figure 8-15. In the DVD Marker dialog box:

✔ Enter a name for the marker in the Name field. This name should be simple and in plain language, because viewers will see this scene name in the DVD's scene selection menu.

✔ Choose a type from the Marker Type menu.

   • A scene marker is the most common type of DVD marker and simply marks the beginning of a new scene.

   • A main menu marker is similar to a scene marker, but it suggests a more important location. Also, when you use this kind of marker, Premiere Elements places a button linking to this marker in the DVD's main menu (as opposed to placing it in the scene selection menu).

      Use a Main Menu marker if your movie project actually contains several unique "mini" movies that are meant to be viewed separately.

   • A Stop marker is usually placed at the end of a movie or wherever you want playback to stop and the main menu to reappear.

✔ Select a thumbnail image for the marker. The DVD's scene selection menu includes thumbnail images for each scene, and by default the thumbnail is always the first frame of the scene. This thumbnail is similar to the poster frames you use in the Premiere Elements Media window. Often, the first frame of a scene doesn't provide a good visual summation of the contents of the scene. Click-and-drag left or right on the timecode under the Thumbnail Offset control until you see a scene that you think would make an appropriate thumbnail. In Figure 8-15 I've chosen a frame that is about 20 seconds into the scene.

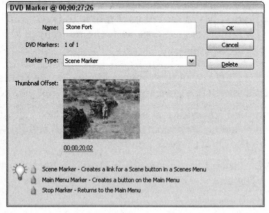

Figure 8-15: Add DVD markers to your project if you plan to record it to DVD.

Automatically generating DVD markers

If you're in a hurry, you can let Premiere Elements automatically generate DVD markers for you. To do so, choose Marker⇨Auto-Generate DVD Markers. The Automatically Set DVD Scene Markers dialog box appears, as shown in Figure 8-16. You have several options:

✔ **At Each Scene.** This option sets a DVD marker at every scene. In most cases I don't recommend this option because creating a DVD marker for every single clip in your movie is probably overkill. Only choose this option if your movie consists primarily of a few long, unedited clips.

✔ **Every *x* Minutes.** You can automatically generate DVD markers at specific time intervals. Use this option if your movie contains several hours of riveting footage of grass growing or paint drying.

✔ **Total Markers.** If you just want to quickly create a few markers — say, five or six — choose this option and enter a number. Premiere Elements automatically creates your markers and spaces them out evenly.

✔ **Clear Existing DVD Markers.** Place a check mark next to this option if you want to get rid of the markers that you created earlier. Only do this if you know that the markers you created earlier are worthless.

Click OK to close the dialog box and automatically generate DVD markers.

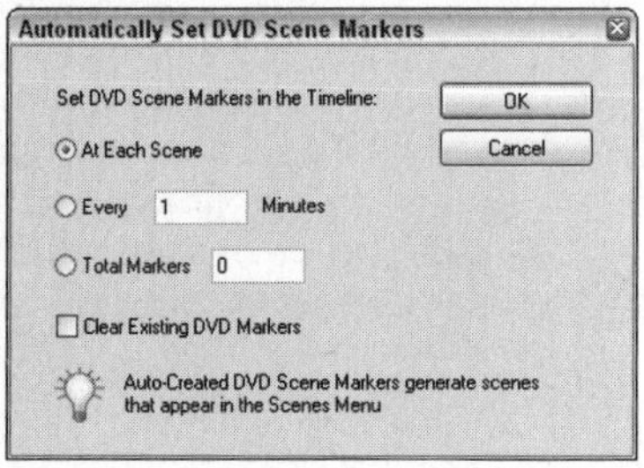

Figure 8-16: Premiere Elements can automatically generate DVD markers for you.

Automatically Set DVD Scene Markers

Set DVD Scene Markers in the Timeline: OK

◉ At Each Scene   Cancel

○ Every [1] Minutes

○ Total Markers [0]

☐ Clear Existing DVD Markers

Auto-Created DVD Scene Markers generate scenes that appear in the Scenes Menu

Moving around with Timeline markers

Moving around in the Timeline is one of my favorite uses for markers. As I'm working through a project (especially a big project with lots of footage) I often say to myself, "I'll probably want to come back to this point." That's my cue to create a marker, and it should be your cue, too. Eventually you end up with a collection of markers that you can use to quickly jump back and forth in the project. There are several methods for moving around in the Timeline using markers:

✔ Choose Marker⇨Go to Timeline Marker and then choose an option from the submenu.

✔ On the keyboard, press Ctrl+Right Arrow to move to the next Timeline marker. Press Ctrl+Left Arrow to move to the previous Timeline marker.

✔ Right-click the Timeline ruler, choose Go to Timeline Marker, and select an option from the submenu.

As you can see in the Marker menus, you can also move around using DVD markers!

Chapter 9

Using Video Transitions

Anyone with two VCRs and a cable can dub desirable bits of video from one tape to another. This is movie editing at its most basic. But making movies like this is inefficient and crude. By using a program like Adobe Premiere Elements you can fine-tune your edits frame by frame, apply your own musical soundtrack, dub in some narration, and add special effects.

If you've followed along in previous chapters — capturing video onto your computer's hard drive, sorting through clips, picking out the parts you want to use, and assembling those clips in the Timeline — you're ready for the next step in your video-editing adventure — dressing up your project with transitions between scenes. You can use Premiere Elements to create transitions that fade in or out, pull open like a stage curtain, spiral down into a vortex, and more. Transitions provide visual breaks between scenes that help the viewer understand that the setting or mood of the movie is changing. This chapter shows you how to choose, apply, and customize transitions in your projects.

Reviewing the Premiere Elements Library of Transitions

One of the trickiest aspects of movie editing (for me, anyway) is making clean transitions between clips. Sometimes the best transition is no transition at all, but a simple, straight cut from one clip to the next. Other times you need a fancy transition — say, one that rotates the image from the old clip in an ever-decreasing radius, like a vortex spinning, spinning towards the center, until — a tiny black dot at the center of the screen — it disappears entirely. Most of your transitions probably fall somewhere in between.

Adobe Premiere Elements comes with 71 unique video transitions that you can use in your projects. You can add even more transitions to Premiere Elements using third-party plug-ins (see Chapter 20 for more on Premiere Elements plug-ins). But for now, you probably agree that 71 transitions, divided into nine categories, are enough to start with. The following sections describe the transitions in each category. To find these categories, choose Window⇨Effects and open the Video Transitions folder in the Effects window. You see a subfolder for each category of transitions.

Three-dimensional transitions

The 3D Motion category consists of ten transitions that apply various kinds of three-dimensional motion to one clip as it disappears to reveal the next one. Most of the transitions here involve getting the exiting clip to swing like a door or spin in a spiral. Figure 9-1 shows the Tumble Away transition, where the outgoing clip appears to be on a plane that is tumbling away from view.

Figure 9-1:
Tumble
Away is
one of the
Premiere
Elements 3D
transitions.

Dissolves

My favorite transition, the Cross Dissolve, can be found in the Dissolve category. It's my favorite not because it is fancy but because it's *not*. The Cross Dissolve is subtle; one clip blends smoothly into the next. It's softer than a straight cut — and if I want the program to be about what's in the clips (and not about fancy transitions), this is the one I choose. Cross Dissolve is just one of six Dissolve transitions available with Premiere Elements.

Iris transitions

The seven Iris transitions are all variations on a theme of one clip starting as a point in the middle and growing to fill the screen. Different Iris patterns include circles, squares, stars, diamonds (I know, it's starting to sound like a breakfast cereal!), and more. Figure 9-2 shows the Iris Shapes transition using diamond shapes. Like many transitions, this transition can be customized by changing the shape and quantity of irises in the transition.

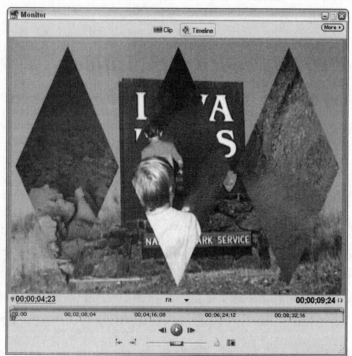

Figure 9-2: The Iris Shapes transition can be easily customized.

Page Peels

The five Page Peel transitions simulate the turning of a page or opening of a book. Use these to make the transition from your "Once upon a time . . ." screen to the story!

Slide transitions

The Slide category is a descriptively named group that contains 12 transitions. All of the transitions in this group are variations on sliding a clip one way or the other. These subtle transitions are also among my favorites. Slide transitions are similar to wipe transitions, which I describe later.

Special Effect transitions

The Special Effect category contains six advanced and varied transitions that apply various combinations of color masks and distortions while moving from one clip to the next.

Stretch and squeeze transitions

The five transitions found in the Stretch category are pretty cool, even though technically some of them *squeeze* rather than stretch the clip image during transition. In Figure 9-3 the outgoing image is squeezed down a funnel using the Funnel transition.

Wipes

Wipe style transitions have been around for a while: One clip appears from the edge of the screen and appears to wipe over the previous clip like a squeegee. Wipe transitions differ from Slide transitions because in a wipe the outgoing image remains static while the incoming image wipes over it. In Slide transitions, the incoming image slides in while the outgoing image slides out. Premiere Elements includes no less than 16 different Wipe transitions.

Transitions that zoom

There are four Zoom transitions, and as you would imagine, they all simulate different camera zooms. An outgoing transition can zoom out into the distance where it disappears, or the camera may appear to zoom in on the incoming clip.

Figure 9-3:
The Funnel
transition
squeezes
the outgoing
image down
a funnel.

Using Transitions Effectively

With so many unique transitions to choose from, selecting just the right one can be challenging. When you consider that most transitions can also be fine-tuned and customized, the endless possibilities may have already started your head spinning. So how do you choose? Because video production is such a creative and personal endeavor, I couldn't possibly recommend a perfect transition for every situation. I do, however, have a few basic transition rules to follow as you develop your own editing style:

- ✔ **Use transitions sparingly.** You don't need to apply a transition between every single clip in your Timeline. That's too much. I try to save transitions for changes of scene. Simple camera angle or position changes in the same scene (for example) usually don't warrant a transition. Watch a typical feature-length movie and you'll probably see just a small handful of simple transitions, even though the movie may be a couple of hours long.

- ✔ **Keep 'em short.** Later in this chapter, I show you how to control the length of a transition. Most transitions should be short in duration, usually one second or less.

✔ **It's all about the pictures.** Editing can help shape the mood and flow of a movie, but ultimately the focus of your project is the video content. The desire to show off your editing skills with fancy transitions can be tempting — but generally speaking, transitions should complement and enhance the video images, *not* overpower them.

Thinking of the mood you want to set may help you narrow down your transition choices. For example, you want to avoid transmogrifying the scene with a high-tech Distortion transition if you're editing a movie that celebrates your grandparents' golden wedding anniversary. Remember, ultimately the movie is about your grandparents, not your incredible movie-editing abilities.

✔ **Follow your inspiration.** You should be familiar with the various transition styles that are available in Premiere Elements, even the ones you seldom, if ever, use. In a moment of late-night, caffeine-induced inspiration, it might come to you: "*This* is the spot for that fancy, spinning, 3D transition!"

Premiere Elements also offers a couple of audio transitions. In this chapter, I mainly want to talk about video transitions, so for more on working with audio transitions, slide, peel, or dissolve your way over to Chapter 13.

Incorporating Transitions into Your Movies

The tricky part of adding transitions to a movie project in Adobe Premiere Elements, in my opinion, is choosing a transition that looks good without detracting from the overall flow of the project. In the previous section, I talk about choosing an effective transition. In this section, I show you how to actually put some transitions to use.

Finding transitions to use

If you're new to video, you may be surprised by how many different transitions are possible between two clips. As I mention previously in this chapter, Adobe Premiere Elements comes with 71 transitions already built in, and you can add even more by using third-party plug-ins.

Premiere Elements stores all its transitions in the Effects window. To open the Effects window, choose Window⇔Effects. The Effects window opens, as shown in Figure 9-4. Transitions are divvied up into 10 subfolders, which you can reveal by clicking the arrow next to Video Transitions. Click an arrow next to a subfolder to see a list of transitions. In Figure 9-4, you can see that six transitions are listed in the Dissolve subfolder.

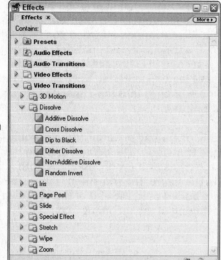

Figure 9-4:
Transitions
are located
in the Video
Transitions
folder of the
Effects
window.

Applying a transition

The software designers at Adobe must really like drag-and-drop because, as with so many other editing actions in Premiere Elements, drag-and-drop is the best way to apply a transition. Simply choose a transition and drag it directly from the Effects tab to the desired spot on the Timeline, as shown in Figure 9-5.

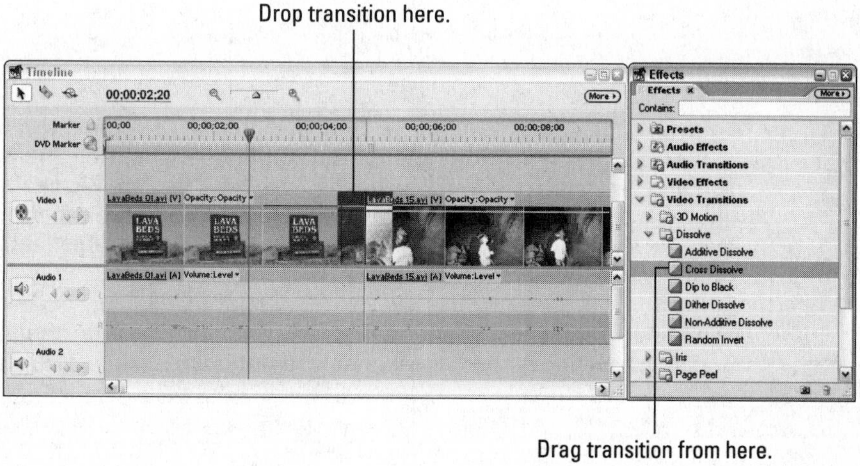

Drop transition here.

Figure 9-5:
Drop
transitions
between
video clips in
the Timeline.

Drag transition from here.

When you add a transition to the Timeline, the In and Out points of adjacent clips are automatically extended to facilitate the transition. Thus, each clip needs some unused frames that were trimmed off when you edited the clip into the Timeline. For example, if a transition lasts one second, the preceding clip must have at least one half-second of trailing material, and the following clip must have one half-second of leading material. Keep this in mind when you set In and Out points as you edit clips into the Timeline (see Chapter 7 for more on setting In and Out points).

If the clips lack sufficient leading or trailing material, you are somewhat limited in how you can position the transition. The default method in Premiere Elements is to drop it so that the transition evenly overlaps both adjacent clips, as shown in Figure 9-6. In the figure, the transition is 30 frames long, which means that 15 frames are added onto the end of the outgoing clip and 15 frames are added to the beginning of the incoming clip.

Transition

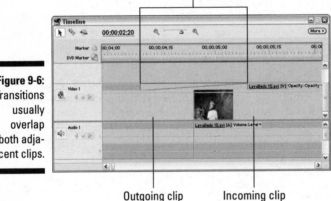

Figure 9-6: Transitions usually overlap both adjacent clips.

Outgoing clip   Incoming clip

If either of the clips doesn't have enough material, Premiere Elements won't let you drop the transition right on the edit line — your Timeline won't look neat and pretty like Figures 9-5 and 9-6. Instead, Premiere Elements may only allow you to drop the transition entirely on one clip or the other. You may even see a warning message as shown in Figure 9-7, advising you that some frames will be repeated.

If you find yourself in a situation in which you have too little media to accommodate a transition, you have a couple of options:

✔ **Skip using a transition at this point in your movie.** Maybe this problem is a sign that you don't really need a transition.

✔ **Shorten the length of the transition.** If the clips have *some* leading and trailing material, but not quite enough for the current transition length, you might be able to make the transition work if you make it shorter. I show you how to adjust transition duration later in this chapter.

✔ **Shorten the length of the clip(s).** Choose the Selection tool in the Timeline (see Chapter 8 for more on ripple edits) and drag the edges of the leading and trailing clips until you've trimmed about half a second from each clip. Because a ripple edit basically trims material off the clip and changes the In and Out points, this should create enough leading and trailing time to facilitate the transition.

If you want to apply a transition between two clips, those clips must be in the same Timeline track. Fortunately, Adobe Premiere Elements allows you to use transitions in any video track. Some older versions of Adobe Premiere, as well as many other consumer-oriented video editing programs, only allowed you to use transitions in the Video 1 track.

Figure 9-7:
You'll need to make some changes if you see this warning message.

Fine-tuning transitions

More often than not, you may just plop a transition down on the Timeline and use it as it sits. Sometimes, however, you may want to fine-tune the transition. You can change the length of a transition by clicking-and-dragging on either side of the transition. For example, you can shorten the duration of a transition to speed it up, or lengthen the transition if you want it to occur more gradually. To change the duration of a transition, first click the Selection tool in the upper-left corner of the Timeline (the Selection tool looks like a single large arrow) and then click-and-drag one side of a transition to lengthen or shorten it.

You can also modify the duration of a clip using the Effect Controls window. To open the Effects Controls window, double-click the transition that you want to modify. The Effects Controls window appears, as shown in Figure 9-8. You can also open the Effects Controls window by choosing Window➪Effect Controls, or choose Window➪Workspace➪Advanced Effects.

The default duration for most clips is one second, but you can make the transition as short or long as your source clips and common sense allow. To adjust the duration of a transition using the Effect Controls, enter a new number in the Duration field. You can also click-and-drag left or right on the Duration field to adjust the time. In Figure 9-9, I have changed the duration of the transition to just 25 frames, which is a little less than one second in NTSC video.

Control transitions in the Effects Controls window.

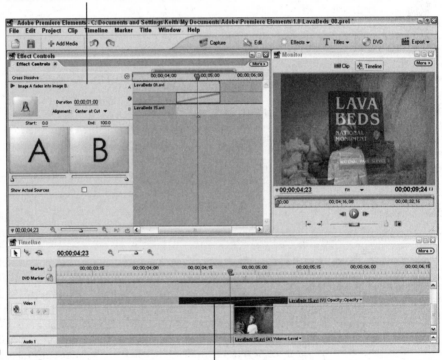

Figure 9-8:
Use the
Effect
Controls
window
to fine-
tune your
transitions.

Double-click transition.

Preview window   Transition

Available leading material   Available trailing material

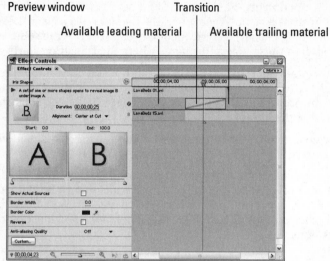

Figure 9-9:
Transition
controls vary
depending
on the type
of transition.

Figure 9-9 shows a number of different controls in the Effect Controls window. Some key settings and features include

- **Split-track Timeline:** The right side of the Effect Controls window contains a small Timeline window showing just the current track. If you've used older versions of Adobe Premiere, you may notice that this looks similar to the split-track Timeline that was used in the old A/B Editing workspace, part of Adobe Premiere 6.5 and earlier.

  The split-track Timeline is useful in Figure 9-9 because it shows how much leading and trailing material is available for each clip. You can roll edit the transition in this Timeline by dragging it back and forth.

- **Alignment:** Use the Alignment menu under the Duration field to control alignment of the transition. By default, a transition uses the Center at Cut setting, but you can also make the transition start or end at the location of the original cut between clips if you want to change the starting or ending frames of the transition.

- **Preview window:** Click the Play button above the preview window in the upper-left corner to see a visual representation of the transition. Some transitions such as slides or wipes allow you to change direction — simply click the arrows around the edges of the preview window to change the transition's direction. The Iris Shapes transition shown in Figure 9-9 doesn't have arrows around the preview window because it is not a directional transition.

✔ **Start/End controls:** The Start and End boxes (you can't miss them; the Start box has a giant "A" in it, and the End box has a giant "B") represent the outgoing clip (A) and the incoming clip (B). Use the slider controls underneath these boxes to change where the transition starts or ends.

✔ **Show Actual Sources:** The giant "A" and "B" are meant to represent clips in your movie. But if these alphabetic metaphors aren't working for you, click the Show Actual Sources option. The actual video clips appear instead of the letters.

✔ **Reverse:** Enabling the Reverse option can reverse the direction of many transitions.

✔ **Other options:** Some transitions have additional options. The transition controls in Figure 9-9 provide options for including a border and smoothing out the edges of the transition (called *anti-aliasing*). Experiment with other options to customize the appearance and function of your transitions.

More than 70 different transitions come with Premiere Elements, all with different settings to adjust, so your Effects Controls window may not look like Figures 9-8 or 9-9. Play around a bit to find the transitions and combinations of settings that work best for you!

Some transition options allow you to specify a color for transition elements (such as borders). To choose a color, click the color swatch to open the Color Picker window. When you choose a color in the Color Picker, watch out for a yellow triangle with an exclamation point in the upper-right corner of the window. If you see the warning icon, it means that the color you chose won't appear properly on video equipment in your area (NTSC or PAL). In that case, your best option is to choose a different color.

Working with default transitions

Premiere Elements knows that a lot of people have one type of transition that they use most of the time. It just so happens that my favorite transition — the Cross Dissolve — is also the default transition in Premiere Elements. (Sorry — it's just so useful I can't resist it.) The default transition is especially handy if you want to quickly apply transitions without having to open the Transitions palette.

Setting the default transition comes in handy when using the Create Slideshow feature in the Media window. (I describe how to create a slideshow in Chapter 6.) When you select a group of clips in the Media window and click Create Slideshow, the Create Slideshow dialog box appears, as shown in Figure 9-10. As you can see in Figure 9-10, the dialog box has an option that allows you to apply the Default Transition. The name of your current default transition is displayed in the dialog box.

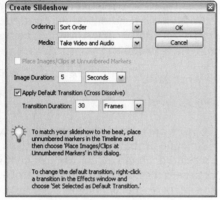

Figure 9-10:
The Default
Transition
option can
be quickly
applied
when you
create a
slideshow.

If the Cross Dissolve is not your favorite transition, I won't hold it against you. In fact, I am even willing to show you how to change the default to *your* favorite transition. To set a new default transition, follow these steps:

1. **Open the Effects window by choosing Window⇨Effects.**

2. **Expand the Video Transitions folder if it isn't already open.**

3. **Locate the transition that you want to use as your default transition, and click the transition once to select it.**

4. **Click the More button in the upper-right corner of the Effects window, and choose Set Selected as Default Transition in the menu that appears.**

You can also change the default transition duration using the Effects window's More menu. When you choose Default Transition Duration from the menu, the Preferences dialog box appears with the General options group displayed. The default duration for video transitions is 30 frames, but you can change it to any length you want. This default duration applies to all transitions, not just the default transition.

Previewing (And Rendering) Transitions

Transitions add a great deal of complexity to a video image. For this reason, a transition must usually be rendered before export, and in some rare cases you may even need to render a transition to preview it properly. When you render a transition or other effect, Premiere Elements creates a new file on your hard drive containing the affected video with your edits incorporated at full quality. If you find that some transitions play back in a rough or jerky manner when you try to previewing them, you need to render to get a smooth preview.

When you place a transition on the Timeline, a red bar appears above it on the Timeline. If you try to preview the transition without rendering it, the transition may play just fine. If it doesn't play acceptably, try rendering the transition. There are two easy ways to render a transition:

✔ Choose Timeline➪Render Work Area.

✔ Press the Enter key on your keyboard.

When you choose to render the work area, Premiere Elements renders the *whole* work area. A lot of your Timeline probably doesn't need to be rendered, but any unrendered areas are rendered when you choose this command. If all you need to render in the work area is a single transition, the process takes mere seconds. If long clips with effects or speed changes need to be rendered, you could be waiting a few minutes. In that case, a progress bar appears on-screen to tell you how many frames must be rendered — and approximately how long it will take. See Chapter 8 for more on adjusting the Work Area bar to reduce the size of the Work Area. I describe rendering in greater detail in Chapter 15.

Part III

Advanced Editing in Premiere Elements

The 5th Wave   By Rich Tennant

DAD ADDS MULTIMEDIA SOUND AND GRAPHICS TO THE TRADITIONAL CAMPFIRE GHOST STORY.

In this part . . .

Virtually all affordable video-editing programs can do the things described in Part II of *Adobe Premiere Elements For Dummies*. Most programs can easily capture video and edit them into a basic movie. (Of course, Premiere Elements does all that with a lot more finesse than the other programs. . . .)

But Part III explores the features of Adobe Premiere Elements that *truly* sets this program apart from other affordable editors. In this part, I show how to improve the light and color in your video images, add special effects, perform advanced animation and video image compositing, work with audio, and add titles.

Chapter 10

Improving and Repairing Video Images

Anyone who has used a camera — be it a still camera or a camcorder — has probably learned some hard lessons about light and color. A scene that looks great to human eyes often turns out poorly when it is photographed. You've probably experienced this before; pictures you take are too dark, colors look weird, or brilliant colors get washed out by bright sunlight. Managing light and color is one of the trickiest aspects of photography and videography.

When you shoot video, there are some things you can do to take advantage of the light and color that is available. In Chapters 4 and 20 I show you some techniques to use to shoot better video. But no matter how hard you try to follow the rules of photography and videography, you're going to wind up with video clips that appear less than perfect when you view them on a TV screen or your computer. Don't feel bad — it happens to the best of us. People often use programs like Adobe Photoshop Elements to touch up light and color problems in still photos, and thanks to some advanced effects and features you can use Premiere Elements to make similar improvements to your video. This chapter shows you how to use the color-correction tools in Premiere Elements to improve the quality of your video images.

Understanding How Video Color Works

Remember back in the old days when many personal computers used regular televisions for monitors? In the early 1980s I had a Commodore 64 hooked up to a TV — it made sense at the time — but these days this setup is hard to visualize, especially when you consider how dissimilar TVs and computer monitors have become. Modern computer monitors offer incredibly high resolution compared to most televisions, and computer monitors today are usually progressively scanned instead of interlaced like TVs. Also, computer monitors of today make up images using square pixels, whereas TVs have rectangular pixels. (I explain interlacing, resolution, and pixel aspect ratios in Chapter 4). On top of all that, TVs and computer monitors use different kinds of color.

Computer monitors utilize what is called the *RGB color space*. RGB stands for *red-green-blue*, meaning that all the colors you see on a computer monitor are combined by blending those three colors. TVs, on the other hand, use the *YUV color space*. YUV stands for *luminance-chrominance*. This tells us two things:

- ✔ Whoever's in charge of making up video acronyms can't spell.

- ✔ Brightness in video displays is treated as a separate component from color. *Luminance* is basically just a fancy word for *brightness*, and *chrominance* means *color* in non-techie speak.

I could go on for pages describing the technicalities of the YUV color space, but there are really only two important things you need to know about color:

- ✔ **Some RGB colors won't show up properly on a TV.** This is an issue mainly when you try to use JPEGs or other computer-generated graphics in a video project, or when you adjust the colors of a video image using effects and color settings in your video-editing program. RGB colors that won't appear properly in the YUV color space are often said to be *illegal* or *out of gamut*. You won't get arrested for trying to use them, but they will stubbornly refuse to look right.

  Generally speaking, illegal colors are ones with RGB values below 20 or above 230. Graphics programs can usually tell you RGB values for the colors in your images. Some graphics programs (including Adobe Photoshop and Adobe Photoshop Elements) even have special filters that help you filter out "illegal" TV colors from your images. In Photoshop Elements, open your image and choose Filter➪Video➪ NTSC Colors to remove out-of-gamut colors from the image.

- ✔ **Video colors won't look exactly right when you view them on a computer monitor.** Because you'll probably do most of your video editing while looking at a computer monitor, you won't necessarily see the same colors that appear when the video is viewed on a TV. In other words, as you use the video filters in Premiere Elements to adjust colors, keep in mind that the changes you see on your computer screen don't necessarily reflect how the video will look when you output it to DVD or tape. If possible, I strongly recommend connecting an external video monitor to your computer, as described in Chapter 15. Using an external video monitor allows you to more properly preview the colors of your video.

Correcting Video Color

Correcting and changing colors in video is much more of an art than it is a science. Every video camera has unique characteristics, every scene is lit differently, and every project has special color needs. I guess this is my way of saying that you won't find a magic formula here to help you make each and every video clip look perfect. When you want to adjust video colors, trial-and-error is an inevitable part of the process. But the following section can help you get started using some of the color and lighting effects available in Adobe Premiere Elements.

Surveying color and light effects in Premiere Elements

Most consumer-oriented video-editing programs now include some sort of provisions for adjusting color and lighting in video clips. Usually such a tool chest consists of a few slider or dial controls that mimic the adjustment knobs on old TVs, with controls for color, tint, brightness, and contrast. Adobe Premiere Elements goes above and beyond with a collection of advanced color and lighting effects that give you capabilities that until now were only found in expensive, professional-grade programs.

To view the selection of effects that Premiere Elements offers up, choose Window⇨Workspace⇨Effects, or click the Effects button on the Premiere Elements toolbar. The Effects window appears, as shown in Figure 10-1. Click the arrow next to Video Effects to reveal the list of subfolders containing effects. You can find the effects that come in handy for fixing light and color by opening the Adjust or Image Control subfolders. In the Adjust folder you find the following effects:

✔ **Auto Color:** This effect quickly adjusts color and contrast by limiting the range of blacks and whites in the image based upon midtones in the image. Use this effect to quickly improve color in high-contrast images.

✔ **Auto Contrast:** This effect adjusts contrast without changing the overall color cast of the image.

✔ **Auto Levels:** This effect adjusts all color levels to soften shadows and highlights, but it can change the overall color cast of the image.

✔ **Brightness and Contrast:** This effect does exactly what the name implies. If you just want to adjust the brightness or contrast of a clip, this effect can do the job.

Before you choose the Brightness and Contrast effect, you may want to experiment with the Shadow/Highlight, ProcAmp, and Color Balance (HLS) effects. Those effects can also fix brightness and contrast problems, often with more favorable results.

✔ **Channel Mixer:** This effect dynamically mixes color channels in the image, and is most useful when converting an image to a black-and-white or sepia tone look. In Chapter 19 I show how to make new video look like old-fashioned film using the Channel Mixer effect.

✔ **ProcAmp:** This effect provides a selection of brightness, contrast, hue, and saturation controls that work like the processing amplifier found on some professional-grade video equipment. This is one of my favorite effects for color correction in Premiere Elements because it provides a variety of useful controls, thereby simplifying the color-correction process. I show how to adjust image color and lightness using the ProcAmp effect later in this chapter.

✔ **Shadow/Highlight:** Use this effect to improve the appearance of heavily-shadowed subjects, or to soften extreme highlights in the image. Use this effect if you find that the Auto Levels effect unfavorably changes the color case in the image.

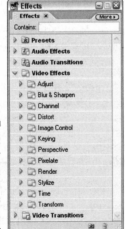

Figure 10-1: Find color and lighting effects in the Effects window.

In the Image Control folder are these effects:

- ✔ **Black & White:** This effect removes color from your video image and turns it to grayscale. Use this effect during dream or flashback sequences. Alternatively, you may want to try the Channel Mixer effect.

- ✔ **Color Balance (HLS):** This effect allows you to adjust hue, saturation, and lightness in the image. It is similar to the Hue/Saturation controls in Adobe Photoshop and Photoshop Elements.

- ✔ **Color Balance (RGB):** You can make direct changes to the levels of red, green, and blue in the image using this effect.

- ✔ **Color Match:** This is one of the most powerful effects in Premiere Elements, and can match colors between video clips. I show how to use the Color Match effect later in this chapter.

- ✔ **Color Pass:** This effect removes all but one color from a video image. Use this effect to place special emphasis on a particular object by making everything except that object grayscale. The Color Pass effect works best if the object contrasts strongly with the background. Say you have footage of a red balloon against a blue wall. Turn everything else grayscale to make the red balloon burst with color.

- ✔ **Color Replace:** Use this effect to replace one color in a video image with another.

- ✔ **Gamma Correction:** This effect adjusts the brightness of midtones in an image without affecting shadows or highlights. I show how to use the Gamma Correction effect in the following section.

- ✔ **Tint:** This effect modifies only the color tint of the image. Use this to change the overall color cast of the image.

In addition to these Adjust and Image Control effects, you can also find a useful effect in the Presets folder at the top of the Effects window. In the Presets folder, open the Color Effects subfolder and select the Increase Saturation effect. This effect quickly increases the color saturation in a clip, giving more vivid colors to an otherwise bland-looking clip. The following sections show you how to use a few of these effects to improve the quality of your video images.

Making color adjustments

In the previous section I list the various effects you can use in Premiere Elements to fix and repair color and lighting in your video images. In all you will find at least 16 different effects to use, each with varying degrees of success. Rather than try to show you how to use all of them, this section focuses on two effects that, in my opinion, are most likely to yield good results with the least amount of fiddling. You might experiment with some of the other effects and find that they work quite well for you. But if you are new to color correction, the following two sections will help you get started.

As you correct colors and light, keep in mind that sometimes less is more. I don't mean less light, but rather less *editing*. Color correction should be done sparingly, or else colors can start to look artificial and cartoonish. Fortunately, Premiere Elements encourages creative experimentation because color corrections and other edits don't make permanent changes to your video clips. If you don't like your changes, simply delete the offending color effect from the Effect Controls window, or use the Premiere Elements History palette (Window⇨History) to step back in time and undo your edits.

Before you start correcting colors, you should set up your Premiere Elements workspace for image correction. I recommend using the Advanced Effects workspace, which you can open by choosing Window⇨Workspace⇨Advanced Effects. This workspace hides the Media window, adjusting the view so that the screen includes the Effects window, Effects Controls window, Monitor, and Timeline. These are the four windows you will need when you correct colors and lighting.

The following sections show how to apply color and light changes to an entire video clip. However, you can also apply changes to only portions of a clip, or have your changes vary as the clip plays. If you don't want to apply your adjustments to the whole video, you must use *effect keyframes*. I show how to use effect keyframes in Chapter 12.

Improving color and lightness with the ProcAmp effect

Video-editing professionals often use a device called a *processing amplifier* — ProcAmp for short — to adjust various aspects of a video signal. If your TV has controls for hue, brightness, or contrast, those controls are actually part of a simple ProcAmp that is built-in to the TV.

The Premiere Elements ProcAmp effect is designed to mimic a professional-style ProcAmp. I like it because this single effect provides controls for brightness, contrast, hue, and saturation all in one place. I have found that a majority of minor video color and light problems can be fixed with a few simple tweaks using the ProcAmp filter.

To apply the ProcAmp filter, open the Adjust subfolder of the Video Effects folder in the Effects window. Click-and-drag the ProcAmp effect from the Effects window and drop it on a video clip in the Timeline. When you drop the effect on the clip, the clip is selected in the Timeline. Controls for that clip appear in the Effect Controls window, as shown in Figure 10-2.

Drag ProcAmp effects from here.

Effects controls appear here.

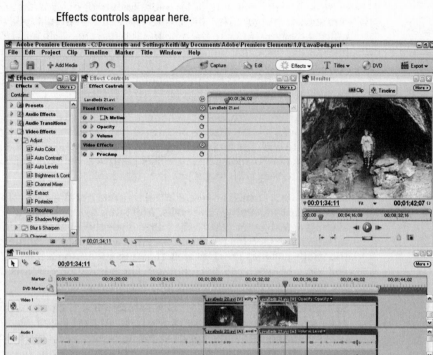

Figure 10-2:
Drag the
ProcAmp
effect to a
clip to apply
the effect.

Drop the effect on a clip.

When you apply effects to a clip, the Monitor window shows previews of your changes in real time. However, when you first drop the ProcAmp effect onto a clip you shouldn't see a change. To start adjusting the image, click the arrow next to ProcAmp under Video Effects in the Effect Controls window. A list of controls appears. Next to each control you see another arrow. Click the arrows to expand each respective control, as shown in Figure 10-3. ProcAmp controls include

✔ **Brightness:** Slide the Brightness slider left to reduce brightness, and slide it right to increase brightness. In most cases I recommend against making large changes to the brightness setting. Be especially cautious about increasing brightness; as you increase brightness, areas of the image that were already bright appear to wash out and lose detail. If you notice that this has happened to your clip, you may want to use the Gamma Correction effect, which I describe in the next section.

✔ **Contrast:** This is another control that you should usually use sparingly, especially if the image includes a lot of white or black areas such as the one shown in Figure 10-3. Increasing the contrast in this type of image quickly causes whites to become too intense and wash out. However, a slight decrease in contrast allows you to slightly increase brightness without light areas becoming too light. In Figure 10-3 I have decreased contrast slightly to 93.6 (the baseline is 100) while increasing brightness to 3.7 (baseline is 0).

✔ **Hue:** The Hue control quickly changes the color cast in the image. The control looks a little strange because it has a dial that you cannot easily manipulate with the mouse. Click-and-drag left or right on the numbers above the dial to adjust the hue. This control is definitely one that you will have to play with to get just the right look.

In Figure 10-3, I used the Hue control to bring out the color of the green lichens growing on the cave walls. Adjusting the Hue control to give a slight greenish color cast to the image gives the right results, but be careful when you use this technique — otherwise the faces of the people in the image will turn green as well. (I had to spend some time working back and forth between the hue, contrast, and saturation controls before I got the improvement I was looking for.)

✔ **Saturation:** This controls the color saturation in the image. You can lose color saturation for a number of reasons, not the least of which is making other color adjustments. For example, in Figure 10-3, I increased saturation to 130.3 (from a baseline of 100) to bring back some of the color lost when I decreased the contrast. Increasing saturation also helps restore color after you make hue adjustments. For example, I was able to restore vitality to the faces of the people in the image; they had taken on a slight greenish cast because of my hue adjustments.

✔ **Split Screen:** The last option in the ProcAmp controls is a split screen feature. Most of the time you won't want to correct colors on just one side of your video image. However, this option can be helpful because it allows you to see a side-by-side comparison of the "before" and "after" appearance of the clip. To test this, place a check mark next to Split Screen and then play the clip. As you can see, half of the clip incorporates your brightness, contrast, hue, and saturation adjustments, and the other half is unchanged.

Move the Split Percent slider to adjust the location of the split in the split screen effect. When you're done previewing your changes, make sure you uncheck the Split Screen option. Otherwise, your final movie may look a little strange because one side of the video image will have nice colors and lighting, and the other side won't.

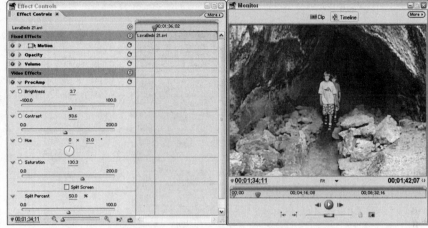

Figure 10-3:
Fine-tune
color and
lighting
settings in
the Effect
Controls
window.

I can't give you a magic formula that will give perfect colors and lighting in every clip. Color correction always involves a lot of trial and error, and it's easy to spend many minutes or even hours playing with color adjustments to create the right look for a single clip!

Make sure you preview your color changes on an external monitor, as described in Chapter 15. As I describe earlier in this chapter, color changes that look okay on your computer screen may not look as nice when viewed on a TV because computer monitors and TVs show color and light differently.

Using the Gamma Correction effect

All of the colors in a video image fall into one of three categories called *tonal ranges*. These tonal ranges are shadows, midtones, and highlights. When you adjust the brightness of a video clip using the ProcAmp or another effect, you usually change the brightness of the whole image. But sometimes this is not desirable.

Consider the image in Figure 10-4, where the subject has just stepped out of a dark cave into a shaft of sunlight. When the subject steps into the sun, his face becomes too bright and detail washes out of the image. This is not an example of exceptional videography, but it is the kind of thing that inevitably happens when you shoot your own video, especially outside where you have almost no control over lighting.

Figure 10-4:
This clip presents a tough lighting situation.

To improve the detail and appearance of the dark cave walls in the background, you could simply increase brightness of the whole video clip, but then the subject's face will turn into even more of a washed out white blob than it already is. Instead, you should brighten the midtones — in my example, the cave walls — without affecting the highlights — the subject's face — or shadows.

Gamma Correction to the rescue! Find the Gamma Correction effect in the Image Control subfolder of the Video Effects folder. As with other effects, simply click-and-drag the effect from the Effects window and drop it on the clip you want to adjust.

The baseline setting for the Gamma Correction effect is 10, but in Figure 10-5 I have adjusted the control to 7. This adjustment has dramatically improved the appearance of the cave in the background, without exacerbating the already too bright face of the subject in the foreground.

The Gamma Correction effect is especially useful for adjusting light when the image looks okay on your computer screen but is too dark or too light when viewed on a TV.

Figure 10-5:
Gamma
Correction
brightens
the back-
ground but
doesn't
change the
bright sub-
ject in the
foreground.

Saving Your Settings as Presets

Adjusting color effect settings can become time-consuming, and you may find that you are making the same changes to many or even all of your video clips. Fortunately Premiere Elements allows you to save and reuse settings as effects presets. To save your settings as presets, follow these steps:

1. **Apply a color-correction effect from the Video Effects folder of the Effects window.**

2. **Adjust your settings to the desired levels.**

3. **When you're satisfied with your changes, right-click the name of the effect in the Effect Controls window and choose Save Preset from the menu that appears.**

   The Save Preset dialog box appears.

4. **Give your preset a descriptive name and click OK to close the Save Preset dialog box.**

   That's it! Your new preset should now appear in the Presets folder in the Effects window.

You can apply this preset just like any other effect; simply drag and drop it to a clip. The settings that are saved in the preset are automatically applied to the clip.

Of course, you can fine-tune the settings if you wish. In fact, I strongly recommend that you preview and fine-tune settings every time you apply an effect or preset to a clip; lighting and color conditions in different video clips often vary.

Matching Colors with the Color Match Effect

Another helpful image enhancement tool provided with Adobe Premiere Elements is the Color Match effect. This effect helps you match the colors in one video clip with the colors in another video clip. This effect is helpful when you have two scenes that were shot with different lighting conditions (or even different cameras) and you want to maintain a common look for both clips.

The Color Match effect uses two clips. The *sample clip* is the clip that has the colors or lighting that you like. The *target clip* is the clip you want to make look more like the sample clip. To use the Color Match effect, follow these steps:

1. **Choose Window➪Workspace➪Advanced Effects if your workspace isn't already set up for color correction.**

2. **In the Effects window, open the Image Controls subfolder of the Video Effects folder.**

3. **Drag-and-drop the Color Match filter from the Effects tab to the target clip.**

4. **Make sure that the target clip is selected, and click the arrow next to Color Match in the Effect Controls window to expand the list of Color Match controls.**

5. **In the Timeline, place the CTI (Current Time Indicator) somewhere in the sample clip.**

   Ideally the CTI should be stopped on a frame of video that shows representative colors that you want to match, as shown in Figure 10-6.

You can use the left and right arrow keys on the keyboard to move frame-by-frame through a clip. Make sure that the target clip remains highlighted in the Timeline, however, so that the Color Match controls are still visible in the Effect Controls window.

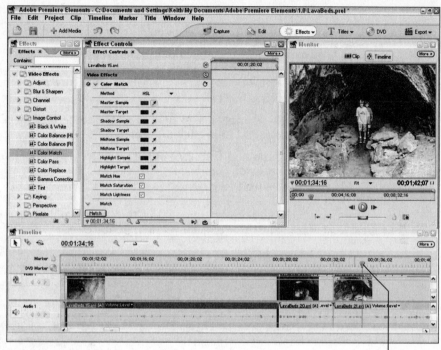

Figure 10-6:
Use the eye-
droppers to
choose sam-
ple colors
from the
sample clip.

CTI

6. **In the Effect Controls window, choose a method from the Method menu under Color Match.**

   HSL (hue, saturation, lightness) is the most common method used for color matching, but you can also choose RGB (red, green, blue) or Curves if you wish.

7. **Choose what you want to match using the check boxes at the bottom of the Color Match settings.**

   If you're using the HSL matching method, you can choose whether you want to match hue, saturation, or lightness individually. For example, you may find that each clip is adequately lit, but that one has better color hue or saturation than the other. In this case, disable the Match Lightness option. If you're using the RGB or Curves matching methods, you can choose whether to match red, green, or blue individually.

8. **Click-and-hold the eyedropper next to Master Sample, and then move the mouse pointer over a representative area of the sample clip.**

   A color is selected when you release the mouse button.

9. **In the Timeline, move the CTI so that it is now in the target clip.**

10. **Use an eyedropper to choose a target color from the target clip.**

    Choose a color from a sample point which you want to match the color in the sample point in the sample clip. For example, in Figures 10-7 and 10-8 I picked spots on the cave walls which should be about the same color in each clip.

11. **Click the right-pointing arrow next to Match at the bottom of the Color match controls, and then click the Match button.**

    The image is modified. If you're not happy with the results, remember that Ctrl+Z (the Undo command) is your friend! You should click the Match button after every change you make.

As with many other color-correction tasks, the Color Match filter requires a great deal of trial and error to achieve the right look.

Figure 10-7: Use the eye-droppers to choose a sample point in the target clip.

Chapter 11

Compositing and Animating Video Clips

*Y*ou can hardly watch a movie or TV show today without seeing something that seems impossible. These scenes may involve superheroes flying among skyscrapers in a major metropolis, giant monsters chasing hapless humans through a jungle, or even a TV weatherman hovering in outer space as he describes the swirling weather pattern seen way down there on Earth, just off the coast and poised to ruin your weekend. Scenes like these are created using a little bit of movie magic called *compositing*.

Guess what? You don't have to be a Hollywood movie mogul with a multimillion-dollar budget to use compositing. With some simple videography tricks and Adobe Premiere Elements, you can create composite scenes with the best of 'em. In this chapter, I show you how. This chapter also shows you how to use the powerful animation features that come with Premiere Elements; these features allow you to move video scenes, titles, and other graphics across the screen.

Compositing Video Clips

Over the years, movie viewers have come to expect sophisticated visual illusions — starships flying into a space battle, lovers standing on the bow of a long-gone ocean liner, or a weatherman standing in front of a moving weather-satellite graphic — and if you ever wanted to create some of these illusions in your own movies, now you can: Adobe Premiere Elements is fully capable of creating such effects. This is a big part of what sets Premiere Elements apart from most other affordable video-editing programs.

One of the great spells you can cast in the magic of moviemaking involves *compositing*. When you composite clips, you combine portions of two or more clips to make a video image that would otherwise be difficult or impossible to capture. Consider this scenario, common in the movies nowadays: an actor appears to be hanging by his fingertips from the fiftieth floor of a skyscraper as cars move like ants on the streets far below. Would the producers risk the actor's life and force him to hang from a tall building? Not likely — think of the insurance costs! But they would shoot some film of him hanging from a prop in a studio and then superimpose that image over a shot taken from an actual skyscraper.

Fundamental to the process of compositing is the careful layering of images. Using Premiere Elements, you can superimpose up to 99 separate video tracks upon one another. Each track contains part of the final image; by making parts of each track either opaque or transparent, you can create a convincing illusion of three-dimensional space. (See Chapter 8 for more on creating new tracks.)

Working with clip transparency

One of the most basic techniques in making realistic superimposition effects is to make a clip less opaque — that is, more transparent. The result is that the more transparent clip becomes a ghostlike image superimposed over the more opaque image behind it. You can change the opacity of an entire clip all at once, or change it gradually as the clip plays. To adjust the opacity of a clip, follow these steps:

1. **Add a clip to the Video 1 track in the Timeline.**

   You shouldn't make clips in the Video 1 track transparent. You might want to think of Video 1 as the background layer. When you layer additional clips over it and make them transparent, the background clip on Video 1 should show through.

2. **Add a clip to a superimpose track in the Timeline.**

   Video 2 and any higher-numbered tracks are all considered *superimpose tracks* because they're the ones you superimpose over a primary or background image. You can think of the video tracks in the Timeline as layers on top of each other. If you superimposed 50 tracks on top of each other, Track 50 would be the very top layer and opaque areas of that track would cover all other tracks.

   After you have added a clip to a superimpose track, the superimposed clip should appear directly above the background clip in Video 1, as shown in Figure 11-1.

3. **Make sure that the words** Opacity:Opacity **appear next to the clip's name in the Timeline.**

   If you see the word Motion instead, click the word Motion. A drop-down list appears. Choose Opacity⇨Opacity.

Notice that a yellow or black line appears across the video clip. This is called the Opacity rubber band, and you can click-and-drag it up or down to change the opacity of the entire clip.

4. **To make the whole clip transparent, drag the rubber band down.**

   To adjust the opacity gradually so that the clip appears to fade in and then fade out, move on to Step 5.

5. **Click the clip that you want to adjust.**

   The clip is selected.

6. **Place the CTI (Current Time Indicator) somewhere in the selected clip.**

7. **Press Page Up on your keyboard to move the CTI to the beginning of the clip.**

8. **Click the Add/Remove Keyframe button on the track header to set a keyframe.**

9. **Move the CTI to a spot about one or two seconds into the clip and click the Add/Remove Keyframe button again to create another keyframe.**

10. **Move the CTI to a spot about one or two seconds before the end of the clip, and click the Add/Remove Keyframe button again to create another keyframe.**

11. **Press the Page Down key to move the CTI to the end of the selected clip and click the Add/Remove Keyframe button again to set another keyframe.**

12. **Click and drag on the keyframes you created to adjust the opacity rubber band.**

    As you drag the rubber band down, the clip becomes more transparent. As you drag it up, it becomes more opaque.

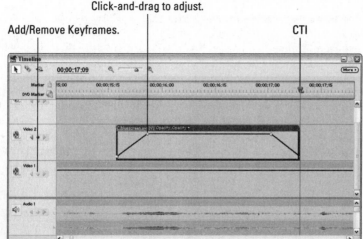

Figure 11-1:
Adjust transparency using the opacity rubber band and keyframes.

If you find that the keyframes are kind of hard to click-and-drag with the mouse, carefully hover the mouse pointer over a keyframe. When the mouse point has a white dot next to it, you can click-and-drag the keyframe.

Using video keys to create partial transparencies

In the previous section, I showed you how to adjust the opacity of a clip to make the entire image transparent or semitransparent. But what if you only want parts of the image to become transparent while other parts of the image remain fully opaque?

You've probably heard of a video technique called *blue screening,* often used in special-effects shots in movies, or during the evening news when a meteorologist appears in front of a moving weather map. In actuality, the announcer is standing in front of a blue screen — usually wearing a color that clashes with the blue. Why the clash? Because you're not supposed to *see* the blue.

Here's how the blue screen becomes a weather map: Video-editing software uses a *key* — an effect that recognizes the special shade of blue. Everything in the video that is this special shade of blue is defined as transparent by the key. Because the wall behind the announcer is the only thing painted that shade of blue, it "disappears." In effect, the image of the meteorologist has been placed on a virtual "glass slide" and superimposed electronically over the image of the weather map. Pretty slick, eh?

Of course, if the meteorologist happens to wear a tie or blouse that *matches* the "transparent" color, you can see chunks of the weather map "right through" the person. (Oops . . .) Editors can only make *so* much movie magic; some careful videography is needed to make blue-screen effects work.

A blue screen key is one of many keys that work by recognizing a specific color in an image. Some keys use an alpha channel instead of a color to define transparent areas of an image. If you've worked with still graphics in Adobe Photoshop Elements or another graphics program, you're probably familiar with alpha channels. An *alpha channel* is basically a layer in the image that defines transparency within the image. Generally speaking, the only time you'll use an alpha key is when you are dealing with a still graphic that was imported from a program like Photoshop or Adobe Illustrator.

The following sections show you how to use different kinds of keys to define transparent areas in your video image.

Reviewing keys in Premiere Elements

Using a blue screen key to replace a blue wall with a moving weather map is one of the most common types of video keys, but the blue screen key isn't the only type of key that comes with Premiere Elements. In fact, Premiere Elements provides seven different kinds of keys for you to use.

To view a list of the keys, choose Window⇨Effects to open the Effects window. Expand the Keying folder under Video Effects. Premiere Elements' keys are

✔ **Alpha Adjust key:** This key works a lot like the opacity controls (described earlier in this chapter); it's for still graphics that have an alpha channel. Use this key to adjust opacity of the whole graphic, ignore the alpha channel, invert the alpha channel, or use the alpha channel as a mask to cover certain parts of the video image.

✔ **Blue Screen key:** Use this key when you've shot video with the subject in front of a blue screen. The blue screen must be well lit and brilliant for this key to be effective. Any shadows that the subject casts on the blue screen reduce the effectiveness of this key.

✔ **Chroma key:** *Chroma* is basically just a fancy word that video professionals use to refer to color. This key enables you to *key out* (make "disappear") a specific color or range of similar colors. With some fine-tuning, you can use this key with almost any clip, and unless you have a professional video studio this is probably the key that will work best for you most of the time. In Figure 11-2, I have applied a Chroma key to the clip on the left to create the superimposition effect shown on the right. (I show how to do this in the next section.) If the Blue Screen or Green Screen keys don't work very well for you, try using the Chroma key instead.

✔ **Garbage Matte keys:** Use the Garbage Matte keys to remove undesired objects that won't key out properly. When you apply a Garbage Matte to a superimposed clip, you can click-and-drag handles around the edge of the screen to (in effect) crop out portions of the image. Premiere Elements includes four-, eight-, and sixteen-point garbage matte effects.

✔ **Green Screen key:** This key works just like the Blue Screen matte except it uses (surprise) green instead of blue. Professional movie makers are starting to use green screens instead of blue screens because with modern films and video technologies green screens often provide superior results.

✔ **Non-Red key:** This key works like the Blue Screen and Green Screen keys, but it keys out both blue and green screens. If you encounter rough edges (called *stair-stepping*) around unkeyed objects with the Blue Screen or Green Screen keys, try using the Non-Red key instead.

✔ **Track Matte key:** Use this key with a black and white image that moves across the screen. Transparency moves with the image. Suppose, for example, that you want to simulate the appearance of looking through binoculars. First create a black-and-white matte image in Photoshop Elements that looks like the outline of binocular lenses. The image would be mostly black, with white circles in the middle to simulate the binocular lenses. Import that image into Premiere Elements, and then place it in a superimpose track in the Timeline. When you apply the Track Matte key to the matte image, the video image shows through the white portion of the image, making it seem as if the viewer is looking through the binoculars.

Figure 11-2:
Use the
Chroma key
to remove
an entire
color from a
video image.

Applying a key

Applying a key to a clip is pretty easy. As I explain in the previous section, a key allows portions of an image to be transparent when it is superimposed over another image. Remember, you can only apply a key to a clip in a superimpose track — that is, the Video 2 track or higher. To apply a key, follow these steps:

1. **Click a clip in a superimpose track to select it, and make sure that the CTI in the Timeline is somewhere over the clip.**

2. **Choose Window⊅Effects to open the Effects window, if it isn't already open.**

3. **Expand the Video Effects folder, and then expand the Keying folder.**

4. **Drag and drop a key from the Effects tab to the selected clip in the superimpose track.**

   You can see a list of keys in the previous section. The easiest key to use if you're a beginner is the Chroma key.

5. **Choose Window⇨Effect Controls to open the Effect Controls window.**

   The effect controls for the selected clip appear. The key you applied in Step 4 is listed under the Video Effects heading.

6. **Click the right-pointing arrow next to the key to expand its controls, as shown in Figure 11-3.**

   If the key uses color information — as with, for example, the Chroma key — you may need to choose a base color for transparency. If you aren't using the Chroma key, you don't need to choose a base color; skip to Step 8.

7. **Click-and-hold the eyedropper next to Color in the Effect Controls, move the mouse pointer over the video image in the Monitor, and release the mouse button over the color you want to key out.**

8. **Adjust any other settings that may be available.**

   Each key is different, so experiment a bit with the settings to achieve the desired result. In Figure 11-3, I had to adjust the Similarity setting to 50% to remove the entire background.

Figure 11-3:
Fine-tune
your keys
using the
Effect
Controls
window.

Creating an image matte

Some of the keys available in Premiere Elements use matte images to define transparent areas. You can create your own mattes by using a graphics program such as Photoshop Elements, and you can even create some mattes within Premiere Elements. You can create mattes for a variety of purposes, as described in the following sections.

Defining transparent areas with a matte

A solid, brightly colored matte can help you key transparency on another clip. To create a matte of a solid color, follow these steps:

1. **Click the New Item button at the bottom of the Media window and choose Color Matte from the menu that appears.**

2. **Choose a color for the matte from the Color Picker.**

   If you see a warning that the picture is out of the color gamut for your video format ("Whaddaya *mean* I can't use fluorescent puce there?"), choose another color.

3. **Place the matte on a track that is under the clip to which you're trying to apply a key.**

   The brightly colored matte shows through to help you identify transparent areas and adjust as necessary.

4. **When you've made all the necessary adjustments, just delete the color matte.**

Using a matte to crop out undesirables

To mask out specific areas of an image, create a "garbage" matte and crop out the undesired object. Using a still graphic as a garbage matte instead of using one of the Garbage Matte keys provided by Premiere Elements allows you to create a matte with much more complex shapes. Consider the matte in Figure 11-4, which creates the shape of a snowflake. You would never be able to create a shape like this using the garbage matte keys in Premiere Elements.

To create a garbage matte, follow these steps:

1. **Create a matte image in a graphics program such as Adobe Photoshop Elements (this will be your "garbage" matte).**

   See the steps in the preceding section for details on creating a color matte.

2. **Import the image into Premiere Elements.**

3. **Place the matte in a superimpose track above the video image that you want to serve as the background.**

   If the matte image has an alpha channel, that channel automatically becomes transparent. Otherwise, apply the Chroma key to the clip and select the color in the image that you want to make transparent.

When preparing a still graphic for importation into a video project, remember the importance of sizing your image to fit properly in the video image. See Chapter 6 for more on preparing still images for use in video.

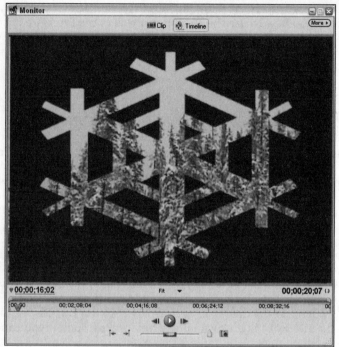

Figure 11-4:
Matte
images can
be used to
create com-
plex video
shapes.

Animating Video Clips

I know what you're thinking when you read this heading — *Why do I need to animate a video clip in which the subjects are already moving?* You may not need to animate the actual *subjects* in the video, but you can move the video image across the screen. For example, a small picture-in-picture image could sail across the screen to give a hint of action that will happen later in the movie. But wait — there's more. You can move a clip across the screen along a fixed path or a zigzag pattern, you can rotate clips, and you can distort them. To begin animating a clip, follow these steps:

1. **Click the clip in the Timeline that you want to animate to select it, and make sure that the CTI is somewhere over the clip.**

   Just about any clip that you animate should be in a superimpose track — that is, the clip should occupy any track above Video 1.

2. **Choose Window⊏>Effect Controls to open the Effect Controls window for the selected clip.**

3. **Under Fixed Effects, click the right-pointing arrow next to the Motion heading to expand the Motion controls.**

Now you're ready to start animating the video clip. The next couple of sections show you how to use the Motion controls in the Premiere Elements Effect Controls window. You can use the Motion controls to change the size or position of the clip, and you can also animate the clip so that it appears to move across the screen.

Resizing a clip with motion controls

You can adjust the Motion controls in a variety of ways. Perhaps the easiest way to adjust a clip is to click the box next to Motion. You can then click-and-drag corners of the video image to shrink it down to a smaller size (see Figure 11-5). To move the clip, click-and-drag on the circle in the middle of the clip. If you want more precise control, use the following controls under Motion in the Effect Controls window:

✔ **Position:** The position of the clip is expressed in pixels along an X (horizontal) and Y (vertical) axis. Zero for the X axis is the left edge of the screen, and zero for the Y axis is the top of the screen. The default position for any clip is right in the middle. For example, in NTSC-format DV video, the default position is 360 by 240. You can change the position of the clip by typing new numbers next to Position, or you can click-and-drag left or right on either Position number.

✔ **Scale:** The default scale for any clip is 100, which means it takes up the whole screen. Reduce the scale to shrink the clip image.

✔ **Scale Width:** If you remove the check mark next to Uniform Scale, you can then adjust height and width independently. With Uniform Scale unchecked, the Scale control adjusts height, and the Scale Width control adjusts width. Just keep in mind that if you adjust height and width independently the video image may become distorted.

✔ **Rotation:** Use this control to rotate the clip. Expand the Rotation control and click-and-drag left or right on the clock-style rotation control to spin the image on its axis.

✔ **Anchor Point:** All of the other controls assume work off the clip's *anchor point*, which is usually in the center of the clip. When you rotate a clip, for example, the rotation axis is the anchor point. If you want to rotate the clip around a corner instead of the center, for example, just move the anchor point.

If you don't like the changes you've made to the Motion controls, just click the Reset button next to Motion in the Effect Controls window. This resets the clip back to the default settings.

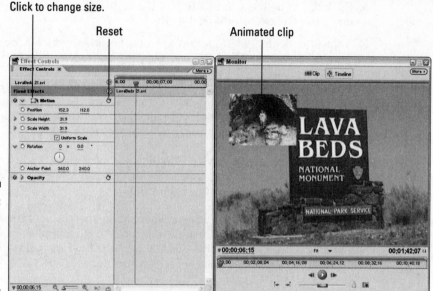

Click to change size.

Reset

Animated clip

Figure 11-5:
Motion
controls can
be used to
resize a
video image.

Animating video clips

The more you play with the Motion controls, the more quickly you will see
how easy it is to change the on-screen position, size, and orientation of a clip.
But what if you want the clip to move across the screen after you've shrunk
it? To do this, you must use *effect keyframes*. Effect keyframes are reference
points used by Premiere Elements to define the starting and ending points for
effects and other changes. I explain keyframes in greater detail in Chapter 12,
but to control motion with keyframes, follow these steps:

1. **Click the clip you want to animate in the Timeline to select it.**

2. **Move the CTI to the beginning of the selected clip.**

   The easiest way to do this is to first position the CTI somewhere over the
   clip and then press Page Up on your keyboard.

3. **In the Motion controls for the selected clip, click the Toggle Animation
   button next to the control you want to animate.**

   For example, Figure 11-6 shows the Position control being animated.

4. **Adjust the Scale, Position, and any other Motion controls you want
   to change.**

   These settings represent what the clip looks like and where it's positioned
   at the start of the animation.

5. **Click the Timeline window to make it active, and press Page Down to move the CTI to the end of the clip.**

6. **Adjust the Scale, Position, and any other Motion controls for the clip.**

As in Step 4, these settings represent what the clip looks like and where it's positioned at the end of the animation.

Premiere Elements automatically creates keyframes at the beginning and end of the clip and automatically calculates how the clip should move and change to steadily go from one keyframe to the next.

In Figure 11-6, the animation in the clip begins off-screen to the upper-left, and ends off-screen to the lower-right. As the clip plays, it appears to move across the screen diagonally from left to right.

You can add additional keyframes anywhere along the path of the clip to make more dynamic changes. Just move the CTI to a position somewhere in the middle of the clip and click the Add/Remove Keyframe button in the Motion controls, and then adjust settings as needed.

Add/Remove keyframes.

Toggle animation

Motion path of clip

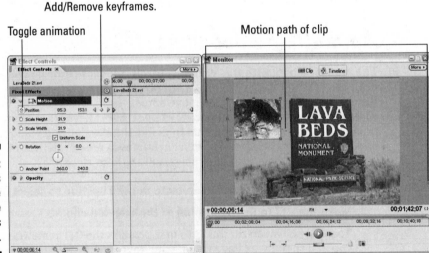

Figure 11-6:
Video clips can move across the screen as they play.

Chapter 12

Adding Special Effects to Your Movies

· ·

· ·

Adobe Premiere was first released in 1993, making it one of the first video-editing programs designed for desktop computers. Over the ensuing years, many other players have come onto the market — Adobe Premiere Elements shares the stage with several other affordable movie-making programs such as Pinnacle Studio, Microsoft Windows Movie Maker, and others.

Not all video-editing programs are created equal, however. Many programs offer special effects you can apply to your video clips, but few offer the quality and variety available with Adobe Premiere Elements — about 70 professional-grade effects. You can add even more effects by using plug-ins from third-party vendors. What's more, each effect in Premiere Elements is fully customizable, allowing you to control the intensity and timing of each effect. The effects in Premiere Elements give you ultimate creative control.

Effects can help you clean up your video or add special touches that amaze and astound your audience. What's really cool about effects is that you can add them to (or remove them from) any clip you want. Effects do not permanently change your clips, so if you aren't happy with a result, you can simply delete the offending effect. Although this book isn't the place to cover each of the effects Premiere Elements has to offer in detail, this chapter does show you the basics of using effects — including the brass-tacks specifics of using several common effects.

Surveying Effects

Adobe Premiere Elements comes with about 70 effects built right in. Some of these effects may not seem immediately useful, but you may be surprised someday to find that what at first seemed like the most obscure effect suddenly comes in handy. You can get a look at all the effects Premiere Elements serves up by choosing Window➪Effects to open the Effects window. Click the arrow next to Video Effects to expand the list of effect subfolders. I describe audio effects in Chapter 13. The following sections provide an overview of the effects available to you in Premiere Elements, as well as the basics of applying effects and adjusting their settings.

Just like transitions and other edits, video effects are meant to enhance the content of your movie, not showcase your off-the-hook editing skills. Too many effects can distract from the purpose of your movie, so choose effects carefully and only when they serve your editing style.

Premiere Elements organizes video effects into 12 categories, represented by subfolders in the Video Effects folder of the Effects window. The categories and effects are covered in the following sections.

Adjust

The nine effects in the Adjust category let you tweak levels of color and light. They can be useful for fixing color- and light-related problems in your video clips. I describe most of the Adjust effects in Chapter 10. One effect that I did not cover in Chapter 10 — the Extract effect — removes all trace of color from a clip as shown in Figure 12-1. This effect can be used to create an interesting background for a title screen.

Figure 12-1: The Extract effect removes all color from a clip.

Blur & Sharpen

The six effects in the Blur & Sharpen effects category run the gamut from blur to sharpen. They include:

- **Antialias:** This effect blends edges together through an *anti-aliasing* process. Anti-aliasing reduces the "stair-step" appearance that sometimes happens to curves in digital images by blending the colors of adjacent pixels along the curve. In some cases anti-aliasing smoothes the appearance of the image and in other cases it just makes the whole image look a little blurry.
- **Fast Blur:** Use this effect to soften the outlines of things to simulate disorientation, or to suggest speed by "unfocusing" parts of the video image.

  A blur effect can be used like a transition to make it appear that the camera starts out blurry and then focuses in on a particular image in the clip. This technique can be effective when simulating the view of a person who is waking up from a slumber or coma. Use keyframes (described later in this chapter) to make the image start out blurry and then gradually come into focus.

✔ **Gaussian Blur:** This effect is similar to Fast Blur, but it also removes *noise* (specs or visual "static") from the image. Gaussian Blur cannot blur an image quite as much as the Fast Blur effect.

✔ **Ghosting:** This effect creates ghost images of moving objects on screen, and can often be used to place increased emphasis on the path of motion.

✔ **Sharpen:** This effect sharpens images that appear too soft or slightly out-of-focus. Be careful when using this effect on clips with a lot of motion — moving objects may appear to have blocky edges.

✔ **Sharpen Edges:** Similar to the Sharpen Edges effect in Photoshop Elements, this effect is a more subtle version of the Sharpen effect because it only sharpens areas of high contrast.

Channel

The Channel category contains only the Invert effect. This effect inverts colors in a clip so that the image looks like a photographic negative. Use this effect to add a psychedelic or "sci-fi" look to a video image.

Distort

The Distort category contains seven effects that bend, twist, exaggerate, or otherwise distort your video images so that they look like they are being viewed through a fun-house mirror. The Distort effects include:

✔ **Bend:** The video image is bent both horizontally and vertically in a series of waves. The waves move as the clip plays, giving viewers the impression that they are viewing the scene from underwater.

✔ **Lens Distortion:** This effect distorts the image to look like it is being viewed through the bottom of a soda pop bottle or another distorted lens.

✔ **Mirror:** Give the appearance that part of your video image rests on a mirror or reflecting pool with this effect. You can adjust the angle and center point of the reflection.

✔ **Polar Coordinates:** If the Bend or Lens Distortion effects don't provide quite enough distortion for your tastes, try this effect. Pixels are adjusted to give the appearance of extreme image distortion, like portions of the video image are being pulled like taffy.

✔ **Ripple:** Similar to the Bend effect, this effect adds ripples to the video image, like ripples in water.

✔ **Transform:** Use this effect to turn or skew the image in the two-dimensional plane.

✔ **Twirl:** Twirl the image so that it appears as if the video clip is caught in a vortex.

Image Control

The eight effects in the Image Control category change the way color is viewed in your clips. They can remove a color (or range of colors) from a clip, convert a color image to black-and-white, or adjust the overall tint of the image (which you will find useful if, for example, you want to transform an ordinary outdoor scene into an alien landscape). Chapter 10 shows you how to use the Image Control effects in greater detail.

Keying

The effects in the Keying effects category allow you to control transparency in clips and perform compositing effects such as blue screening. (See Chapter 11 for more on using keys in your video projects.)

Perspective

The four effects you find in the Perspective category add a three-dimensional feel to your clips. They include:

✔ **Basic 3D:** This effect turns and tilts your image on a plane. Using this effect you can move the corners of the video image to give the appearance that the image is on a plane that is not parallel with the viewing screen.

✔ **Bevel Alpha:** If an image doesn't fill the entire screen, use this effect to smoothly bevel the edges of the image.

✔ **Bevel Edges:** This is similar to Bevel Alpha effect, except that the edge bevels are rectangular rather than softly rounded.

Pixelate

The Pixelate category contains only the Facet effect, which modifies the pixels in your video image to create a textured appearance.

Render

The three Render effects allow you to simulate various properties of real light. They are

- **Lens Flare:** This effect simulates lens flares — momentary bright circles that often occur in video footage when the sun reflects or glares on the lens. Although you probably work hard to avoid *real* lens flares when you shoot video, well-placed *simulated* lens flares can have a dramatic effect, especially if you are depicting a sunrise or sunset.

- **Lightning:** The Lightning effect is kind of cool because it creates realistic lightning on-screen. Simulated lightning created by this effect is much safer to work with than the real thing.

- **Ramp:** This effect creates a color gradient on the screen. Adjust the Blend With Original setting to make the original video image show through the gradient. This effect is of limited use, though in some cases you may find it helpful when you want to put titles on the screen and want to slightly soften or darken the background image without totally hiding it.

Stylize

The ten effects in the Stylize effect category create a variety of image modifications:

- **Alpha Glow:** If your image includes a masked alpha channel (usually a still graphic from Adobe Photoshop Elements with a transparent layer), this effect creates a glow around the alpha channel.

- **Color Emboss:** This effect creates an embossed appearance to the clip without changing any of the clip's original colors. Even a slight application of the Color Emboss effect can give the video image a cartoonish appearance.

- **Emboss:** The image is given an embossed appearance, and most color information is removed.

✔ **Find Edges:** Major edges in the image are identified and replaced with black lines, and the rest of the image information is discarded. This is another effect that is most useful when creating a background for a title screen.

✔ **Mosaic:** The image is blurred in a block pattern for a pixelated appearance.

✔ **Noise:** Do not attempt to adjust the transmission! This is just an effect that adds artificial video noise to the image, as if the viewer has poor antenna reception.

✔ **Replicate:** Turn a single video image into many, as shown in Figure 12-2.

✔ **Solarize:** This effect blends the image with its negative. It is similar to the Invert effect, except that you can adjust the blend along a scale from zero (normal) to 100 (full negative).

✔ **Strobe Light:** Flash your video image on and off using this effect. Just be careful not to give your audience members seizures!

✔ **Texturize:** This effect applies the apparent texture from one clip to another clip.

Figure 12-2:
The Replicate effect creates many copies of your video image.

Time

In the Time category you can find two effects. The Echo effect creates visual echoes (or a double-image) of a picture. Look here also for the Posterize Time effect, which modifies the apparent frame rate of a clip. Use this effect to make it look like you are a cable news channel correspondent broadcasting via video phone from the other side of the world.

Transform

The nine effects in the Transform category transform the view of your clip in a variety of interesting and sometimes humorous ways:

- **Camera View:** Simulate various camera angles and views with this effect.

- **Clip:** This basic effect trims off portions of the video image. This may come in handy if you want to create a black bar on the side of the screen to insert some bulleted points.

- **Crop:** This effect is similar to the Clip effect, but it adds the zoom feature, which appears to zoom the image off the edge of the screen.

- **Edge Feather:** Use this effect to create a feathered frame around the edge of your video image.

- **Horizontal Flip:** The image is flipped horizontally.

- **Horizontal Hold:** This effect simulates a horizontal hold problem on a TV.

- **Roll:** The image appears to roll horizontally across the screen.

- **Vertical Flip:** The image is flipped vertically.

- **Horizontal Hold:** Use this effect to simulate a vertical-hold problem on a V (you can have a lot of fun with this one; just imagine your friends banging on their TVs trying to figure out why the vertical hold is messed up).

Introducing the Effect Controls Window

To apply an effect to a clip, you simply drag the effect from the Effects window to a clip in the Timeline. (Choose Window⇨Effects to open the Effects window.)

You can adjust attributes of an effect using the Effect Controls window. To reveal this window, click the clip in the Timeline to select it and then choose Window⇨Effect Controls. The Effect Controls window appears, as shown in Figure 12-3.

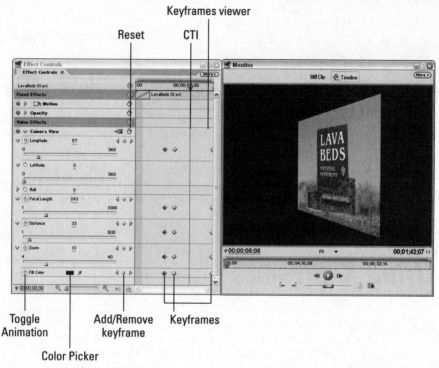

Figure 12-3:
Fine-tune
your effects
using the
Effect
Controls
window.

Key features of the Effect Controls window include:

✔ Each effect applied to a clip is given a separate listing under the Video Effects heading. Click the arrow to expand the view of options for each effect.

✔ On the left side of the Effect Controls window, next to the effect's title, is a tiny circle. To disable an effect, click to remove the tiny circle.

✔ Each effect has its own unique controls. Click the right-pointing arrow next to an effect control to view more specific controls.

✔ To enable keyframing so that the effect can change over the duration of a clip, click the Toggle Animation button, as shown in Figure 12-3. I show you how to use keyframes in the next section.

✔ The Effect Controls window includes a keyframe viewer, which, as you can see in Figure 12-3, looks like a miniature Timeline, complete with its own CTI (Current Time Indicator).

✔ To add a keyframe for a control at the current location of the CTI, click the Add/Remove Keyframe button. Use the arrows on either side of any Add/Remove Keyframe button to move the CTI to the next (or previous) keyframe.

✔ Some effects have Color Pickers. For example, if you're using the Camera View effect, as shown in Figure 12-3, you must use the Color Picker to choose a fill color for the background after the camera view has been modified.

Some Color Pickers have eyedroppers next to them. Eyedroppers are used to choose a color from the video image in the Monitor. To use an eye-dropper, click-and-hold the mouse button on the eyedropper icon, drag the mouse pointer over the desired color in the video image, and release the mouse button. Your desired color is selected when the mouse button is released.

✔ To quickly reset all effect settings back to default, click the Reset button. (I use this button a lot, especially when I'm working with keyframes because the button quickly resets all of the effect controls back to the default settings.)

Using Keyframes

Effects can have a variety of, er, *effects* on clips in Premiere Elements. You can blur, recolor, distort, and more. If you don't believe me, read the first few pages of this chapter. You can apply an effect with its default settings intact to an entire clip, or you can set the effect up so that it changes over time. To do the latter, however, you need to give Premiere Elements a way to determine exactly how and when to make such changes. For this purpose the program uses reference points called *keyframes*. If you want an effect to change over time, you use keyframes to specify when those changes occur. Premiere Elements automatically extrapolates how the effect should progress from one keyframe to the next.

The types of keyframes I am talking about in this chapter are *effect keyframes*. Video codecs (the compression/decompression schemes used to make video files smaller) use another kind of key frame called a *compression key frame*. Although the names sound familiar, the two terms refer to very different subjects. (See Chapters 15 and 16 for more detailed explanations of compression key frames.)

After you have applied an effect to a clip, you can adjust that effect using keyframes. To set keyframes, follow these steps:

1. **Locate in the Timeline the clip that has the effect you want to modify.**

2. **Select the clip, and then open the Effect Controls window for the clip (Window⇨Effect Controls) if the window isn't already open.**

3. **Click the Toggle Animation button next to each control that you want affected by keyframes.**

The Toggle Animation button enables the use of keyframes for the effect. If the Toggle Animation button is disabled, the effect is applied evenly across the entire clip.

4. **Move the CTI in the keyframes viewer to the exact frame where you want to set a keyframe.**

   You can move the CTI using the playback controls in the Monitor window, or you can use the J, K, and L keys on your keyboard. Use the left- and right-arrow keys to move a single frame at a time.

5. **In the Effect Controls window, click the Add/Remove Keyframe button next to an effect control.**

   You need to add a keyframe for each control that you want to change. For example, if you apply the Camera View effect to a clip (refer to Figure 12-3), and you only want the camera view to change after the clip has played for a few seconds, then at the first two keyframes you should set all the controls to their defaults. At the third keyframe, adjust the Longitude, Focal Length, Distance, and Zoom controls to the desired settings. And at the last keyframe, which is at the very end of the clip, set the exact same settings as at the third keyframe. The effect of these changes is that the clip plays normally from the beginning until it reaches the second keyframe. At that point, the camera angle starts to morph until it gets to the settings you specify at the third keyframe. At that point, the camera angle remains morphed until the end of the scene.

6. **Set additional keyframes as desired.**

   Don't forget to use those Previous and Next Keyframe buttons. They provide an easy way to move from keyframe to keyframe. If you want to remove a keyframe, simply move to the keyframe and click the Add/Delete Keyframe button to remove the check mark. When you remove that check mark, you'll notice that the keyframe also magically disappears from the clip.

 If you apply multiple effects to a clip, each effect gets its own keyframes. Thus, if you set a keyframe for one effect, don't assume that it applies to the other effects on that clip as well. To view the keyframes for an effect, click that effect in the Effect Controls window to select it.

Removing Effects

You'll probably change your mind about some of the effects you apply to your clips. Don't feel bad; this is perfectly natural. In fact, you'll find that a lot of time in video editing is spent on good ol' trial and error. You'll try an effect, you won't like it, and then you'll try something else.

To get rid of an effect, click the clip in the Timeline to select it and then choose Window⇨Effect Controls to reveal the Effect Controls window. You have two options for removing effects from a clip:

- ✔ **Temporary disability:** You can temporarily disable an effect by clicking the little circle next to the effect's listing in the Effect Controls window. This can be a handy option because any settings that you changed for the effect are preserved. With the circle removed, the clip is disabled so you can review the clip without the effect in action. When the effect is disabled, it's not applied to the clip when the movie is rendered or output.

- ✔ **Permanent leave:** To delete an effect from a clip, right-click its title in the Effect Controls window and choose Clear from the menu that appears. Don't worry! You're only removing the effect from the current project and restoring the affected clip back to normal. The effect is not deleted from Premiere Elements.

Working with Effect Presets

Before Premiere Elements was released, I spent some time talking to the team over at Adobe that developed this program. In our conversations the team members repeatedly talked about the desire to make Premiere Elements a program that is easier to use than Premiere Pro. The idea was that Premiere Elements should appeal more to entry-level video enthusiasts who may not be comfortable with advanced video-editing tasks. And let's face it, adjusting multiple effect controls and setting keyframes can be a complex, time-consuming process.

To make using and modifying video effects easier, Premiere Elements comes with a collection of effect presets. Each preset is basically a collection of settings that perform common tasks like panning across a still image or creating a picture-in-picture (PiP) effect. Rather than spending minutes or even hours fine-tuning motion controls, keyframes, and other effect settings, you just drop a preset onto the clip, thereby applying a raft of pre-determined settings instantly. These presets are incredible time-saving tools that I think even veteran video professionals could appreciate.

Using a preset is easy. Simply drag-and-drop a preset from the Effects window to a video clip, just as you would with any other effect. All settings related to the preset are applied to the clip; however, you can always fine-tune the settings if you wish.

Surveying Premiere Elements effect presets

You can find Effect presets in the Effects window (Window⇨Effects). The Presets folder in the Effects window contains several subfolders. Presets that come with Premiere Elements include:

- **Bevel Edges:** The two presets in this subfolder quickly bevel the edges of the video image, providing a beveled picture frame appearance.

- **Blurs:** The Fast Blur In preset causes the clip to start out extremely blurry. The picture quickly comes into focus and the clip plays normally to the end. Use this preset to give the appearance that the camera is focusing in on the scene in the clip. The Fast Blur Out is similar, but the image goes blurry at the end of the clip.

- **Color Effects:** These 13 presets quickly apply color changes to a clip. For example, if you want to quickly give a radically red tint to the clip, apply the Hyper Tint Red preset. The Increase Saturation preset quickly increases color saturation in a clip and is a great way to improve the appearance of clips that are sun washed or otherwise lack color depth without having to do too much time-consuming effect tweaking.

- **Horizontal Image Pans:** If you've ever used Apple's iMovie, you may be familiar with the Ken Burns effects that come with later versions of that Macintosh-only program. The Horizontal Image Pan presets available with Premiere Elements are similar to Apple's Ken Burns effects; for example, you can pan across a still image that would otherwise sit static and lifeless on the screen. If you have ever watched a film by renowned documentarian Ken Burns, you have probably seen this technique used many times in his work. The historical subject matter of Burns' films usually requires many still images, and panning slowly across those images restores a sense of motion and action that viewers expect from a video presentation.

- **Horizontal Image Zooms:** Similar to the image pan presets, the Horizontal Image Zoom presets zoom in or out on an image. I find that these presets are especially fun and useful when used on titles. Titles that zoom in or out of view as you read them are very cool when they aren't overdone.

- **Mosaics:** These two presets are much like the Blur presets, but the image "mosaics" in or out rather than blurs.

- **PiPs:** These are my favorite presets. PiP stands for picture-in-picture, an effect that I use quite often. Until the release of Premiere Elements, creating picture-in-picture effects was a time-consuming process that required lots of fine-tuning of motion settings. What used to take minutes or even hours now takes mere seconds. Just drop a PiP preset onto a clip and you have an instant picture-in-picture image. I show you how to use these fabulous presets in greater detail later in this chapter.

✔ **Solarizes:** As mentioned earlier in this chapter, the Solarize effect blends an image with its negative. The two Solarize presets make a clip "solarize" in or out as it plays.

✔ **Twirls:** Do you want a video image to twirl into view or twirl out in a vortex? Apply one of the Twirl presets to quickly create this effect.

✔ **Vertical Image Pans:** These presets are just like the Horizontal Image Pans, but they pan vertically rather than horizontally.

Maybe you're wondering whether you can use the vertical and horizontal image zooms and pans together to apply a diagonal effect. Well, it seemed like a good idea to me, but when I tried it, I realized that — alas — it doesn't work. The problem is that these presets change motion settings, so when you apply one preset it displaces motion settings made by another preset. A diagonal effect would require manual adjustment of existing presets. Play around with it if you've got a few hours to spare.

✔ **Vertical Image Zooms:** Yep, you guessed it. Vertical Image zooms are just up-and-down versions of the left-and-right Horizontal Image Zooms.

Saving your own presets

If you have your own custom effect settings that you like to use on a regular basis, you can save those settings in a preset of your own. For example, if you apply a horizontal image pan preset to an image and then fine-tune the Motion settings so that the image actually pans diagonally, you may want to save your own "diagonal pan" preset. To save a preset, follow these steps:

1. **Adjust your effect settings the way you like them.**

2. **In the Effect Controls window, right-click the name of the effect under Video Effects and choose Save Preset from the menu that appears.**

   The Save Preset dialog box appears, as shown in Figure 12-4.

3. **Enter a descriptive name for the preset in the Name field.**

   If you're creating a Camera View preset, for example, that might make a good name for the preset.

4. **Choose a Type setting for the preset.**

   Your options are Scale, Anchor to In Point, and Anchor to Out Point. In Figure 12-4 I have chosen Anchor to In Point, which means that the effect will begin at the clip's In point. If I choose Anchor to Out Point, the preset will automatically be applied to the end of the clip. Scale simply scales the effect settings to encompass the entire clip.

5. **Enter a description for the preset in the Description field.**

   This information is important because several months from now you may forget exactly what this preset does — even if you have given it an exciting and descriptive name.

6. **Click OK to save the preset and close the dialog box.**

When you save your own preset, the preset appears at the top of the Effects window. Simply drag-and-drop the preset to a clip to quickly apply it, just as you would with any other effect or preset.

Figure 12-4:
Presets can be scaled or anchored to the In or Out point.

Using Some Common Video Effects

Lots of effects are available with Premiere Elements, and I couldn't possibly describe them all here. That's not simply because there are so many effects, but also because there are so many unique video projects. You have to choose the effects that best complement your movie through a process of trial and error.

What I *can* do is provide detailed instructions on how to apply a few of the most common video effects. You can adapt the techniques described here when using many other effects.

Twirling video

Adobe Premiere Elements comes with a plethora of effects that you can use to distort your video. Some of the best ones can be found in the Distort and Transform folders. Distortion effects range from mild to wild. Consider the clip in Figure 12-5. I have applied the Twirl effect, found in the Distort folder under Video Effects. The Twirl effect twirls the video image into a spiral or vortex.

Toggle Animation

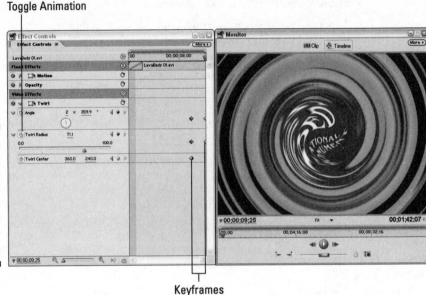

Keyframes

Figure 12-5:
The Twirl
effect has
distorted
this video
clip in a
most pecu-
liar way.

In this section I show you how to make a video image appear to play normally until the end, at which point the image twirls away into nothing. You can quickly apply this effect using one of the Twirl presets (see the discussion of presets earlier in this chapter) but for now I'm going to show you how to do it the old fashioned way. If you've never applied a video effect to a clip before, these steps are a good way to practice working with effect settings and keyframes. Follow these steps:

1. **Open the Effects window by choosing Window⇨Effects. Expand the Video Effects folder and the Distort subfolder.**

2. **Click-and-drag the Twirl effect and drop it on a clip in the Timeline.**

3. **Close the Effects window and then open the Effect Controls window by choosing Window⇨Effect Controls.**

4. **Arrange the Effect Controls and Monitor windows so that both are visible, as shown in Figure 12-5.**

5. **Under Video Effects in the Effect Controls window, click the right-pointing arrow next to Twirl to expand the list of controls.**

   If you don't see Twirl or other controls in the Effect Controls window, click the clip in the Timeline to make sure that the clip is selected.

6. **In the keyframes viewer, move the CTI so that it is about one second from the end of the clip.**

You can use the J, K, and L keys on your keyboard to play backwards, pause, or play forward, respectively. You can also use the left and right arrow keys to step back or forward one frame at a time.

7. **Click the Toggle Animation button next to each of the three controls under the Twirl effect.**

   Keyframes for each control appear in the keyframes viewer.

8. **Press the Page Down button on your keyboard to move the CTI to the end of the clip.**

   If the first frame of the next clip appears, press the left arrow key once to move back one frame. Make sure you are positioned to see the last frame of the clip you are actually modifying.

9. **Adjust the Angle and Twirl Radius controls.**

   The Angle control has a dial that's a little confusing; I don't recommend that you try to figure it out. Instead, just click-and-drag right on the numbers above the dial to increase the angle setting. The angle setting can go up to 360 degrees, but there is a multiplier in front of that, so if you want to twirl the angle 720 degrees simply change the numbers to 2 × 359.9. (I know, technically speaking, that equals 719.9 degrees, not 720, but I figure it's close enough.) The Twirl Radius setting is a much easier to use slider control.

After you adjust these settings, new keyframes appear at the end of the clip in the keyframes viewer. When you are done making changes, press PgUp on your keyboard to move the CTI to the beginning of the clip, and then press L to play the clip and preview your special twirl effect.

Disorienting your audience

Suppose a subject in a movie is sick or disoriented. What is the best way to communicate this to the audience? You could have someone in the movie say, "Hey, you don't look well. Are you sick?" Then the unwell person can stumble and fall down. That may be effective, but an even better way to convey a feeling of illness or confusion is to let your audience see through the subject's blurry and distorted eyes.

You can begin by shooting some footage from the subject's point of view. Hand-hold the camera and let it move slightly as you walk. You probably don't need to exaggerate the movement, but the camera shouldn't be tripod-stable either. As you shoot, pan across the scene — but not too quickly — as if the subject were looking around the room, confused by his surroundings. Occasionally you may want to dip the camera slightly left or right so the video image appears to tilt. A tilting video image has a strong disorienting effect on the viewer.

Now that you have some footage to work with, you can perform the real magic in Premiere Elements. One effect that can provide a feeling of illness or disorientation is Fast Blur (found in the Blur & Sharpen folder). Use keyframes to adjust camera blur throughout a clip, as if the subject's vision were moving in and out of focus. Another good one is Ghosting (also in the Blur & Sharpen folder). Ghosting produces ghost images of moving objects. Similar to Ghosting is the Echo effect, found in the Time folder, which is used in Figure 12-6. Echo gives you a bit more control over the number and timing of echoed images.

Figure 12-6: The Echo effect can be used to disorient the viewer.

Flipping video

Do you ever wish you could produce a mirror image of a video clip, or maybe rotate it and change its orientation on the screen? Such modifications are easy to make with Premiere Elements. Effects that you can use to flip video can be found in the Transform subfolder of Video Effects. These effects include two classics:

- ✓ **Horizontal Flip:** This effect flips the video left to right, as shown in Figure 12-7.
- ✓ **Vertical Flip:** This effect flips the video top to bottom.

When flipping video, watch out for letters and numbers that appear in the frame. Backward or upside down letters stick out like sore thumbs (or rude gestures) when your audience views the movie.

Figure 12-7:
The Horizontal Flip effect was applied to the clip on the left.

Creating a picture-in-picture effect

If you have a somewhat fancy TV, it might have a *picture-in-picture* (PiP) feature. This feature allows you to watch your favorite show in a small window on the screen while your significant other watches another show on the main screen.

Picture-in-picture effects come in handy for a variety of purposes in your movies. For example, if you're interviewing a star soccer player, you may want to show a small picture in the corner of the screen which shows the subject playing a game and scoring a goal. Making picture-in-picture effects has always been possible in Adobe Premiere, but thanks to some handy new presets in Premiere Elements it's not only possible, it's easy.

Applying a PiP preset

Before you can create a picture-in-picture effect, you must set up the video clips properly in your Timeline. Place the main background image in the Video 1 track. Then place another clip in Video 2 or a higher video track, as shown in Figure 12-8 (remember, tracks Video 2 and higher are also called *superimpose* tracks). In this example, I show a small clip of cave exploration in the corner of the introductory scene for my Lava Beds project.

After you have placed the picture-in-picture clip in a superimpose track, follow these steps:

1. **Open the Effects window by choosing Window⇨Effects.**

2. **Open the Presets folder and then open the PiPs subfolder.**

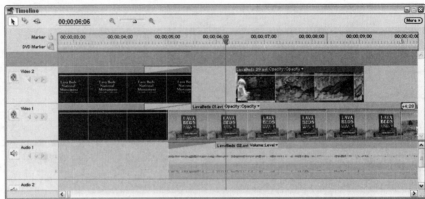

Figure 12-8:
The picture-in-picture clip should be placed in a superimpose track.

3. **Open the 25% or 40% PiPs subfolder, as appropriate.**

   The 25% PiP presets create picture-in-picture clips that are 25% of their original size, and the 40% PiP presets create images that are 40% of their original size.

4. **Open the subfolder for the orientation that you want to use.**

   Presets are divided into LL (lower-left), LR (lower-right), Motion (these move from one orientation to another), UL (upper-left), and UR (upper-right).

5. **Find the preset that best matches the effect you want to create, and click-and-drag it to the clip in the superimpose track.**

   In this example, I am using the preset PiP 25% UL Scale Out. This preset creates a picture-in-picture effect that is 25% of its original size. The image will be positioned in the upper-left corner of the screen, and at the end of the clip it will scale down to a point and disappear.

Adjusting the picture-in-picture image

Premiere Elements' PiP presets greatly simplify the process of creating a picture-in-picture effect, but you may find that some fine-tuning is still necessary. For example, in Figure 12-9 the picture-in-picture effect is ruined by the fact that the smaller picture slightly blocks the words on the sign. Moving the smaller image slightly to the left is no problem.

You can adjust picture-in-picture settings using the Motion controls in the Effect Controls window. Click the picture-in-picture clip in the Timeline to select it, and then choose Window➪Effect Controls to reveal the Effect Controls window, as shown in Figure 12-10. Click the arrow next to Motion to reveal the Motion controls. In Figure 12-10, I have changed the horizontal position to 175.0, which moves the clip over to the left just a bit so that it no longer blocks the letter "L" in the "Lava Beds" sign. In addition to the Position settings, you can also change the size of the picture-in-picture image by adjusting the Scale control.

Figure 12-9:
This picture-in-picture effect is less than perfect because of the slightly blocked sign in the background image.

Figure 12-10:
Use the Motion controls to adjust the position of picture-in-picture effects.

Adding Web links to movies

The term *multimedia* is used pretty loosely these days, although few types of media are as "multi" as the movies you can create with Premiere Elements. Not only can your movies contain audio, video, and still graphics, but they can also include links to the World Wide Web. Of course, for the link to work, your audience must be watching the movie on a computer that is connected to the Internet. Also, the movie needs to be output in a format that supports Web links, such as QuickTime. Web links can be handy if you want a specific Web page to open during or after playback. To create a Web link, follow these steps:

1. **Move the CTI to the point in the Timeline at which you want the link to be activated.**

2. **Choose Marker⇨Set Timeline Marker⇨Unnumbered.**

   A marker appears on the Timeline ruler. Actually, you can make it a numbered marker if you wish.

3. **Double-click the marker.**

   The Marker dialog box appears.

4. **In the URL field, type the complete URL (Uniform Resource Locator) for the link target.**

   The URL is the Web address for the site that you want to open. To be safe, it should include the `http://` part of the address.

   Consider the URL that you enter here carefully. Does it point to a page that will still be online several months (or even a year) from now? Consider how long users might be viewing copies of your movie.

5. **Click OK to close the dialog box.**

6. **Test your Web link in the final output format.**

   If it works, the desired Web page opens in a Web browser. Some formats (such as QuickTime) support Web links; others don't.

Be really, really careful when you type the address for your Web URL. Exact spelling and syntax is crucial or else your Web link is broken — and that creates a bad impression with your audience. Furthermore, because most Web servers run a UNIX-based operating system, everything after the `.com`, `.org`, or `.net` part of the Web address is probably case-sensitive. Watch that capitalization!

Chapter 13

Adding Sound to Your Movies

*W*hen you think about movies you probably think primarily of the pictures in the video image. And when you edit your video clips together
in a movie project, you probably spend most of your time working with the
visuals by placing video clips in the Timeline, adding transitions, and even
using a special effect or two. The audio portion of a movie is, sadly, often
treated only as an afterthought.

Fortunately, you are reading this chapter, which means you probably want to
make sure that great audio is incorporated into your movie projects from the
very beginning. Many video experts will tell you that while audiences tend to
be forgiving of flaws and mistakes in a video image, they find poor-quality
audio almost immediately noticeable and off-putting. This speaks volumes
(pun intended) about the importance of audio.

If you really want to create high-quality, well-rounded movies you need to
spend some time tweaking audio levels, smoothing audio transitions between
clips, and maybe adding some narration or a musical soundtrack. This chapter
introduces you to the basics of audio and shows you how to work with audio in
your Premiere Elements projects.

What Is Audio?

Consider how audio affects the feel of a video program. Honking car horns on
a busy street; crashing surf and calling seagulls at a beach; a howling wolf on
the moors; these are sounds that help identify a place as quickly as visual
images can, if not quicker. If a picture is worth a thousand words, well-done
audio can be worth a thousand pictures.

Understanding sampling rates

For over a century, humans have been recording sound waves using analog devices, ranging from wax cylinders to magnetic tapes. But nowadays most audio is recorded digitally, just as with many modern video recordings. Because a digital recording can only contain specific values, it must approximate a continuous stream of sound. A digital recording device *samples* a sound many times per second. The more samples per second, the more closely the recording can approximate the live sound.

The number of samples per second is called the *sampling rate*. As you might expect, a higher sampling rate provides better recording quality. CD audio typically has a sampling rate of 44.1 kHz — that's 44,100 samples per second — and most digital camcorders can record at a sampling rate of 48 kHz.

When you create a new project in Premiere Elements it always has a sample rate of 48 kHz, but when you export your project you can sometimes choose a lower sample rate.

You may have to use a lower sample rate when exporting a movie for the Web because a small file size is usually more important than CD-quality audio, especially when you're dealing with iffy and often-changing Internet connection rates. Higher audio sampling rates during export usually mean much larger movie files.

Delving into bit depth

A term you'll hear bandied about in audio editing is *bit depth*. The quality of an audio recording is affected by the number of samples per second, as well as the amount of information (or bit depth) in each of those samples. More bits equal more information. Many digital recorders and camcorders offer a choice between 12-bit and 16-bit audio; set your camcorder to the 16-bit audio setting whenever possible.

Conforming audio

When you first import audio into Adobe Premiere Elements — whether you're importing music from a CD or capturing audio and video from a DV tape — Premiere Elements *conforms* the audio to match the audio settings of your project. For example, when you start a new project in Premiere Elements it always has an audio sample rate of 48 kHz (see Chapter 5 for more on starting a new project). But suppose you want to import audio from a music CD, which has a sample rate of 44.1 kHz. When you import that audio, Premiere Elements automatically converts the CD audio to 48 kHz (the sample rate of your project).

Where do conformed files go?

When audio is conformed, Premiere Elements doesn't actually change the audio file that is being imported or captured. Instead, Premiere Elements creates new conformed audio files, which are, by default, stored in the following subfolder of your My Documents folder:

```
Adobe\Premiere Elements\1.0
    \Conformed Audio Files
```
Within this folder are subfolders, one for each of your projects.

When you first import some audio that doesn't conform to the project, Premiere Elements automatically starts creating conformed audio files. Conformed audio serves two important purposes:

- ✔ Audio quality remains consistent throughout your project.
- ✔ Conformed audio files are essentially rendered audio files, meaning that audio effects and other edits can be previewed in real time.

You may notice that some audio files won't play immediately after you import or capture them. That's because Premiere Elements isn't done conforming the audio. The process happens quickly, so you shouldn't have to wait long. When a waveform appears on an audio clip (it looks like a jagged, wavy line), that means the audio has been conformed.

Conformed audio files are almost always huge, which means they use up a lot of disk space. For example, when I recently imported a three-minute MP3 file, the resulting conformed audio file was 70MB, even though the original MP3 file was less than 3MB. If you're trying to clean up old files and recover some disk space, you may want to delete the conformed audio files left over from old projects that you aren't working on any more. Happily, if you decide to work on that project again later, Premiere Elements can automatically regenerate conformed audio files (see the sidebar in this chapter about conformed audio files).

Recording Sounds

When you shoot video, you probably spend extra time and effort making sure the shot is composed just right and that the lighting is favorable. You want to shoot the best quality video that is possible so that you have less editing work to do later on. You should also spend some time making sure that the audio you record is top quality. The following section offers basic tips on recording better audio. I also show you how to record audio using your computer.

Making better quality audio recordings

Recording great-quality audio is no simple matter. Professional recording studios spend thousands or even millions of dollars to set up acoustically superior sound rooms. You probably don't have that kind of budgetary firepower, but you can get still nearly pro-sounding results if you follow these basic tips:

- ✔ **Use an external microphone whenever possible.** The built-in microphones in modern camcorders have improved greatly in recent years, but they still aren't ideal. They often record undesired *ambient* (or background) sound near the camcorder, such as coughing or chatting audience members; some mics even pick up the mechanical whirring sounds from the camcorder's tape drive. If possible, connect an external microphone to the camcorder's mic input. Chapter 21 provides some recommendations on finding a good-quality microphone.

- ✔ **Eliminate unwanted noise sources.** If you *must* use the camcorder's built-in mic, be aware of your movements and other possible causes of loud, distracting noises on tape. Problem items may include a loose lens cap banging around, your finger rubbing against the mic, wind blowing across the mic, and the *swish-swish* of those nylon workout pants you decided to put on this morning.

    When you're recording audio in your studio (a.k.a. your office), be especially wary of ambient noise. Subtle sounds like the cooling fans inside your computer, air rushing through heating ducts, and someone playing video games in the next room all create ambient noise that *will* show up on audio recordings. If you're using your computer to record narration, you won't be able to do much about the computer's fans, but if you have other computers in the room, you definitely want to shut those down.

    Do not try to disable the cooling fans in your computer, not even for just a few minutes! Modern computer processors run so hot that they can be ruined in mere seconds if they're not properly cooled.

- ✔ **Try to minimize sound reflection.** Audio waves reflect off any hard surface, which can cause echoing in a recording. Hanging blankets on walls and other hard surfaces is one way to significantly reduce reflection. If the floor isn't carpeted, cover it with blankets as well.

- ✔ **Obtain and use a high-quality microphone.** A good mic isn't cheap, but it can make a huge difference in recording quality. A high-quality mic may be worth the investment if your project necessitates it. (Doing a movie on the history of yodeling?)

- ✔ **Watch for trip hazards!** In your haste to record great sound, don't forget that your microphone cables can become a hazard on scene. Not only are loose wires a safety hazard to anyone walking by, but if someone snags a cable, your equipment could be damaged as well. If necessary, bring along some duct tape to temporarily cover cables that run across the floor.

Recording audio with your computer

Narration is an important part of many of my movie projects, and I usually find that the easiest way to record narration is to simply record it using my computer. Premiere Elements does not include provisions for recording audio directly, but fortunately any computer running Windows XP can easily record audio. All you really need is a sound card and a microphone. Those cheap microphones that come free with many computers aren't very good, and if your budget allows I strongly recommend a good microphone (see Chapter 21 for more on choosing a good microphone).

When you have a microphone connected to the microphone port on your computer's sound card, you are ready to record audio using the Windows XP Sound Recorder program. Follow these steps:

1. **To open Sound Recorder choose Start⇨All Programs⇨Accessories⇨ Entertainment⇨Sound Recorder.**

   The Sound Recorder program opens.

2. **Choose File⇨Properties.**

   The Properties for Sound dialog box appears.

3. **Click Convert Now.**

   The Sound Selection dialog box appears.

4. **In the Attributes menu, choose 48.000 kHz, 16 Bit.**

   Notice that the Attributes menu contains two 48.000 kHz, 16 Bit options, one for mono, and one for stereo. If you have a stereo microphone choose Stereo. Otherwise, choose the Mono option.

5. **Click OK to close the Sound Selection dialog box. Then click OK to close the Properties for Sound dialog box.**

6. **In the Sound Recorder, click Record and briefly record some sample narration.**

   If you plan to record narration, speak a few sentences into the microphone.

7. **Click Stop after you've recorded a few seconds of sample narration, and then click Play to listen to the recording.**

   Does the recording sound the way you want? Listen for unwanted ambient sounds and other problems. Did the microphone pick up breathing or clothing sounds? If so, consider suspending the microphone overhead. You may also need to vary your distance from the microphone before you get the optimal recording quality. Go ahead and re-record samples as often as necessary.

8. **When you are done recording samples and are ready to record the real thing, choose Edit⇨Delete Before Current Position, and then click OK in the Sound Recorder warning message that appears.**

   The sample recordings you made are deleted forever.

9. **Click Record and record your narration for real.**

   If you make a mistake and need to start over, click Stop and repeat steps 8 and 9 as often as needed.

10. **When you're satisfied with your recording, choose File⇨Save and save your recording.**

    The recording is saved as a .WAV file, which can be quickly imported into Premiere Elements. Chapter 6 shows how to import media files.

Working with Audio in Your Movies

As I mention in the introduction to this chapter, the importance of good audio is easy to underestimate when you edit video. But audio is a crucial ingredient when you make movie magic, so you'll want to spend some time tweaking and adjusting the audio in all of your movie projects.

Premiere Elements doesn't have a workspace specifically designed for working with audio, but you can easily set up your workspace for audio editing. I recommend that you start by switching to the Edit workspace by choosing Window⇨Workspace⇨Edit. Next, open the Audio Meters window by choosing Window⇨Audio Meters. The Audio Meters help you measure sound levels in your audio.

You may need to move windows around the screen to get a workspace that you can use. In Figure 13-1 I've closed the How To window to make room for the Audio Meters window. I show how Audio Meters come in handy later in this chapter. The following sections show how to work with audio in your Premiere Elements movie projects.

Editing audio visually

Although audio is something we hear with our ears, Premiere Elements lets you edit it using your eyes. It sounds crazy, I know, but there's often a good reason to edit audio by looking at it. Using Premiere Elements you can look at the audio waveform for an audio clip. A waveform like the one shown in Figure 13-2 is simply a visual representation of the audio waves in a file.

Figure 13-1:
This work-
space is
ready to
edit audio.

CTI

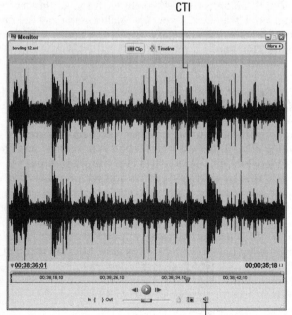

Figure 13-2:
Waveforms
allow you
to edit
audio with
your eyes.

Toggle Take Audio and Video

The waveform shows two sets of waves because it is a stereo audio file. Each wave is called a *channel*. The waveform on top is the left stereo channel, and the waveform on the bottom is the right stereo channel.

To view a clip's waveform, first double-click the clip in the Media window to load it into the Monitor window. In the Monitor, click the Toggle Take Audio and Video button until the waveform appears.

Spikes in the waveform indicate louder audio events. Sometimes when you work with audio you need to be able to time edits to those particular events, but identifying the exact frame when one of those events occurs can be difficult if you're only listening to the clip. But when you look at the clip's waveform, identifying the exact location of audio events is easy. Waveforms also appear on audio clips in the Timeline. I show you how to work with audio clips in the Timeline later in this chapter.

I like to use clip markers to identify important audio events in a clip. When you are previewing a clip's waveform in the Monitor, use the left and right arrow keys on your keyboard to move back and forth a frame a time. When you have the CTI on the exact location of an audio event, choose Marker⇨ Set Clip Marker⇨Unnumbered. An unnumbered clip marker appears at the location of the CTI. This will come in handy later when you try to line up video clips with this audio event.

Before you edit a clip into the Timeline, click the Toggle Take Audio and Video button again so that the Monitor is set to edit both the audio and video portions of the clip into the Timeline. If you try to click-and-drag the clip to the Timeline while the waveform is still shown, only the audio portion of the clip will be added to the Timeline.

Setting audio In and Out points

When you first start putting a movie together, you begin by sorting through your captured video clips to decide which clips you want to use. For each clip, you also decide which portions of the clip you want to use. As I show in Chapter 7, you do this by setting in points and out points for the clips.

Usually when you set an In point or Out point for a clip, you set them for both audio and video. However, you can set separate In points and Out points for audio and video. Why? Consider the video clip in Figure 13-3. In this clip, the subject throws a bowling ball down a bowling lane. My plan is to cut from this clip to the clip in Figure 13-4, which shows a ball traveling down the bowling lane and hitting some pins.

Figure 13-3:
This video
clip will be
shown first.

The audio portion of this bowling sequence presents an interesting editing challenge. I want the sequence to play the sound of one bowling ball rolling all the way down the lane and hitting the pins. To do this, I'm going to use the audio recorded with the clip in Figure 13-4 instead of the clip in Figure 13-3. This means that when I edit the clip in Figure 13-4 into the Timeline, I'm going to have to set separate In points for the audio and video. To set separate In points for audio and video, follow these steps:

1. **Find the point where you want to start using the audio portion of the clip, and make sure the CTI in the Monitor window is stopped on that point.**

2. **Choose Marker➪Set Clip Marker➪Audio In.**

   An audio In point is set, and a green band across the bottom of the Monitor's time ruler shows the audio portion that you plan to take.

3. **Move the CTI to the spot where you want to start taking video, and choose Marker➪Set Clip Marker➪Video In.**

   A blue band appears across the top of the Monitor's time ruler, as shown in Figure 13-4. The blue band indicates the video portion of the clip that will be used.

Figure 13-4:
This video clip contains the audio I will use in the whole sequence.

You can also set Out points separately by using the same method described here. Simply choose Audio Out or Video Out from the Set Clip Marker submenu in the Marker menu.

Unlinking audio and video in the Timeline

When you insert into the Timeline a clip that contains both audio and video, the audio and video tracks for that clip are usually linked together. If that's the case, then you'll notice that they both become selected when you click one of them in the Timeline. Usually this is a handy function, but sometimes you may want to unlink the two and edit them individually. For example, you may decide that you want to delete or ripple edit (see Chapter 8 for more on ripple edits) the audio portion of a clip, while leaving the video portion of the clip alone. To unlink audio and video for a clip, select that clip in the Timeline and choose Clip⇨Unlink Audio and Video. You can now select the audio and video portions of the clip individually.

Premiere Elements provides a visual clue to tell you which clips are linked and which ones are not. Linked clips have underlined names in the Timeline. The names of unlinked clips are not underlined.

Adjusting audio volume

I like to use a lot of different audio tracks in a project. If you like to use a lot of audio too, I suggest that you try to insert each new audio element on a different track. This trick gives you greater flexibility when you make adjustments to things such as volume. Different bits of audio get recorded at different levels, and you may find that one audio clip is too loud whereas another is not loud enough.

The volume of audio in video projects is measured in volume units (VU). Audio Meters in Premiere Elements (Window⇨Audio Meters) provide VU meters that may appear similar to the volume meters on a tape deck or other recording device you've used before. If you've ever recorded audio on tape using an analog tape deck, you probably made sure that the audio levels got above 0 and into the red zone of the VU meter once in a while, but that average volume was below 0. When you're working with digital audio, 0 is the maximum volume level you can have before distortion occurs. That's why if you look at the Audio Meters, you notice that the VU meter scales stop at 0.

When adjusting volume — also sometimes called *gain* — for an individual track, keep an eye on the Audio Meters. If the meters reach 0, you'll probably get audio distortion in the final program. If 0 is reached, the red indicator at the top of the VU meter lights up red.

Besides watching for audio peaks that are at above 0, you should also keep an eye on the average audio levels. The VU meters dance up and down quite a bit as you play the project, and you should adjust volume so the average levels are between –12 and –18 on the VU meter.

When you adjust the volume of an audio clip, you can adjust the overall volume for the entire clip, or you can adjust it variously throughout the clip. To adjust volume for a whole clip at once, follow these steps:

1. **Select the audio clip in the Timeline and choose Clip⇨Audio Options⇨Audio Gain.**

   The Audio Gain dialog box appears.

2. **Click-and-drag left on the dB number to reduce gain; click-and-drag right to increase gain.**

   Alternatively, click Normalize. Doing so automatically adjusts the gain to the highest possible level without creating distortion. To reset the clip to its original gain level, restore the gain value to 0 dB.

3. **Click OK to close the dialog box.**

In addition to adjusting the overall volume of an audio clip, you can also adjust volume at individual points within the clip. Here's how:

1. **Click an audio clip in the Timeline to select it.**

2. **Move the CTI to a spot in the Timeline where you want to start adjusting volume.**

3. **Click the Add/Remove Keyframe button.**

   A round keyframe appears along the yellow volume rubberband.

4. **Move the CTI to a new location in the clip and click the Add/Remove Keyframe button again.**

   Repeat this step to create additional keyframes.

5. **Click-and-drag on keyframes to move the volume rubberband.**

   Moving the rubberband up increases volume, and moving it down decreases volume. In Figure 13-5 I have adjusted the volume rubberbands on two audio clips so that one fades out as the other fades in. The effect is barely noticeable to the listener and provides a seamless audio experience for the sequence. Also notice that audio waveforms appear on audio clips in the Timeline.

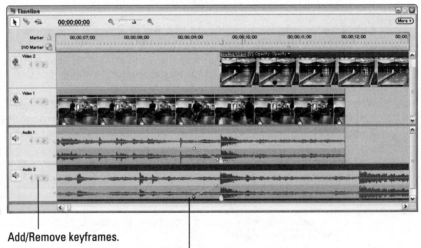

Figure 13-5:
Use volume rubberbands to dynamically adjust volume throughout a clip.

Add/Remove keyframes.

Click-and-drag rubberbands to adjust volume.

If you adjust the volume rubberbands upward on any audio clips, make sure that you play the clip using Audio Meters and keep an eye on the VU meters. If the audio levels exceed 0, you need to reduce volume a bit.

Using Audio Effects and Transitions

Adobe Premiere Elements comes with a valuable selection of audio effects and transitions. Just like video effects and transitions, you can access audio effects and transitions in the Effects window. If you don't see the Effects window, choose Window⇨Effects. The following sections describe audio effects and transitions available in Premiere Elements. I also show how to use the Balance effect.

Reviewing the Premiere Elements audio effects

Premiere Elements comes with a good selection of audio effects that allow you to improve and modify your audio clips. Some of these effects can be used to make audio seem distorted or surreal; other effects simply help you repair problems in an audio track. Premiere Elements' audio effects live in the Effects window, which you can reveal by choosing Window⇨Effects. Audio effects offered in Premiere Elements include:

- **Balance:** Controls balance between the left and right channels in a stereo clip. I show how to use the Balance effect later in this chapter.

- **Bass:** Provides control over bass response in the clip. Bass sounds are the deeper, low frequency sounds in an audio clip.

- **Channel Volume:** Allows you to control the volume of stereo channels independently.

- **Delay:** Echoes the clip. Echoes the clip.

- **DeNoiser:** Removes unwanted background noise during quiet parts of the clip. This effect works kind of like the Dolby noise reduction found on audio cassette tape players by removing pops and hisses from the audio.

- **Fill Left:** Moves the audio completely to the left stereo channel.

- **Fill Right:** Moves the audio completely to the right stereo channel.

- **Highpass:** Removes lower frequencies from the audio clip.

- **Invert:** Inverts the audio phase (or delay) between the left and right audio channels in a stereo clip. For example, if the audio in the left channel is slightly delayed behind the right channel, the Invert effect inverts the phase so that the right channel is delayed instead of the left.

- **Lowpass:** Removes higher frequencies from the audio.

- **Notch:** Removes sound at a frequency you specify. Use this effect if the audio clip has a constant hum caused by a nearby power line or a flaw in the recording device.

- ✔ **PitchShifter:** Adjusts pitch in an audio clip. For example, if you speed up a clip and as a result the voices have an unnaturally high pitch, you can use this effect to make the voices sounds more normal.

- ✔ **Reverb:** Makes the audio clip sound as if it's being played in a large hall or room.

- ✔ **Swap Channels:** Swaps the left and right stereo channels, if for some reason you decide that the sound in the right channel should be on the left, and vice versa.

- ✔ **Treble:** Provides control over treble (the higher frequency sounds) in the clip.

- ✔ **Volume:** Allows you to adjust volume with an effect rather than the Audio Mixer or the volume rubber bands.

A complete course on how to use each effect would take up nearly another whole book (each effect differs considerably from the others). Some general instructions are in order, however: To apply an audio effect to a clip, simply drag it from the Effects window and drop it onto your audio clip in the Timeline. Depending on which effect you chose, you can manipulate audio effect settings using the Effect Controls window (Window⇨Effect Controls); you can also adjust the effect dynamically using keyframes (see Chapter 12 for more on working with the Effect Controls window and with effect keyframes). Make sure a clip is selected in the Timeline if you want to view its controls in the Effect Controls window.

Using audio transitions

One of the most common reasons for adjusting volume on a clip (at least, in my experience) is to fade a clip in as it begins and fade it out as it ends. When done well, fading sound in and out is barely perceptible to the viewer. This fading — called cross-fading — takes a distinct "edge" off the transition as a loud noise gradually starts or stops. I like to apply audio transitions to fade between virtually all audio clips in a project, even though I usually don't use video transitions between every video clip.

The idea behind audio transitions is to make the audible transition between clips virtually imperceptible, and audio transitions can do that.

The process of fading in or out between clips has never been easier. Premiere Elements provides two audio transitions that you can apply to audio clips to quickly fade them in or out. If two clips are adjacent, the transition cross-fades the two clips. You can access the transitions under Audio Transitions in the Effects window (choose Window⇨Effects if you don't see the Effects window). There are two Cross Fade transition effects available in Premiere Elements:

✔ **Constant Gain:** Audio fades in or out at a constant, linear level.

✔ **Constant Power:** Audio fades in a manner that sounds linear to the human ear, although from a purely mathematical standpoint, it is not linear.

I use the Constant Power transition most often, but you may want to experiment to get the best results for your projects. To apply a transition, simply drag-and-drop it from the Effects window to the edge of a clip or a spot between clips. As you can see in Figure 13-6, audio transitions appear in the Timeline much like video transitions.

Video transitions

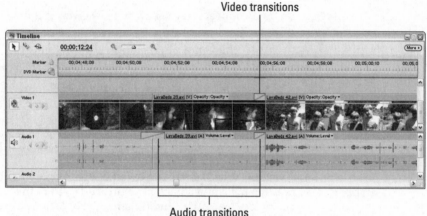

Figure 13-6: Audio transitions make cross-fading audio a snap.

Audio transitions

Adjusting audio balance

Most audio clips have more than one channel. Stereo clips — the most common type — have left and right channels. Sounds in the left channel play out of the left speaker of a stereo system, and sounds in the right channel play out of the right speaker.

You can also easily adjust the balance of mono or stereo clips using the Premiere Elements Balance effect. Moving the audio balance over to one channel or the other is sometimes called *panning*. Using this effect you can pan audio to the left or right channels (just as you might pan the camera to the left or right side of a room), and using effect keyframes you can change the effect as the clip plays. For example, if the subject exits to the left side of the screen you may want to pan audio to the left so that the sound seems to exit to the left with the subject. To adjust audio balance, follow these steps:

1. **Open the Effects window if it isn't already open (Window⇨Effects) and expand the Audio Effects folder.**

2. **Click-and-drag the Balance effect from the Effects window and drop it on the audio clip in the Timeline that you want to adjust.**

3. **Click the clip in the Timeline to select it, and then choose Window⇨ Effect Controls to open the Effect Controls window, as shown in Figure 13-7.**

4. **In the Effect Controls window, click the arrow next to Balance to expand the controls for the Balance effect.**

5. **Place the CTI at a spot where you want to start panning the audio balance, and then click the Toggle Animation button next to the Balance heading.**

   An effect keyframe appears in the keyframes viewer, as shown in Figure 13-7.

6. **Adjust the Balance slider left to pan audio left, or adjust the slider right to pan right.**

7. **Move the CTI to a new location, and click the Add/Remove Keyframes button.**

   Another effect keyframe appears in the keyframes viewer.

8. **Adjust the Balance slider again to adjust balance at the new keyframe.**

In Figure 13-7, I panned audio heavily to the left at the first keyframe because an object (the bowling ball shown back in Figure 13-4) enters the scene from the left side of the video image. The audio then quickly pans back to normal (a balanced setting) as the bowling ball comes into view.

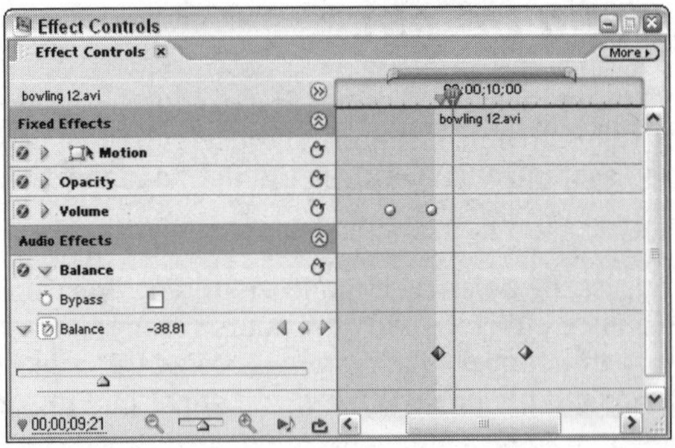

Figure 13-7: Pan audio between stereo channels using the Balance effect.

Chapter 14

Adding Titles to Your Movies

· ·

· ·

*I*n a rush to get to the pictures, folks who are new to video editing often overlook the importance of good audio (see Chapter 13). The same could also be said of titles — the subject of this chapter. Titles — the words that appear on-screen during a movie — are critically important in many different kinds of projects. Titles tell your audience the name of your movie, who made it, who starred in it, who paid for it, who made the titles, and who baked cookies for the cast. Titles can also clue the audience in to vital details — where the story takes place, what time it is, even what year it is — with minimum fuss. And, of course, titles can reveal what the characters are saying if they're speaking a different language.

Adobe Premiere Elements includes a powerful titling tool called the Adobe Title Designer. Few video-editing programs offer the creative control and power over on-screen text that you get with the Adobe Title Designer. In this chapter, I show you how to create beautiful and functional titles using the Adobe Title Designer, as well as show you how to integrate those titles into your projects.

Introducing and Setting Up Adobe Title Designer

Sure, you can think of titles as just words on the screen. But think of the effects, both forceful and subtle, that well-designed titles can have. Consider the *Star Wars* movies, which all begin with a black screen and the sentence, "A long time ago, in a galaxy far, far away. . . ." This simple title screen quickly and effectively sets the tone and tells the audience that the story is beginning. And then, of course, you get those scrolling words that float three-dimensionally off into space, immediately after that first title screen (I show you how to create this exact effect in Chapter 19). A story floating through space is far more interesting than white text scrolling from the bottom to top of the screen, don't you think?

To begin creating titles for a project, open that project and choose File➪New➪Title. The Adobe Title Designer window appears. Before you begin creating text for your titles, spend some time setting up the view.

Revealing the Safe Title Margin

One of the first things you should do before creating titles is make sure that the Safe Title Margin is visible. To do so, choose Title➪View and make sure that Safe Title Margin has a check mark next to it. You know the margin is visible if you see a thin margin line in the title area on-screen.

If you look closely you might also see a second line slightly outside the Safe Title Margin. The outer line is the Safe Action Margin. The Safe Action Margin is less important when designing titles because all your titles should fall within the smaller box drawn by the Safe Title Margin anyway. The Safe Action Margin is a bit bigger than the Safe Title Margin because if action in the video image gets too close to the edge, that is at least more tolerable than words that get cut off at edges of the screen. If you want to hide the Safe Action Margin, choose Title➪View➪and click Safe Action Margin to remove the check mark next to it. You can always view the Safe Action Margin later if you are worried about video activity being too close to the edge of the screen.

The Safe Title and Safe Action Margins are especially important if you're producing a movie that will be viewed on TV screens. Most TVs *overscan* images (they allow some of the video image to be cut off at the edges of the screen). Some TVs overscan more than others; fortunately, you don't have to concern yourself with knowing how bad each TV might be. Just know that anything inside the Safe Title Margin is going to appear on just about any TV screen — with some room to spare. If you place titles outside that margin, you're taking a chance that some text may run off the screen and be unreadable.

Displaying video images in the Adobe Title Designer

If you're creating a title to superimpose over a video image, I recommend that you display the actual image in the Adobe Title Designer window as you work on the title. Doing so helps you decide exactly where to position the text.

To display a video image in the Adobe Title Designer, simply place a check mark next to the Show Video option, as shown in Figure 14-1. Video from your current project appears. You can move to a specific point in the Timeline using a couple of methods:

- ✔ Click (once) on the timecode next to the Show Video option and then enter a specific timecode to which you want to jump.
- ✔ Click-and-drag left or right on the blue timecode next to Show Video. The video image jogs back and forth as you drag.

In Figure 14-1, the Timeline is set at 00;00;20;03. Creating titles over the real video image is pretty important because you need to be able to see how your text contrasts with different parts of the image.

Show video   Current timecode

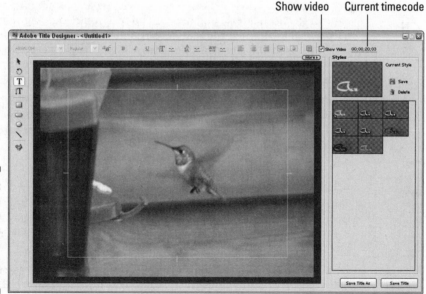

Figure 14-1: Previewing video images makes title creation a lot easier.

Important Title Formatting Rules for Video

If you've ever worked in print or Web design, you've probably spent some time changing the size, color, style, and font of text. You may know some of the general rules for text on the Web or in print: Use dark text on light backgrounds; use serif typefaces for large bodies of text; don't use too many different typefaces on a page.

Video has some text rules too, although they differ considerably from print. One of the things you must take into consideration when creating text for video is the effect that interlacing has on your text. Interlacing on NTSC or PAL TV screens causes thin lines to flicker or crawl on-screen. To prevent this headache (literally), make sure that you follow these important Do's and Don'ts:

- ✔ **Do make sure that all the lines in your text are thicker than 1 pixel.** Lines that are only 1 pixel thick will flicker on most TVs because of interlacing (see Chapter 4 for more on interlaced TV displays).

- ✔ **Do avoid using serif typefaces in video, especially for smaller text.** Serif typefaces — such as Times New Roman — have those extra little strokes at the ends of characters, while sans serif typefaces — like Arial — do not. Those little strokes in serif typefaces are often thin enough to cause interlacing flicker. The text you're reading right now uses a *serif face*, while the text in the caption for Figure 14-2 uses a *sans serif face*. To be on the safe side, always carefully preview your titles on an external video monitor and check for flickering or other appearance problems.

- ✔ **Don't assume that dark text is better.** In print and on the Web, dark text over a light background usually looks best because it provides good contrast. Although adequate contrast is important in video, light text usually works better.

The best possible combination for video is white text on a dark background.

- ✔ **Do experiment with shadows and graphics.** Simpler isn't always necessarily better. If the background of the video clip is light or has mixed color, you can use shadows or graphics to create a dark background just for your titles.

- ✔ **Do stay within the boundaries.** *Always* keep your titles inside the Title Safe Margin. Not only does this prevent text from running off the screen on TVs that badly overscan the image, but it also means that your text isn't running right up against the edge of the screen.

Creating and Manipulating Text

After you have revealed the Safe Title Margin and made sure that the video image displays in the Adobe Title Designer, you can start adding text. From the toolbar on the left side of the Title Designer window choose either the Type Tool or the Vertical Type Tool. Then click in the Adobe Title Designer window and start typing. Your text appears on-screen. As you can see in Figure 14-2, the text probably doesn't look exactly the way you want it at first.

To begin with, you probably want to move the text after you're done typing it. Click the Selection tool (it looks like an arrow) and then click-and-drag the text box to a new location. Don't get too picky at this point; you'll probably move the text again later after you adjust some text attributes.

If you want long lines of text to automatically wrap to a new line when space runs out, right-click the text and choose Word Wrap from the menu that appears. I have enabled word wrap for the text in Figure 14-2.

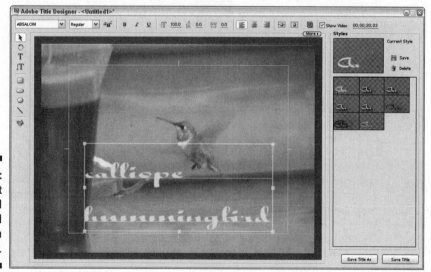

Figure 14-2: Arrghh! Text can be hard to read when you first type it.

Using title templates

One simple way to start creating titles is to use one of the built-in title templates. Premiere Elements comes with over a hundred pre-designed templates that can save you oodles of time when you're creating complete titles. To use a title template, follow these steps:

   1. **Open the Title Designer (File⟶New⟶Title).**

2. **Choose Title⇨Templates, or choose Recreate Title From Template in the More menu in the Title Designer.**

   The Templates window appears.

3. **To preview a template, click it in the Templates list on the left side of the window and preview it on the right side of the Templates window.**

   If you want to use a template, it's best to make that decision before you start entering text for your titles. When you apply a template to a title, any text you've already entered is replaced by the stock placeholder text that comes with the template. Any other frills you added or modifications you made disappear when you apply a template to them.

4. **Preview a template or two, or maybe three or four.**

   The templates are arranged into folders and subfolders by themes and styles. Many designs are available, so you may want to spend some time exploring the Templates window to preview them. For example, in the Travel folder you can find a subfolder called Topo. Here, you'll find a collection of titles that would work well in, say, a video about a hiking excursion.

5. **After you've chosen the title you want to use, click OK in the Templates window.**

   The Templates window closes and the template is applied to your title.

Setting text properties

Regardless of whether you use a template (as described in the previous section), you'll probably want to adjust the attributes of the text in your titles to make them more to your liking. For example, you can pick a font that's consistent with the project's style (and is easy to read), pick a color that contrasts adequately with the background, adjust the size and scaling of the text, and more.

To adjust text properties, click the text object once to select it, and then adjust the text attributes using the menus and controls along the top of the Adobe Title Designer window.

One of the coolest new features in the Premiere Elements Adobe Title Designer is the Font Browser. Click the Browse button next to the font menu in the upper-left corner of the Title Designer window to reveal the Font Browser, which appears. The Font Browser makes it easy to visualize font appearance. When you find a font that you like, click it once to select it in the Font Browser and click OK.

Other controls along the top of the Adobe Title Designer help you change the style of text, adjust the text size, fine-tune spacing between characters and lines, control alignment, and change the color.

Coloring and shadowing text

If you want to apply a different color and perhaps a drop shadow to some text, the Adobe Title Designer provides a great deal of control. To change the color of text or apply a drop-shadow, click the Color Properties button along the top of the Adobe Title Designer window. The Color Properties dialog box appears. With this dialog box you can control several important text attributes:

- ✔ **Color:** Use the Color Picker at the top of the Color Properties dialog box to select colors for text fill and stroke.

- ✔ **Stroke:** Stroke is an outline around text characters. A thin stroke often greatly enhances the appearance of text. Click the Stroke Color button to pick a color for the stroke, and then adjust the Stroke Weight to change the thickness.

- ✔ **Gradient:** In addition to solid color text, you can also make text that is a color gradient. Choose a gradient style from the Gradient menu and pick colors for the gradient in the controls that appear. Depending on the type of gradient you choose, you can usually adjust the angle of the gradient as well.

- ✔ **Drop Shadow:** Place a check mark next to this option if you want your text to have a drop shadow.

- ✔ **Angle:** Adjust this setting from 0 to 360 degrees to precisely set the angle of the drop shadow.

- ✔ **Distance:** The distance should be greater than 0, but it shouldn't be so great that the shadow makes the text appear blurry and difficult to read.

- ✔ **Softness:** Use this setting to soften the shadow's appearance.

Click OK to close the Color Properties dialog box and apply your changes.

A shadow can help offset text from the video image somewhat, especially if the title appears over a light- or mixed-color background.

Using styles

If a title template seems too fancy and manually adjusting title attributes is too time-consuming, try using one of the Adobe Title Designer's pre-designed styles. Various styles are available in the Styles menu on the right side of the Title Designer window. To apply a style to some text that you have already typed, simply click the text object to select it, and then click a style in the list on the right side of the Title Designer window. The style is automatically applied to the text.

Styles can be thought of as starting points. Even if one of the styles doesn't exactly match what you need, choosing one that is close can still save you a lot of time. After you've applied the style, you can always fine-tune attributes such as color, size, and shadows.

Making a rolling or crawling title

Titles are often animated in video productions. Text can fly onto the screen, crawl along the bottom like a stock ticker, or scroll from bottom to top as you roll the credits at the end of your movie. You can animate text using one of two methods:

✔ Animate the title clip in the Timeline using the animation tools that come with Premiere Elements. (For more on animating titles and other clips in the Timeline, see Chapter 11.)

✔ Use the animation tools built into the Adobe Title Designer.

The second method is the less complex of the two, so it's a good general choice. To create animated titles using the Adobe Title Designer, follow these steps:

1. **In Premiere Elements, choose File⇨New⇨Title.**

2. **Open the Title menu on the Premiere Elements menu bar and choose Roll/Crawl Options.**

   The Roll/Crawl Options dialog box appears, as shown in Figure 14-3.

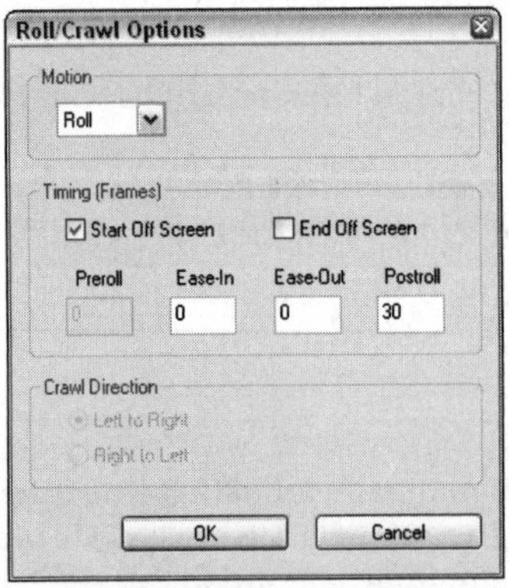

Figure 14-3: Use this dialog box to create titles that roll or crawl across the screen.

3. **If you want the rolling or crawling title to begin off-screen, select the Start Off Screen option. If you want the title to end out of view, choose the End Off Screen option.**

In Figure 14-3 I've selected the Start Off Screen option, which means the titles will appear from the bottom and scroll up into view. I've left the End Off Screen option unchecked, however, which means that the titles will stop scrolling when the end of the text appears.

4. **If you want the title to remain static for a while before it starts to roll or crawl, enter a time in frames in the Preroll field.**

   If you enter 15 in the Preroll field, the title appears on-screen for 15 frames before it starts to roll or crawl off the screen. This field is not available if you choose the Start Off Screen option.

5. **If you want the title to roll or crawl on-screen and then stop, enter a time in the Postroll field.**

   Like Preroll, Postroll is measured in frames. In Figure 14-3 I've entered a Postroll value of 30 frames, which means the titles will roll up the screen and then stop, staying in view for 30 frames, which is about one second.

6. **If you want the title to gradually increase speed as it starts to move or gradually decrease as it stops, enter times in the Ease-In and Ease-Out fields.**

   Like Preroll and Postroll, Ease-In and Ease-Out are expressed in frames. If you enter an Ease-In time of 15 frames, the title starts moving slowly and gradually builds up to full speed within 15 frames.

7. **If you are creating a crawling title, choose whether you want the title to crawl Left to Right or Right to Left.**

8. **Click OK when you're done.**

   The Roll/Crawl Options dialog box closes.

You can now create text objects in the Adobe Title Designer window. If you are making a rolling title, simply scroll down the work area as you add more items as shown in Figure 14-4. If you are creating a scrolling title, scroll left or right in the work area.

The copyright symbol is commonly used in movie titles, but unfortunately there isn't a key for it on the keyboard. To enter the copyright symbol in your own title, hold down the Alt key on your keyboard and type 0169. Voilà! The copyright symbol appears.

Although you can scroll in the work area of the Adobe Title Designer to see all the contents of your titles, you cannot preview the actual roll or crawl in the Title Designer. This is because Premiere Elements dynamically adjusts the speed of the roll or crawl based on the length of the clip in the Timeline. The entire title rolls or crawls past, whether you have the title set to play for five seconds or five minutes in the Timeline. Obviously, the more time you give the title to play, the slower it rolls by. To quickly increase the amount of time that a title plays in the Timeline, choose the Time Stretch Tool in the Timeline and then click-and-drag an edge of the title to change its duration.

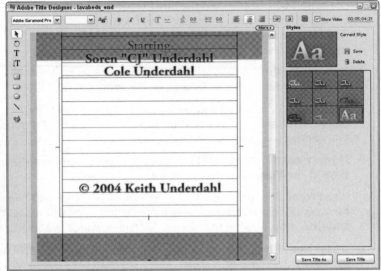

Figure 14-4:
Scroll down in the Title Designer work area to create rolling titles.

Adding Graphics to Titles

In addition to inserting text into your movies, Adobe's Title Designer also enables you to draw some basic graphics and shapes in your titles. The drawing tools can serve a variety of useful purposes, including

✔ Drawing a line under some text, thus making the text stand out a bit more on the screen. This is often done when identifying a speaker or subject on-screen. Drawing a line with the Adobe Title Designer's drawing tools gives you more control over the size and appearance of the line than simply using the Underline text formatting option.

✔ Including a solid-colored box behind the text to create adequate contrast between words and the background image.

You can find the drawing tools along the left side of the Adobe Title Designer window. Their functions are pretty self-explanatory; simply click a tool and then click-and-drag the shape on-screen. Use the Color Properties button to adjust colors and other attributes of the objects you draw. In Figure 14-5, for example, I've drawn a line underneath a row of text using the Line tool, and created an oval using the Rounded Rectangle tool to provide a contrasting background for the title.

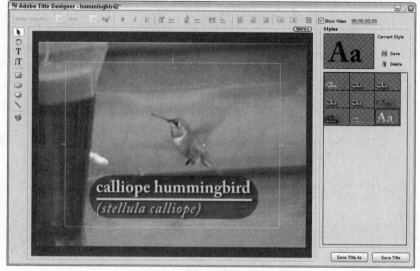

Figure 14-5:
Subtle
graphics
can make
your text
much more
readable.

You may want to adjust several other attributes of your graphics as well. When you select a graphic object using the Selection tool, the Title menu (located up on the main Premiere Elements menu bar) provides access to a couple of important options:

✔ **Arrange:** If you want some objects in a title to overlap with other objects (say, for example, you want text to appear over a background graphic), you need control over which objects are arranged on top of others. To move an item forward or back relative to other objects in the title, select that item and choose Title➪Arrange. Then select an option from the sub-menu that appears. In Figure 14-5, I created a black, rounded, rectangular background graphic for the text and chose Send to Back from the Arrange menu to ensure that the graphic was behind the words.

✔ **Opacity:** By default, all graphics you create in a title are opaque, which means you can't see through them. You can reduce the opacity of graphic objects, thereby making them more transparent. To adjust opacity, select a graphic object and choose Title➪Transform➪Opacity. Enter a percent-age less than 100 to make the object less opaque. In Figure 14-5, I placed a black oval behind the text. An opaque black oval looked like a heavy black blob — but with its opacity reduced to 40 percent, the background oval gained some subtlety. Now it still helps the text stand out, but it doesn't completely blot out the action going on in the video image.

Opening and Saving Titles

When you're done creating and tweaking a title, click Save Title in the bottom-right corner of the Adobe Title Designer. The title then appears in your Media window. If you want to modify a title, simply double-click it in the Media window to re-open the title for editing in the Adobe Title Designer. To help keep things organized, I recommend that you create a special folder in the Media window just for titles (call it `Titles` or something similarly creative), and store all your titles there. For more on creating folders in the Media window and organizing your media, see Chapter 6.

Try to keep a consistent appearance to all of the titles that appear in a single movie project. Rather than create each title from scratch and adjust the font, size, and other attributes every single time, simply double-click an existing title in the project's Media window. The title opens in the Adobe Title Designer. Then click Save Title As in the lower-right corner of the Adobe Title Designer. Give the title a new name, and then make your changes.

Adding Titles to Your Movie

Creating titles in the Adobe Title Designer is just one part of the job of working with titles. After you're done creating titles, you need to add them to your movie project just like other images, sounds, and video clips. The following sections show you how to add your saved titles to your movies.

Adding titles to the Timeline

To add a title to a project, you basically just drag it from the Media window to a video track on the Timeline. Usually you add titles to an overlay track, which is Video 2 or higher. This is because titles are often meant to appear over other video. I recommend that you create a separate track specifically for titles. To add a title to the Timeline, follow these steps:

1. **Create a new video track specifically for titles.**

   To do so, choose Timeline➪Add Tracks. In the Add Tracks dialog box, add one video track. Click OK to close the Add Tracks dialog box.

2. **Right-click the name of your new track and choose Rename from the menu that appears.**

Type a new name for the track. Titles should work fine, but if you have more than one group of titles you may want to be more specific (Opening Credits).

3. **Drag the title from the Media window and drop it on the title track in your Timeline, as shown in Figure 14-6.**

   As with still graphics and many other elements, the default duration for a title to appear on-screen is five seconds.

4. **Fine-tune your title to fit the needs of your project.**

   - **To change the duration of your title:** Click-and-drag the edge of the title clip to increase or decrease its duration.

   - **To fade a title in or out:** Expand the title track and use the Opacity handles to control opacity. (See Chapter 11 for more on working with clip opacity.) You can also add a cross-dissolve transition (see Chapter 9) to the beginning and end of a title to make it appear to fade in and out.

Drag title from here.   Title overlays video clip.

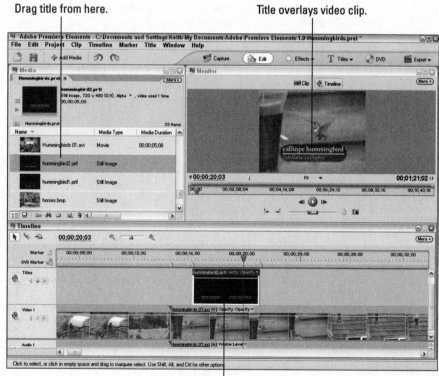

Figure 14-6: Add titles to the Timeline and manipulate them like you would any other clip.

Drop title here.

Previewing titles

Previewing your titles is critical; presenting a movie with a half-obscured (or otherwise mangled) title is like playing an orchestral concert under the approach path to a busy airport. Preview your titles and look for the following:

- ✔ Check the timing of the appearance and disappearance of the titles.

- ✔ Review the positioning of your titles as action takes place behind the text.

- ✔ Make sure that the action in the video clip doesn't conflict with or obscure your titles while they are on-screen.

- ✔ Double-check to make sure that your titles are inside the Safe Title Margins.

Titles that come from the Adobe Title Designer are generated automatically, but like effects and transitions they have to be rendered before you export your project. To render your titles, choose Timeline⇨Render Work Area. Titles render pretty quickly. After a few adjustments (and/or a few moments to gaze admiringly at your work), you can rest assured that your titles will make a competent entrance into your film.

Part IV
The Finishing Touches

The 5th Wave   By Rich Tennant

Here, boy.

MULTIMEDIA

In this part . . .

The ultimate goal of video editing is to make movies that other people will enjoy. The chapters in Part IV of *Adobe Premiere Elements For Dummies* show you how to prepare and share your movies. I show you how to make sure your movie is ready for "prime time," and then I show you how to share your movies on the Internet, on video-tape, or on DVD.

Chapter 15

Wrapping Up Your Movies

. . . .

. . . .

*Y*ou may find as you work on more movie projects that you have a really hard time finishing a movie project. Some clip always lasts a few frames too long, or an effect keyframe isn't in exactly the right spot, or a title font doesn't look exactly right. There's always *something* — no matter how miniscule — that could be improved upon. Moviemaking is like that. But at some point, you have to give up tweaking your masterpiece and decide that it is "good enough."

Before you can actually stick a fork in your movie and call it done, you have a few tasks to do to finalize the movie and get it ready for output. You should sit back and preview the whole thing, of course, and also add elements to the beginning and end of the movie to prepare it for broadcast or delivery. Finally, you need to make sure that the project is rendered and ready for output. This chapter helps you put the finishing touches on your project and shows you how to export audio or still images from Premiere Elements.

Previewing Your Movie

I could start and end this section by simply telling you to click Play in the Monitor window to preview the current project. As an "oh-by-the-way," I could also mention the effects and edits may need to be *rendered* before you can play them properly.

Thanks to the powerful real-time features of Adobe Premiere Elements, rendering (the process where Premiere actually applies your edits and creates preview files on the hard drive) usually isn't necessary unless your computer is below the recommended system specifications I detail in Chapter 2. Any portion of a movie that has to be rendered — but isn't yet — shows a red line under the Work Area bar, as shown in Figure 15-1. A green line means that you have already rendered a section that needed it. To render the unrendered portions of the Timeline, choose Timeline➪Render Work Area (or just press the Enter key on your keyboard).

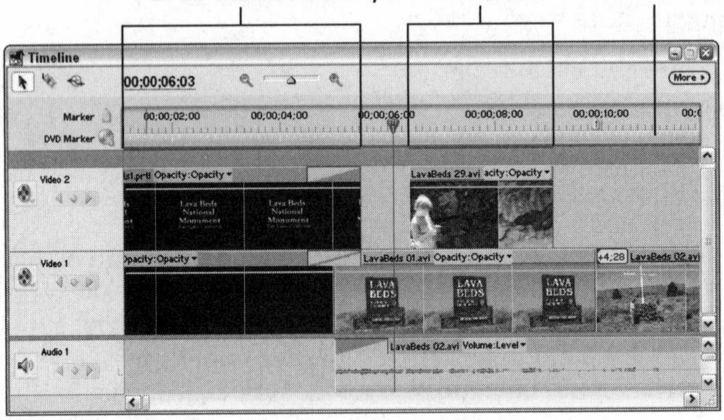

Red bars indicate that you must render.   Work Area bar

Figure 15-1:
The Work
Area bar at
the top of
the Timeline
shows you
whether the
project must
be rendered.

Even if your computer seems to have no trouble playing effects, transitions, and other edits in real time, those edits still need to be rendered before the movie can actually be output to tape, DVD, or the Internet.

Critiquing your project

Of course, there's more to previewing your project than simply rendering the Timeline and clicking Play. Consider carefully what you are actually previewing when you play a movie. Here are some ways to get the most out of previewing your project:

✔ **Watch the whole program from start to finish.** You may be tempted to periodically stop playback, reverse, and repeat sections, perhaps making a few tweaks to the program as you run it. This is fine, but to get a really good feeling for the flow of the project watch the whole thing from start to finish — just as your audience would. Keep a notepad handy and jot down quick notes if you must.

✔ **Watch the program on an external television monitor.** If you plan to export your movie to tape, previewing on an external monitor is crucial. (See the next section in this chapter for a more detailed explanation.)

✔ **Have trusted third parties review the project.** Moviemakers and writers are often too close to their creations to be totally objective; an outside point of view can help a lot. Though I worked hard to write this book (for example), my work was reviewed by various editors and their feedback was invaluable. Movie projects benefit from a similar review process. Even if you want to maintain strict creative control over your project, feedback from people who were not involved with creating it can help you see it afresh.

Looking at your movie on an external monitor

Even if you expand the Premiere Elements Monitor window to a really big size, it still probably won't be as large as some of the displays that your audience is likely to use. A larger external monitor reveals camera movements and other flaws that might not be obvious on your computer screen. But an even more important element is color: Your computer monitor uses the RGB (red-green-blue) color space to generate color, but television screens generate colors differently. Properly previewing the colors of your project on a computer monitor is virtually impossible. The best way to accurately preview a project is to view it on an actual TV.

How you connect an external TV monitor to your computer varies depending on your hardware. If you have a video card with analog outputs, you should be able to connect your external monitor to those outputs. However, keep in mind that Premiere Elements cannot play video directly to those analog video outputs. You will need to export the movie as an AVI or MPEG file and preview it using the software that came with your analog capture card.

Premiere Elements can play video out through your computer's FireWire port. All you need is a device that can connect to the FireWire port and also has analog video outputs. For this you could use an external video converter, or you could purchase a high-end video deck that supports FireWire. But the much easier solution is to just use your digital camcorder. Connect your camcorder to your computer's FireWire port, and then connect a TV monitor to the analog outputs on your camcorder. Turn the camcorder on to VTR (player) mode, and video from the Premiere Elements Timeline should play right out to the camcorder and through to the TV as well. Sure, you'll have a mess of cables strewn all over the place, but this method should still be effective.

If you preview your project on an external DV device, the preview playback in the Monitor window might not play back at full quality. Also, keep in mind that some older digital camcorders cannot play video through their analog connectors at the same time that video comes in via the FireWire port. If connecting a TV to the camcorder doesn't seem to work, check your camcorder's documentation.

After you have your hardware set up, make sure Premiere Elements is configured to play out to your external monitor. Here's how to check:

1. **In your project, choose Project⇨Project Settings⇨General.**

   The General page of the Project Settings dialog box appears.

2. **Click the Playback Settings button.**

   The DV Playback Settings dialog box opens.

3. **Place a check mark next to Play Video on DV Hardware (under Video Playback).**

4. **Under Audio Playback, choose whether you want to play audio on your DV Hardware or Audio Hardware.**

   This setting only applies to video previews as you play the Timeline to preview it.

5. **Choose whether you want real-time effects to play out to DV hardware or only on your desktop.**

   If you have some DV hardware hooked up to your computer and turned on, you may notice that transitions and effects play on the external monitor during previews, even though they haven't been rendered. Behold the real-time playback power of Premiere Elements! If real-time effects don't seem to play smoothly on your external monitor, choose the Desktop Only option.

6. **When you're done, click OK twice to close the two settings dialog boxes.**

If you find that your preview doesn't play smoothly, especially during transitions and effects, go back and adjust settings so that previews only play to the DV hardware and not on the desktop. This adjustment preserves some processing power if your computer barely meets the system requirements outlined in Chapter 2.

If you aren't able to or don't feel like connecting an external monitor to your computer, you could simply use your camcorder. (It's better than nothing!) However, your camcorder is not the ideal preview monitor.

Making Final Additions to Your Video

Movies and videos usually have a few elements that you may take for granted (or never consider at all) if you've never worked with professional-style video before. Broadcast engineers use some special video elements to help adjust video equipment. These include counting leaders and color bars and tone. A third element that I discuss in the following sections seems like nothing at all: black video. Do you need these elements? Not necessarily. Unless you're producing video for a local public access cable TV channel or other broadcast outlet, you probably don't *need* bars and tone or a counting leader. But they can sometimes come in handy, and when used creatively they can lend a cool Hollywood feel to your movies.

Creating a counting leader

Have you ever seen one of those spinning countdowns at the beginning of a video program? That's called a *counting leader* and it's used by video engineers to ensure that the playback speed is correct and that audio and video are synchronized. The leader counts down from eight, and when the count reaches two, a blip sounds. This blip helps the broadcast engineer synchronize the audio with the video.

If your project is for use in broadcast or another professional environment and you will be delivering it on videotape, you should include a counting leader at the beginning of the tape. But even if you're just making home video projects, you may decide that a counting leader is a cool way to start a movie.

Premiere Elements can generate a Universal Counting Leader. It is 11 seconds long and must be placed in the Timeline. Ideally, you should plan ahead and leave 11 seconds open at the beginning of the Timeline; however, it is possible to insert that time later. To create a counting leader and place it in your project:

1. **In your project, choose the New Item button at the bottom of the Media window and choose Universal Counting Leader from the menu that appears.**

   The Universal Counting Leader Setup dialog box appears as shown in Figure 15-2.

2. **Review the settings in the Universal Counting Leader Setup dialog box.**

   In general, I recommend that you maintain the default colors and settings unless you are just creating the leader because you think it looks cool and you'd like to use some custom colors.

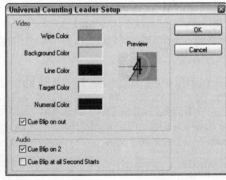

Figure 15-2: Choose colors and settings for your counting leader here.

You see two audio options in the Counting Leader dialog box. Leave the first one — Cue Blip on 2 — enabled unless you are not concerned about audio synchronization.

Alternatively, if you're *really* concerned about synchronization, enable the Cue Blip at all Second Starts option. Doing so creates a blip at the beginning of each second during the countdown.

3. **Click OK to close the dialog box.**

   The counting leader is generated, appearing in the Media window when it's ready.

4. **Click an empty area in the Timeline window to make it the active window, and press Home on your keyboard.**

   The CTI moves to the very beginning of the movie project.

5. **Drag the Universal Counting Leader clip from the Media window and drop it on the very beginning of Track 1, as shown in Figure 15-3.**

   Premiere Elements automatically shifts everything in your project over by 11 seconds, making room for the inserted counting leader. Your project now has an 11-second counting leader at the beginning.

You'll probably have to render your entire Timeline again to create all new preview files. You should play through the whole Timeline to ensure that all of the clips still play correctly.

Adding color bars and tone

Two more important movie elements — especially if you plan to export to a public access cable channel or other professional broadcast environment — are color bars and a 1 kHz tone. The pattern for color bars is standardized by the Society for Motion Picture and Television Engineers (SMPTE) and can be used to calibrate the colors on a TV monitor or other broadcast equipment. The 1 kHz tone serves to calibrate audio levels.

To generate bars and tone, click the New Item window at the bottom of the Media window and choose Bars and Tone from the menu that appears. A five-second bars-and-tone clip now appears in the Media window. As with the counting leader described in the previous section, you can drag the bars and tone clip to the beginning of the Timeline.

The bars and tone don't necessarily need to appear for long, although you should consult with the video engineers you are working with at the broadcast facility or production house to find out exactly what they want. In some cases, they may only need a single frame of bars and tone, but in other cases, they may want up to 30 seconds of bars and tone at the beginning of the tape.

New Item button   Universal Counting Leader

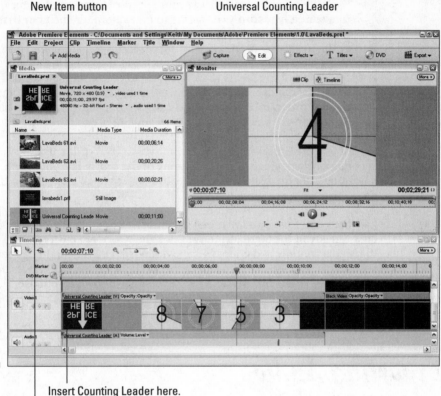

Figure 15-3:
Insert the
11-second
Universal
Counting
Leader at
the begin-
ning of your
project.

Insert Counting Leader here.

Drag Counting Leader from here.

Generating black video

Let's talk about nothing for a moment, shall we? By "nothing," I mean *black
video* — as in "fade to black." Black video is a surprisingly important element
for almost any movie project, often overlooked precisely because it seems
like there's, well, nothing to overlook. Black video actually serves several
important purposes:

✔ At the beginning of a movie, a stretch of black video gives the viewer a
chance to get comfortable or "in the mood" after pressing Play. If the
movie starts immediately after Play is pressed, the initial perception of
the movie can be abrupt and unsettling for the viewer.

✔ At the end of the movie, black video gives the viewer some cushion space
to press Stop after the credits stop rolling but before the static at the end
of the tape starts. Without a bit of black video at the end of the program,
that static could put viewers' eyes out if they're not expecting it (well,
maybe it won't be *that* drastic, but you get the idea).

✔ Black video provides splicing room at the beginning of a tape. If you plan to eventually record your movie to a videotape, remember that one of the most common mechanical failures on VHS tapes is the tape snapping at the beginning of the reel during rewind. You can repair this breakage using a razor blade and some sticky tape, but some videotape from the beginning of the reel is usually cut off in the process. It would be better if a few seconds of black video were cut rather than the first few seconds of your program. If you're outputting for VHS tape, I recommend at least 60 seconds of black video at the beginning of the tape.

Even if you are only outputting your movie to DVD or the Internet, a couple seconds of black video at the beginning of the movie is a good idea. As I said, if nothing else, the black video helps the viewer relax and get into the right mood to enjoy your movie.

Like bars and tone or a Universal Counting Leader, black video can be generated quickly in the Media window. Click the New Item button at the bottom of the Media window and choose Black Video from the menu that appears. A five-second black video clip appears in the Media window. To change the duration of the black video clip, select it in the Media window and choose Clip⇨Time Stretch. The Time Stretch dialog box appears. I suggest changing the duration of your black video clip to 45 seconds.

Exporting Audio

Many people think of Adobe Premiere Elements as a video-editing program, but you can also edit and export audio with it. You can export audio in several different formats, including QuickTime, Windows Media Audio (WMA), Windows waveform (WAV), and others.

If you want to export audio in QuickTime or WMA format, see the sections in Chapter 16 on exporting movies in those formats. When you export the movie you can choose to export only audio if you wish. If you just want to quickly export some audio in WAV format, follow these steps:

1. **Select a clip in the Media window that you want to export, or click the header of the Timeline window if you want to export the Timeline.**

2. **Choose File⇨Export⇨Audio.**

   The Export Audio dialog box appears.

3. **Click Settings.**

   The Export Audio Settings dialog box appears, as shown in Figure 15-4.

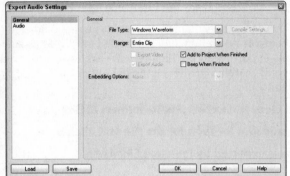

Figure 15-4:
Choose
audio export
settings
here.

4. **Choose Windows Waveform in the File Type menu if it is not already selected.**

5. **Select the desired export range in the Range menu.**

   If you're exporting a clip from the Media window, you'll probably want to choose Entire Clip. Alternatively, you can export just the area between In and Out points if you have set any. If you're exporting from the Timeline, you can export the Entire Timeline or just the range covered by the Work Area Bar.

6. **Click Audio on the left side of the Export Audio Settings dialog box to reveal Audio settings.**

7. **Choose an option from the Compressor menu.**

   I generally prefer to just choose the Uncompressed option from the Compressor menu because doing so ensures that the WAV file will be compatible with virtually any other program. Most CD-burning programs like Nero Burning Rom and Roxio Easy CD Creator can instantly convert an uncompressed WAV file into CD audio format and burn an audio CD with your exported WAV file. The audio CD can then be played by virtually any CD player.

8. **Choose a Sample Rate.**

   Higher-quality audio produces larger file sizes. CD-quality audio usually has a sample rate of 44,100 Hz, although 48,000 Hz is a good sample rate to choose since it matches the audio recorded by most digital camcorders.

9. **Choose a Sample Type.**

   Use the Sample Type menu to choose the bit depth for your audio. I explain bit depth in Chapter 13. CD-quality audio is usually 16-bit.

10. **Choose Stereo or Mono from the Channels menu.**

    The Audio Export Settings dialog box includes a menu labeled Interleave. This menu controls how often audio is loaded into RAM as a movie plays. If you are only exporting audio the Interleave setting doesn't really matter, so I recommend that you just leave the default setting of 1 Frame in the Interleave menu.

11. **Click OK to close the Export Audio Settings dialog box.**

12. **Choose a name and location for the file and click Save.**

    The WAV file is exported by Premiere Elements.

Exporting Still Images from Your Project

Premiere Elements enables you to export still graphics from your movies, which comes in handy for a variety of reasons. For example, you may want to display some stills from the movie on a Web page, or use stills as background images in DVD menus. Just keep in mind that stills extracted from video are of much lower quality than stills shot with a conventional still camera (film or digital).

If you want poster-quality promotional shots of your movie, bring a high-quality still camera along with you during a video shoot and use it to take some pictures of the scenes or subjects in the movie.

Adobe has also designed Premiere Elements to work in conjunction with Adobe Photoshop Elements. Photoshop is a renowned editing program for still images, and Adobe offers Premiere Elements and Photoshop Elements together in a package at a bargain price. In the following sections I show you how to export still images from Premiere Elements and improve the way they look in Photoshop Elements. I also show you how to take a collection of still images from Photoshop Elements and create a slideshow DVD using Photoshop and Premiere Elements together.

Exporting stills from Premiere Elements

Premiere Elements lets you quickly export still images from any clip in the Media window or the Timeline itself. To export a still image from Premiere Elements, follow these steps:

1. **Move the CTI in the Timeline to the exact frame that you want to export.**

   If you want to export a frame from a clip in the Media window, double-click the clip to open it in the Monitor and then play the clip in the Monitor until you find the frame that you want to export.

You can use the J, K, and L keys on your keyboard to control playback. Press K to pause playback, and then use the left and right arrow keys to step forward or back a single frame at a time. You may find that you have to search around to find a good frame to export, especially if the clip includes a lot of motion. Often, you may simply have to settle for whichever frame is the least blurry.

2. **Choose File⇨Export⇨Frame.**

   The Export Frame dialog box appears.

3. **Click Settings to open the Export Frame Settings dialog box.**

4. **Choose an export format from the File Type menu.**

   The available export formats for still frames are Windows Bitmap (BMP), GIF, JPEG, Targa, and TIFF. Bitmap or TIFF will provide the highest quality, but JPEG and GIF are more Web-friendly. I recommend that you export in Windows Bitmap or TIFF format, because you can always resave the image in a Web-friendly format after improving it in Photoshop Elements.

5. **Click OK.**

6. **Choose a location and name the file, and then click Save.**

   The still image is saved. The still image also shows up in the Media window.

You should edit any still images exported from video, especially if the image comes from interlaced video. Fast-moving objects in the image may have *interlacing jaggies*. This is a non-technical term that describes the horrid horizontal distortions that occur in an image that has been interlaced. Also, if the video comes from a rectangular-pixel video image, it will appear stretched or squeezed on computer screens. I show you how to improve images using Adobe Photoshop Elements in the next section.

Correcting still images from your movie with Adobe Photoshop Elements

Adobe Photoshop has long been the world standard for image-editing software. Photoshop has become so ubiquitous, in fact, that you will sometimes hear people use the word "Photoshop" as a verb, as in, "Hey Bill, can you Photoshop this image for me?"

Photoshop has been popular for a long time, but traditionally it has also been quite expensive. Several years ago Adobe released a more affordable version of Photoshop called Photoshop Elements, and Version 3 of Photoshop Elements was released about the same time as Premiere Elements Version 1. Adobe offers Premiere Elements and Photoshop Elements together in a package that retails for about $130, which represents one of today's great software bargains. If you have not purchased Premiere Elements, I strongly suggest that you spend the extra $30 above and beyond the Premiere Elements purchase price so that you can also get this excellent image-editing program.

You'll probably find Photoshop Elements to be an invaluable tool as you work. Photoshop includes a variety of filters that allow you to apply special effects to images and fix various problems. Of special interest are the video filters. Consider the image shown in Figure 15-5 — a frame I exported from a video file in Premiere Elements (see the previous section in this chapter for details on how to export video frames). Look carefully at the image and you'll notice that it has a couple of problems:

✔ The image appears elongated, and the subjects seem slightly distorted. This is because the DV footage from which the frame was exported has rectangular pixels, but Photoshop Elements works with square pixels. This problem occurs with any still image that you export from a DV-based movie project.

✔ The image has interlacing jaggies. Because the original footage was inter-laced, fast-moving portions of the image have an ugly pattern of horizontal distortions. The interlacing problems in the image in Figure 15-5 are so bad that it appears to be a blurred double-image. This problem is espe-cially prevalent on fast-moving subjects.

Figure 15-5:
Still graph-ics exported from inter-laced video footage appear distorted in Photoshop Elements and other graphics programs.

Both of these problems are easily fixed in Photoshop Elements. First, you can fix the elongation problem by simply adjusting the size of the picture:

1. **In Photoshop Elements, choose Image➪Resize➪Image Size.**

   The Image Size dialog box appears.

2. **In the Image Size dialog box, remove the check mark next to Constrain Proportions.**

If the frame was exported from DV footage with a 4:3 aspect ratio, the image size will be 720 x 480 pixels. All you need do is change the image size so it conforms to a 4:3 aspect ratio. I describe aspect ratios in greater detail in Chapter 4.

3. **Change the Width value from 720 pixels to 640 pixels. Make sure that the Height is still 480 pixels.**

4. **Click OK.**

The image shape should now be more natural, but there are still those interlacing jaggies to get rid of.

5. **Choose Filter⇨Video⇨De-Interlace.**

The De-Interlace dialog box appears. Here you can choose to eliminate odd or even fields and decide whether to generate the replacement fields by duplication or interpolation. I generally recommend that you choose Interpolation, but the Odd or Even choices may need some experimentation on your part.

When Photoshop Elements de-interlaces an image, it actually deletes every other horizontal line of the image and replaces each deleted line with a new line. It can generate these replacement lines in one of two ways: *duplication* or *interpolation*. If the lines are generated through duplication, the line above (if you deleted the even lines) or below (if you deleted the odd lines) is copied to create the new replacement line. If the lines are generated through interpolation, Photoshop Elements compares the lines above and below the deleted line and generates a new line that is halfway between in terms of appearance. Interpolation usually gives a smoother appearance to the image.

6. **Click OK and view the results.**

If you're not satisfied, choose Edit⇨Undo, and then open the De-Interlace filter again and choose different options. My finished result looks like Figure 15-6.

Figure 15-6: The picture looks much better after using Photoshop Elements to adjust the size and de-interlace the image.

Exporting AVI and MPEG Files

Besides making movie editing easy, Premiere Elements also makes it easy to record your movies to tape, to DVD, or to the Internet. You can also export your movies directly to a file in AVI or MPEG format. AVI and MPEG files are generally too big to share online (see Chapter 16 for more on exporting your movies in a Web-friendly format) but on some rare occasions you may find it necessary to export in one of these formats. For example, if you plan to export your movie to an analog VCR using another program, or if you need to send your movie somewhere else for further editing, you'll probably need to export the movie as an AVI or MPEG file.

Neither format offers a distinct advantage over the other. Which format you choose depends on the requirements of the program to which you are exporting. For example, if you plan to edit your movie further on a Macintosh, many Mac programs support the MPEG format — but not the AVI format. The following sections show you how to export a movie as an AVI or MPEG file from Premiere Elements.

Exporting AVI files

AVI is short for Audio-Video Interleave and is also sometimes called Video for Windows. It has been a common Windows multimedia format for years. When you capture video using Premiere Elements, the captured video footage is stored on your hard drive in AVI format. To export a movie in AVI format, follow these steps:

1. **Choose File⇨Export⇨Movie.**

2. **In the Export Movie dialog box, click Settings.**

   The General options section of the Export Movie Settings dialog box appears.

3. **Choose Microsoft AVI or Microsoft DV AVI in the File Type menu.**

   In general, I recommend that you choose Microsoft DV AVI so that the movie is exported in full DV quality. On the other hand, if you choose Microsoft AVI, you can reduce the frame size, frame rate, and other settings to produce a smaller file size.

   If small file size is a priority I recommend that you use the QuickTime or Windows Media formats described in Chapter 16.

4. **In the Range menu, choose whether you want to export the Entire Timeline or just the Work Area Bar.**

   I describe the Work Area Bar in Chapter 8.

5. **Choose whether you want to export audio and/or video using the check boxes in the General options.**

6. **Click Video on the left side of the Export Movie Settings dialog box to open the Video settings, and review and adjust video settings.**

   If you are exporting in Microsoft DV AVI format, you won't be able to change many video settings, but if you are exporting in standard Microsoft AVI format you can change the frame size, frame rate, color depth, and other settings to yield a smaller file size.

7. **Click the Keyframe and Rendering settings.**

   Under Rendering Options you can change whether you want the video rendered with the Upper Field First, Lower Field First, or No Fields. I recommend that you leave this setting alone unless you know specifically that you need to export progressive scan (no fields) video. See Chapter 4 for more on video fields.

   Keyframe Options are only available if you are exporting in Microsoft AVI format. Rendering keyframes control how Premiere Elements compresses video. The default setting of keyframes every 15 frames is adequate most of the time, but if your video images don't contain a lot of movement you may want to increase it to 30 frames. If your video contains many fast-moving images, setting keyframes every 10 frames offers better video quality — and a larger file size.

8. **Click Audio to adjust audio settings.**

   Audio settings have a huge effect on the file size of the movie you output. If file size is more of a concern than audio quality, you can reduce the Same Rate or Sample Type settings.

9. **Click OK to close the Export Movie Settings dialog box.**

10. **Give your movie a filename and choose a save location in the Export Movie dialog box, and click Save.**

    The movie is exported. Depending on the size of the movie, rendering and output may take a while.

Exporting MPEG files

MPEG — short for Motion Pictures Experts Group — is a popular export format that is widely supported by multimedia programs. Virtually any media player program on any type of computer can play an MPEG file. To export a movie in MPEG format:

1. **In Premiere Elements choose File⇨Export⇨MPEG.**

2. **In the Export MPEG dialog box, choose a preset.**

   If you plan to eventually export your movie to videotape or DVD, you should choose one of the DVD Compatible presets. Conversely, if you want to record your movie to a VCD or SVCD, choose one of the VCD or SVCD presets. If you have a CD burner but not a DVD burner, you can still create short DVD-style movies, but the video quality is somewhat reduced. An SVCD provides near-DVD quality video, but it can only hold about 20 minutes of video.

Premiere Elements cannot create VCDs or SVCDs directly. However, using MPEG export you can export a movie in VCD or SVCD format. You can then use a third-party CD burning program to burn your VCD or SVCD. Just remember that some older DVD players don't support VCDs and SVCDs.

You can also choose one of the Multimedia Compatible presets, but keep in mind that these presets reduce output quality and *still* produce files that are probably too big to share on the Internet. If you want to share a movie online, see Chapter 16 to find out how to use the Windows Media or QuickTime formats.

 3. **Click OK to close the Export MPEG dialog box.**

 4. **In the Save File dialog box, choose a location and give your movie a file name.**

 5. **In the Export Range dialog box, choose Entire Sequence if you want to export the entire Timeline, or choose Work Area if you just want to export the range covered by the Work Area Bar.**

    See Chapter 8 for more on working with the Work Area Bar.

 6. **Click Save to save your movie.**

Chapter 16

Preparing Movies for Online Viewing

In This Chapter

▶ Using the Internet as your screening room

▶ Choosing a movie player program

▶ Exporting movies for online viewing

Making movies with Adobe Premiere Elements is so fun and easy that it's easy to forget the most important part: Sharing your movies with others. This is, after all, one of the main reasons for manipulating raw video clips into an interesting and creative movie.

You can share your completed movies with the world in many different ways. This chapter shows you how to share your movie projects in the online world of the Internet. I help you identify some of the special problems involved with putting movies online, I help you choose a player program for your movies, and I show you how to export your movies in a variety of Web-friendly formats directly from Adobe Premiere Elements.

Entering the World's Largest Screening Room

It's hard to believe, but the World Wide Web has been with us for over a decade now. As for the Internet (of which the World Wide Web is a part), it will soon reach middle age. The good folks who built the foundations of the online world envisioned it as a staging ground for efficient global information exchange, though I doubt they envisioned folks like you and me exchanging full-motion video online. Video, and especially streaming video, is at odds with the fundamental design of the Internet for two key reasons:

✔ **Bandwidth:** A majority of Internet users still have slow dial-up connections. In the United States (for example), about two-thirds of all Internet users were still using dial-up connections in mid-2004. That's potentially a problem because video files tend to be large — so large that even broadband users still can't watch full broadcast-quality video over the Internet. For most of us, many video files — even those with drastically reduced quality — are simply too big to download in a reasonable amount of time.

Even if you have a high-speed Internet connection and you only want to cater to other high-speed users, keep in mind that large movie files also increase the bandwidth demands on your Web server. Most commercial Web hosting services place a limit on how much bandwidth your site is allowed to use in a given month. If you exceed that limit they may charge you additional fees or place a limit on your services. Large movie files can quickly eat up your monthly bandwidth allotment, especially if your movies become popular with other Internet users.

✔ **Packet delivery:** Data is transmitted over the Internet in packets rather than in steady streams. This makes data transfer over the Internet reliable, but not fast.

Data is broken down into packets before being transmitted over the Internet. These packets can travel over many different pathways to the destination, where they are reassembled in the correct order to form a Web page, e-mail message, or any other file that is shared online. Compare this to, say, a radio or television broadcast, which transmits data in a continuous wave. Packet delivery is very reliable because it does not require a single unbroken connection between the sender and the receiver. Confused? Imagine you want to give your phone number to someone across a crowded room. You could try yelling across the room (a broadcast), but because of all the other noise, the other person might miss a number or two. A more reliable method would be to write your phone number on a piece of paper and send it via messenger to the other person. The paper method would be slower, but at least you know the recipient will get the correct phone number.

So what's the point of all this technical discussion about bandwidth and packets? I bring it up because you must be aware of the potential problems before you start sharing video over the Web. Video for the Web must be highly compressed, the frame size must be reduced, and you must accept some sacrifices in quality.

Video can be distributed over the Internet in one of two ways:

✔ **Download:** Users download the entire movie file before it can be viewed. Most current video player programs can start to play the movie before it is all downloaded. The program calculates when enough of the movie has been received so that playback can begin and continue without interruption. This type of download playback is called *progressive playback* or *progressive download*, and it does a fair job of mimicking streaming video.

✔ **Stream:** The movie plays as it downloads to the user's machine. Some of the video is *buffered* (portions of the file are temporarily stored on the user's hard drive or computer memory) to provide uninterrupted playback. The three predominant formats for streaming video are Apple QuickTime Streaming, RealMedia, and Windows Media Streaming Video. In each case, special server software is required to host streaming media.

Regardless of which distribution method you choose, the export process for the movie from Adobe Premiere Elements is still the same. You export the movie as a file that resides on your hard drive. Whether that file is later streamed is determined by whether you use streaming server software on your Web server. For information on choosing a Web server on which to host your movies, see Chapter 21.

If possible, I recommend that you produce several different versions of your movie for the Web. Produce a lower-quality movie for people on slow dial-up connections and a higher-quality movie for folks with broadband access. You may also want to offer versions for several different players. For example, you may want to offer both an Apple QuickTime version and a Windows Media version. Let's face it. Some people are very touchy about using software from certain companies. In practical terms, offering your movie in only one format is sure to limit the size of your audience.

Choosing Player Software

Distributing your movie digitally actually means distributing it as a file — so you have to make sure your intended audience can open that file. If you're distributing on a DVD, this usually isn't a problem; DVD players have their own built-in software for playing movies. But if you're distributing a movie file over the Internet, your audience has to have the right program to play your movie. As the moviemaker, you have two basic choices:

✔ Assume that your audience already has the necessary software installed.

✔ Direct your audience to download the necessary software from a Web site.

The following sections describe Apple QuickTime and Microsoft Windows Media Player, two common movie player programs. These are not by any means the only movie player programs that are available. But they are easily the most common, and they are also both directly supported by Adobe Premiere Elements. You can export movies in Apple QuickTime or Windows Media format directly from Premiere Elements without having to use any additional software. Versions of Apple QuickTime and Windows Media Player are available for computers running either the Macintosh or Windows operating systems.

Apple QuickTime

Apple QuickTime is an almost-ubiquitous media player in the personal computer world — which makes it a good overall choice for your audience. Although QuickTime is developed by Apple, it is available for all versions of Windows, and it is widely used on Windows PCs. Apple QuickTime can play MPEG and QuickTime media formats. The QuickTime Player also supports *progressive download*, allowing files to begin playing as soon as enough of the content has been downloaded to allow continuous playback. The free Apple QuickTime Player is available for download at

```
www.apple.com/quicktime/download/
```

Apple also offers a version of QuickTime called QuickTime Pro. Key features of QuickTime Pro include

- ✔ Full-screen playback
- ✔ Additional media-management features
- ✔ Simple authoring tools
- ✔ Advanced import/export options

As an owner of Adobe Premiere Elements, you don't need the extra features of Apple QuickTime Pro; it doesn't do anything that Premiere can't do already. Your audience really doesn't need QuickTime Pro either (unless of course they want to watch movies in full screen.) The standard Apple QuickTime Player should suffice in most cases. QuickTime-format files can be exported directly from Premiere Elements.

Windows Media Player

Microsoft's Windows Media Player can play many common media formats. Windows Media Player comes preinstalled on computers that run Windows Me or Windows XP. Although the name says Windows — and contrary to the belief of some Macintosh users — versions of Windows Media Player are also available for Macintosh computers that run OS 8 or higher. In fact, Figure 16-1 shows Windows Media Player being used in Mac OS X. Windows Media Player is even available for Pocket PCs and countless other devices. Windows Media Player is available for free download at

```
www.microsoft.com/windows/windowsmedia/download/
```

Figure 16-1:
This is the Macintosh version of Windows Media Player.

Windows Media Player can play video in MPEG and AVI formats. Premiere Elements can output both of these formats, but they're not terribly useful for online applications because they're big and have an appetite for resources. I show how to export MPEG or AVI files in Chapter 15. Windows Media Player can also play the Windows Media Video (WMV) format, and Premiere Elements can output that as well. I like the WMV format because it provides decent quality (for Web movies) with incredibly small file sizes.

What are the compelling reasons for choosing Windows Media Player (shown in Figure 16-1) over other players? Choose Windows Media Player as your format if

✔ **Most or all of your audience members use Windows.** Most Windows users already have Windows Media Player installed on their systems, so they won't have to download or install new software before viewing your Windows Media-format movie.

✔ **You want the look, but not the expense and complexity, of streaming media.** If you don't want to deal with the hassle of setting up and maintaining a streaming-media server, Windows Media-format files can provide a workable compromise. Like Apple QuickTime, Windows Media Player does a decent simulation of streaming media with progressive download: When downloading files, Windows Media Player begins playing the movie as soon as enough of it is downloaded to ensure uninterrupted playback.

✓ **You're distributing your movie online and extremely small file size is more important than quality.** The Windows Media format can offer some remarkable small file sizes, which is good if your audience downloads your movie over slow dial-up Internet connections. I recently placed a three-and-a-half-minute movie online in Windows Media format, and the file size was only 5.5MB (megabytes). Of course, the movie wasn't broadcast quality. It had 32 kHz stereo audio, a frame size of 320 x 240 pixels, and a frame rate of 15 frames per second (fps). Although the quality was relatively low (compared to, say, DVD), it was superior to the quality offered by other formats, given the file size and length of the movie.

Exporting Your Movie

When you have decided which online format you want to use for your movies, exporting them in your preferred format is easy. Before you export your movie, however, you should make sure that all effects and other edits are rendered. Click somewhere in the Timeline window to make it active, and then press the Enter key on your keyboard. Alternatively, choose Timeline⇨Render. The rendering process may take a few minutes, especially if your movie is long and includes many titles, transitions, and effects. This would be a good time to go refill that coffee cup.

Eventually, the render process will finish. (Trust me!) When rendering is complete, you are ready to export it in either Apple QuickTime or Windows Media format. The following sections show you how to export your movies in either format.

Exporting an Apple QuickTime movie

Apple QuickTime is a very popular format for sharing movies online because it provides a good balance of file size and quality. Before you can export to QuickTime format, you must have QuickTime Player 6 or later installed on your computer. See the section on Apple QuickTime earlier in this chapter for information on downloading this software.

The process of exporting a movie in QuickTime format is simple. First, make sure that your movie has been rendered in the Timeline, as described in the previous section. Then follow these steps:

1. **Click somewhere in the Timeline window to make it active, and choose File⇨Export⇨QuickTime.**

Alternatively, click Export on the Premiere Elements toolbar and choose QuickTime from the menu that appears. If the Timeline window isn't active, the Export submenu may not be available in the File menu.

2. **In the Export QuickTime dialog box, shown in Figure 16-2, choose a preset.**

   Presets are listed on the left side of the Export QuickTime dialog box and are divided into three basic categories. When you click a preset on the left, a description of the preset appears on the right. The presets offer different combinations of frame size, frame rate, and audio frequency to suit a variety of bandwidth needs. The highest quality preset is the LAN preset, which includes a frame size of 320 x 240, a frame rate of 29.97 fps (NTSC) or 25 fps (PAL), and an audio frequency of 44 kHz, which is roughly CD-quality. Contrast this with the lowest-quality preset, which is the 56K Modem preset. This preset has a frame size of 160 x 120, a frame rate of just 6 fps, and 8 kHz audio. Obviously the LAN preset gives much better playback quality, but it also yields a much bigger file size.

   If none of the presets seem to exactly match your needs, click Advanced in the lower-left corner of the Export QuickTime dialog box to customize your export settings. I describe advanced QuickTime settings in the next section.

   Although the QuickTime presets are named for specific Internet connection speeds or wireless devices such as a Pocket PC or Smartphone, anyone with Apple QuickTime Player should be able to view your movies. For example, if you export your movie using the Cable Modem/DSL preset, users with slow dial-up connections will still be able to watch the movie; it will just take them longer to download it.

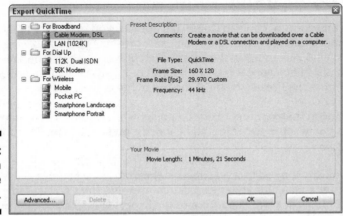

Figure 16-2:
Choose a
QuickTime
preset here.

3. **When you have chosen a preset, click OK.**

   A Save File dialog box appears.

4. **Enter a filename for your movie in the File Name field.**

   If you plan to export your movie in several different sizes to accommodate a variety of online viewers, make sure that the filename reflects the preset used for this version. For example, if this version of a movie about hummingbirds uses the Cable Modem/DSL preset, you might name the file `hummingbirdsDSL`. A second version which uses the 56K Modem preset might be called `hummingbirds56K`.

5. **Choose an option from the Export Range menu.**

   In most cases, you'll want to export the Entire Sequence, but you can also choose to export just the Work Area if you have specified a work area that only encompasses part of your Timeline.

6. **Choose a location in which to save the movie and click Save.**

   When you click Save, the movie is exported. A Rendering dialog box appears to let you know the progress of the export. The dialog box also estimates the remaining time; saving the file might take a while, especially if this is a long project.

In the next few sections, I help you sort out some of the specific settings for each export format.

Choosing advanced export settings for Apple QuickTime

When you export a movie in QuickTime format, you may want to customize your export settings rather than just use a preset. To customize the export settings, click Advanced in the Export Timeline dialog box. The Transcode Settings dialog box appears, as shown in Figure 16-3. You can select QuickTime presets from the Presets menu at the top of the dialog box.

I recommend that you first choose a preset which most closely matches the settings you want to use. After you choose a preset you can fine-tune other settings.

When you are done adjusting settings in the Transcode Settings dialog box, click Save. Enter a name for your new custom preset in the Choose Name dialog box, and then click OK. You return to the Export QuickTime dialog box, where you can finish exporting your movie as described in the previous section.

Adjusting general QuickTime settings

To review and adjust settings, first click a category on the left. First click General to reveal the general settings as shown in Figure 16-3. General settings include:

- ✔ **Loop:** Check this option if you want the movie to loop back to the beginning and start playing again when the movie is finished.

- ✔ **Compress Movie Header:** Check this option if the movie will be served on a streaming media server.

- ✔ **Autoplay:** This option causes the movie to start playing as soon as it is opened.

- ✔ **For Streaming Server:** This option enables streaming as well as progressive download, which means the movie starts to play before the entire file has been downloaded. The player program calculates the amount of download time remaining and starts playback when it figures that the whole thing will be downloaded before the movie reaches the end.

- ✔ **Hint Movie:** In the Hint Movie menu, choose Self Contained to ensure that the whole movie occupies a single file. Any movie you share online should be self contained. If the movie will be on a streaming server with a lot of bandwidth, choose Self Contained & Optimized. Optimization allows more people to access the file simultaneously. Optimization greatly increases the file size, however.

- ✔ **Video Hinter Track:** If the file will be streamed, this option must be checked.

- ✔ **Payload Encoding:** The Realtime Transport Protocol (RTP) is part of a streaming movie file that tells the player what kind of data is being sent. In general, you should choose the Use Native Encoding if Possible option, but if your audience seems to have a lot of problems opening and playing your movie, you may want to try choosing the Always Use QuickTime Encoding option.

- ✔ **Packet Size Limit/Packet Duration Limit/Interval:** If your audience seems to have a hard time downloading a streaming movie with acceptable quality, smaller or shorter packets should provide more reliable streaming.

- ✔ **Audio Hinter Track:** As with the Video Hinter Track, this option should be checked for streaming movies. Note that you can also set packet size, duration, and interval limits for audio.

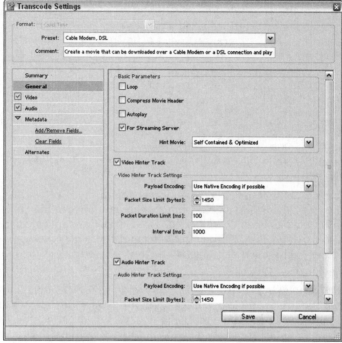

Figure 16-3:
Review and adjust advanced settings in the Transcode Settings dialog box.

Adjusting QuickTime video settings

I know what you're thinking: Some of those General settings didn't seem too general. Fortunately, the QuickTime video settings are easier to sort through. Click Video in the left pane of the Transcode Settings dialog box and review these settings:

- **Codec:** As described in Chapter 4, the codec is the compression/decompression scheme used to compress the movie to a smaller file size. There are many, many choices in the Codec menu, but for online use, one of the Sorensen codecs is probably best.

- **Spatial Quality:** This setting controls how the video image is compressed. Higher quality results in larger file sizes. (I'll bet you didn't see that one coming!)

- **Frame Rate:** Broadcast-quality video usually has a frame rate of 25 or 29.97 frames per second (fps). Online movies often use a frame rate of 15 fps to help reduce file size.

- **Field Order:** For online movies you'll usually want to choose None (Progressive). However, if you find that the movie you output has interlacing *jaggies* or other interlacing problems, choose Upper or Lower here. Some experimentation may be necessary. I explain interlacing in Chapter 4.

✔ **Pixel Aspect Ratio:** The Square Pixels option is the most common choice here, though if your video image appears stretched or squeezed you may need to choose one of the rectangular pixel options in this menu. Choose the option that matches the format of your original source footage.

✔ **Width/Height:** These boxes control the size of your video image. Remember to maintain the same aspect ratio (usually 4:3) of your source footage so as not to distort the video image. See Chapter 4 for more on aspect ratios. Keep in mind that larger video sizes mean larger files. (Is there an echo in here? Is there echo in here?)

✔ **Set Bitrate:** A higher bitrate means higher video quality, and of course higher file sizes.

✔ **Set Key Frame Distance:** Compression keyframes help video compress more efficiently. A longer interval between keyframes often reduces file size and quality. The Advanced Mode checkbox must be enabled for the Set Key Frame Distance option to be available.

Although they share a name with effect keyframes, compression key frames are entirely different. Basically, a compression key frame is a picture of the entire video image. When video is compressed, a key frame might only occur once every one, five, or even ten seconds. All of the frames between those key frames — the in-between frames are called *delta* frames — contain information about only the things in the video image that have changed.

Adjusting QuickTime audio settings

Apple QuickTime's audio settings are actually pretty simple. You can choose an audio codec from the Codec menu (the QDesign Music 2 codec works well), select mono or stereo output, and specify a frequency. A frequency of 44 kHz provides CD-quality audio, but keep in mind that high-quality audio can inflate the size of your files in a big hurry.

If your exported files are too big, you may want to start here to whittle down the file size. A simple reduction of the audio frequency, as well as switch from Stereo to Mono, can make a big difference in the size of the file.

Adjusting QuickTime metadata settings

Metadata is extra data that goes along with the movie. This data can include the name of the movie, the author, a copyright notice, and other information. The metadata is displayed by QuickTime as the movie plays. When you click Metadata on the left side of the Transcode Settings dialog box, the area to the right will probably be empty. To add metadata, click Add/Remove Fields. The Select Metadata dialog box appears.

Place a check mark next to the metadata fields that you want to use. When you click OK, the metadata fields appear in the Transcode Settings dialog box. Type information in each metadata field, as shown in Figure 16-4. If you wish to remove a metadata field, click Add/Remove fields again and remove check marks next to the fields you want to remove.

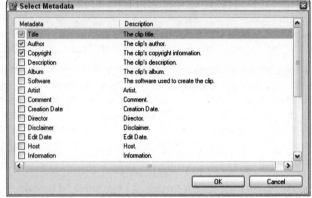

Figure 16-4:
Enter meta-
data in the
Transcode
Settings
dialog box.

Exporting Windows Media

Another Web-friendly export option available in Adobe Premiere Elements is Windows Media. This export option produces Windows Media Video (WMV), an efficient export format for online media. WMV-format video supports progressive download (also called *hinted download*), which means it starts to play as soon as a sufficient amount of data has been received to ensure continuous playback from start to finish. Versions of Windows Media Player — the only program that can play Windows Media Video — are available for both Windows and Macintosh systems.

Exporting Windows Media video is a lot like exporting QuickTime movies. To export Windows Media video, make sure that the movie has been rendered in your Timeline as described earlier in this chapter. Then follow these steps:

1. **Click somewhere in the Timeline window to make it active, and choose File➪Export➪Windows Media.**

   If the Timeline window isn't active, the Export submenu may not be available in the File menu.

2. **In the Export Windows Media dialog box, choose a preset.**

   Presets are listed on the left side of the Export Windows Media dialog box, and like QuickTime presets they are divided into three basic categories. When you click a preset on the left, a description of the preset appears on the right.

   As with QuickTime, presets that offer a higher frame rate, a larger frame size, or greater audio quality tend to produce larger movie files. If you want to customize your Windows Media export settings, click Advanced. I describe advanced settings in following section.

3. **When you have chosen a preset, click OK.**

   A Save File dialog box appears.

4. **Enter a filename for your movie in the File Name field.**

   If you plan to export your movie in several different sizes to accommodate a variety of online viewers, make sure that the filename reflects the preset used for this version. For example, if this version of a movie about hummingbirds uses the Cable Modem/DSL preset, you might name the file `hummingbirdsDSL`. A second version which uses the 56K Modem preset might be called `hummingbirds56K`.

5. **Choose an option from the Export Range menu.**

   In most cases, you'll want to export the Entire Sequence, but you can also choose to export just the Work Area if you have specified a work area that only encompasses part of your Timeline.

6. **Choose a location in which to save the movie and click Save.**

   When you click Save, the movie is exported.

You'll see a Rendering dialog box that tells you the progress of the export. A "remaining time" estimate is given; the saving process might take a while, especially if you're exporting a long project.

Choosing advanced export settings for Windows Media

The Windows Media format allows you to customize export settings, although there aren't nearly as many items to adjust as there are with QuickTime. In the Export Windows Media dialog box, click Advanced to customize export settings. The Transcode Settings dialog box appears. Click a settings category on the left side of the Transcode Settings dialog box to review and adjust the following settings:

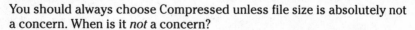

✔ **General:** You can choose whether the exported movie will be compressed or uncompressed.

   You should always choose Compressed unless file size is absolutely not a concern. When is it *not* a concern?

✔ **Video:** Several Windows Media codecs are available in the Codec menu. You can choose older versions of the Windows Media codec (such as 7 or 8) if you wish to make your movie compatible with older versions of Windows Media Player. If a user tries to view a Windows Media Video 9 movie using Windows Media Player 7 or 8, the movie may play improperly or not at all. For example, in many cases the audio portion of the movie may play but not the video. Windows Media Player 9 has been available since 2003 and it is becoming increasingly common. The default codec, Windows Media Video 9, is a pretty good choice.

The Video settings also allow you to specify interlaced processing. Choose this if your exported videos have interlacing jaggies or other interlacing-related problems.

Under Bitrate Settings, you probably want to choose Two Encoding Passes. This choice increases the time it takes the movie to export, but it also helps the movie compress more efficiently. Only choose one encoding pass if you're in a hurry to export the movie. The Variable Unconstrained option is probably your best bet in the Bitrate Mode menu.

✔ **Audio:** As with video, here you can choose a specific codec and bitrate settings.

✔ **Metadata:** Metadata consists primarily of descriptive information about the movie like the title, the name of the author, and copyright information. Click Add/Remove Fields under Metadata to add metadata fields and then enter metadata.

✔ **Audiences:** The Windows Media 9 codec supports multiple audience levels. When a Windows Media Player 9 user tries to download your Windows Media 9 movie, the software automatically detects the user's Internet connection speed. If your movie is set up for multiple audiences, dial-up users will get a low-quality version and broadband users will automatically get a higher-quality version.

To add an audience, choose a new preset from the Add Audience menu. Each audience for your movie is listed in the space below the Add Audience menu. For example, you can create two versions of my movie — one version is for dial-up modem users, and the other version for broadband users with cable modems or DSL. You can fine-tune settings for each audience in the lower-right section of the Transcode Settings dialog box.

When you're done reviewing and adjusting Windows Media transcode settings, click Save to close the Transcode Settings dialog box. Provide a name for your new custom preset in the Choose Name dialog box that appears. Click OK in the Export Windows Media dialog box, and then continue saving your movie as normal.

Chapter 17

Burning Your Movies on DVD

. . . .

. . . .

*I*n 1997 a new medium for distributing video came onto the market. That new medium was the *digital versatile disc*, more commonly known as DVD. DVDs packed full length, high-quality movies in digital format onto relatively small laser discs that were exactly the same size as ubiquitous CD-ROMs and audio CDs. Offering better playback quality and greater long-term durability, in 2003 DVDs surpassed VHS videotapes as the most common movie distribution method, and today they are *the* world standard for video recording.

Of course, during the first few years on the market, DVDs had one distinct disadvantage compared to VHS tapes. That disadvantage involved recording for the average consumer. Videocassette recorders (VCRs) have been common and affordable for decades, but until recently DVD burners were expensive and difficult to use. In 2001 Apple released a version of its G4 PowerMac that included a DVD burner called the SuperDrive, and at $5,000 it was considered the best and most affordable DVD burning system of its time. Fortunately, prices continued to plunge, and by 2004 DVD recording drives were widely available for less than $100. Today, DVD burners are so common that if you have purchased a new computer recently there's a good chance that it already has a DVD burner built-in. Not only are DVD burners useful for moviemaking, but the huge capacity of DVDs makes them great for data storage as well.

If your computer has a DVD burner, Adobe Premiere Elements is ready to put that burner to use. With just a few mouse clicks you can burn your Premiere Elements movie projects onto DVDs, complete with menus that can be used to navigate to the difference scenes in your movies. This chapter shows you how to record DVDs using Premiere Elements. But first I introduce you to the fundamentals of DVD technologies. If you're new to DVD, start with the next section to get the full scoop on what makes DVDs work, because understanding DVD technology will help you record better DVDs.

Getting on the DVD Bandwagon

Chances are you already have a DVD player or two around the house and you have been watching movies on DVD for a couple of years now. Watching DVD movies is easy, but until recently, the process of recording a DVD movie was complex, and the hardware for recording (a.k.a. *burning*) DVDs was prohibitively expensive. And then of course there were the precious blank recordable DVDs; when I worked on my first DVD-ROM software project in 2000, the blank recordable DVDs that we used during testing cost $40 *each*.

Thankfully, all that has changed. Consider:

- ✔ DVD burners are now widely available for less than $100.

- ✔ Blank recordable DVD discs are almost as cheap as blank CD-Rs. In fact, recordable DVDs are now cheaper than VHS tapes.

- ✔ DVDs are lighter and easier to mail than VHS tapes, meaning that sending copies of your movies to friends and family has never been easier or more affordable.

Decrypting DVD Standards

One of the things everyone loves about VHS tapes is that when you record a movie onto a tape, you can be sure that it'll play in just about any VCR. Likewise, you can usually look at the tape and immediately know how much video it holds. For example, a tape labeled T-120 is going to hold about 120 minutes of NTSC video.

Alas, DVDs are a little more complicated. Although many DVD players can play the DVDs that you record yourself, some players have trouble with them. And of course, the amount of space on a blank DVD is usually listed computer-style (gigabytes) rather than human-style (minutes). If a blank DVD says it can hold 4.7GB, how many minutes of video is that, exactly? The next few sections answer the most common questions you'll have about recording DVDs.

How much video can you cram onto a DVD?

A standard recordable DVD of the type you are likely to record yourself has a capacity of 4.7GB, which works out to a little over two hours of high-quality MPEG-2 video (MPEG-2 is the codec used by DVD video). Two hours is an approximation; as I show later in this chapter, quality settings greatly affect how much video you can actually squeeze onto a disc. If you are willing to sacrifice some quality you can squeeze quite a bit more than two hours of video into a disc.

Some DVD formats can hold more than 4.7GB because they are double-sided or have more than one layer of data on a single side. Table 17-1 lists the most common DVD capacities.

Table 17-1	DVD Capacities	
Type	*Capacity*	*Approximate Video Time*
Single-sided, single-layer	4.7GB	More than 2 hours
Single-sided, double-layer	8.5GB	4 hours
Double-sided, single-layer	9.4GB	4.5 hours
Double-sided, double-layer	16GB	More than 8 hours

You've probably seen double-sided DVDs before. They're often used to put the widescreen version of a movie on one side of the disc, and the full-screen "pan-and-scan" version on the other. Unfortunately, there is currently no easy way for you to make double-sided DVDs in your home or office. These types of discs require special manufacturing processes, so (for now) you're limited to about two hours of video for each DVD you record, unless you have a special double-layer DVD burner, as described in the next section.

The capacities listed in Table 17-1 assume standard-size DVDs, which are about 12cm in diameter. Some companies now offer miniature recordable DVDs, and of course these smaller discs also have a smaller capacity. For example, Verbatim's 8cm miniature DVD-R discs hold about 1.4GB of material.

How much video can you cram onto a double-layer DVD?

Until recently, conventional DVD burners could only make single-sided, single-layer discs with a maximum capacity of 4.7GB. Traditionally, double-layer discs were actually glued together (I'm not making this up) using a special transparent glue. This gluing was a highly technical process performed by technicians clad in white lab coats and working in advanced "clean room" manufacturing facilities.

But in 2004 double-layer DVD burner drives came onto the market, and Verbatim released recordable double-layer discs. If you have a double-layer DVD burner and the proper double-layer media, you can record double-layer discs that will hold 8.5GB, and you don't even have to wear a white lab coat. 8.5GB is a lot of space. A double-layer disc can hold about four hours of video at the highest DVD quality, or about 16 hours of video if you ramp the quality back to about what you get on a VHS tape. Like I said, that's a lot of video for something that easily fits in your hand!

What is the deal with the DVD-R/RW+R/RW alphabet soup?

When it comes to buying a drive to record DVDs, you're going to see a lot of similar — yet slightly different — acronyms thrown around to describe the various formats that are available. The basic terms you'll encounter are

- ✔ **DVD-R (DVD-Recordable):** Like a CD-R, you can only record onto this type of disc once.

- ✔ **DVD-RW (DVD-ReWritable):** You can record onto a DVD-RW disc, erase it later, and record something else onto it.

- ✔ **DVD-RAM (DVD-Random Access Memory):** These discs can also be recorded on and erased repeatedly. DVD-RAM discs are only compatible with DVD-RAM drives, which pretty much makes this format useless for movies because most DVD players cannot play DVD-RAM discs. DVD-RAM drives are quickly disappearing from the market.

The difference between DVD-R and DVD-RW is simple enough. But as you peruse advertisements for various DVD burners, you'll notice that some drives say they record DVD-R/RW, whereas others record DVD+R/RW. The dash (-) and the plus (+) aren't simply a case of catalog editors using different grammar. The -R and +R formats are unique standards. If you have a DVD-R drive, you must make sure that you buy DVD-R blank discs. Likewise, if you have a DVD+R drive, you must buy DVD+R blank discs.

Fortunately, many manufacturers now offer dual-format DVD burners that can handle either DVD-R or DVD+R discs. These drives are usually marked as DVD+/-R drives, and if you're still shopping for a DVD burner I strongly recommend that you choose a dual-format drive. A dual-format drive eliminates the headache of accidentally buying the wrong type of blank DVD discs.

One more thing: When you buy DVD-R discs (that's *-R*, not +R), make sure you buy discs that are labeled for General use, and not for Authoring. Not only are DVD-R for Authoring discs more expensive, but they are not compatible with most consumer DVD-R drives. This shouldn't be a huge problem because most retailers only sell DVD-R for General discs, but it's something to double-check when you buy blank media, especially if you are mail-ordering your blanks.

What are VCDs and SVCDs?

You can still make DVD movies even if you don't have a DVD burner.

Yes, you read that correctly. Okay, technically you can't make *real* DVDs without a DVD burner, but you can make discs that have menus just like DVDs and play in most DVD players. All you need is a regular old CD burner and some blank CD-Rs to make one of two types of discs:

- ✔ **VCD (Video CD):** These can hold 60 minutes of video, but the quality is about half that of a DVD.

- ✔ **SVCD (Super VCD):** These hold only 20 minutes of video, but the quality is closer to (though still a little less than) DVD quality.

The advantage of VCDs and SVCDs is that you can make them right now if you already have a CD burner but not a DVD burner. Unfortunately, Adobe Premiere Elements cannot export movies in VCD or SVCD format. However, you can "burn" your movie to a folder from Premiere Elements, and then use another program such as Nero Burning Rom to create a VCD or SVCD from that folder.

A great resource for compatibility information is a Web site called VCDHelp.com (www.vcdhelp.com). Check out the Compatibility Lists section for compatibility information on specific brands and models of DVD players.

Getting Your Movie Ready for DVD

Perhaps the best thing about DVDs is the high-quality play back you can achieve, regardless of whether the movie has been played once or a hundred times. The digital nature of DVDs means they don't suffer from the generational loss problems of analog videotapes (see Chapter 4 for a detailed explanation of generational loss).

Viewers expect very high quality from DVD movies. They're more likely to buy high-quality TVs so that they can watch their DVDs on crisp, bright displays. Viewers also expect DVDs to be easy to use, with features such as scene markers and navigation menus. This means you're going to have to work especially hard to make sure that your movies are properly prepared for DVD. There are two basic things you can do to better prepare your movies for DVD:

✓ **Make image quality superb:** Spend some time improving the colors and lighting in your video images. Chapter 10 shows you how to use the Premiere Elements video effects to fix lighting problems, improve washed out colors, and more.

✓ **Use effective scene markers:** If you create DVD scene markers in the Timeline whenever an important new scene begins, the movie will be easy to navigate in a DVD player. All viewers will need to do is click the Next Scene or Previous Scene on their DVD remotes to quickly jump between scenes. I show you how to add DVD markers to the Timeline in Chapter 8.

The basic image resolution and audio quality of your movie project should be adequate for DVD. All Premiere Elements movie projects are in full-quality DV format, which is desirable for DVD playback.

Recording DVDs with Premiere Elements

Until recently, recording a DVD on a computer was a complex, time-consuming process. The software designers at Adobe wanted to eliminate most of that complexity from Premiere Elements, and overall I think they've done a good job.

In fact, Adobe decided that easy DVD creation is so important that they included a special DVD workspace in Premiere Elements. To open the DVD workspace, click the DVD button on the Premiere Elements toolbar or choose Window⇨Workspace⇨DVD. The following sections show you how to choose a DVD template, customize your DVD menus, and record your DVD.

Choosing a DVD template

If you have ever watched a movie on DVD — I'm probably not going out on a limb here — you are probably familiar with DVD menus. DVD menus are graphically-attractive screens that appear on your TV. Using your DVD remote you can select a link in the DVD's main menu to play the movie, or you can go to submenus for scene selection or special features. Creating DVD menus can be a time-consuming process, but not with Adobe Premiere Elements.

Premiere Elements comes with a nice selection of DVD menu templates to help you quickly and easily create nice looking, easy-to-use menus. Each template includes both a main menu and a scene selection menu, complete with pre-configured menus for navigating the contents of the DVD.

Of course, you don't have to choose a template if you don't want. Premiere Elements can also create an "auto-play" DVD with no menus. An auto-play DVD automatically starts playing your movie as soon as it is placed in the DVD player.

When you first open the DVD workspace (Window⇨Workspace⇨DVD) you might see the DVD Templates dialog box, as shown in Figure 17-1. If you do not see this dialog box, click the Change Template button in the DVD Layout window.

Figure 17-1:
Premiere
Elements
comes with
many built-
in DVD
templates.

To select a template, follow these steps:

1. **In the DVD Templates window, choose whether you want a disc with or without menus.**

   If you just want to create an auto-play disc without menus, choose the Auto-play DVD with no Menus radio button at the top of the DVD Templates dialog box. If you're creating an auto-play disc, just click OK and proceed to the section "Burning your DVD," later in this chapter. But if you want to create a DVD with menus, choose the Apply a Template for a DVD with Menus radio button.

2. **Choose a theme from the Theme menu.**

   Premiere Elements' DVD templates are divided up into themes such as "Happy Birthday" and "Wedding." In Figure 17-1 I'm selecting a template from the "Travel" theme.

3. **Scroll down the list of templates and click a template to select it.**

   When you select a template, details about the template appear on the right. In Figure 17-1 I have chosen a template named "World Travel." The Template Details on the right side of the screen list two buttons in the main menu and three buttons in the scenes menu. Don't get too hung up about how many scene links are listed for the scenes menu — you can customize the number of buttons there later if you wish.

4. **When you have chosen a menu, click OK to close the DVD Templates dialog box.**

   DVD menus are automatically generated for your project, and the menus appear in the DVD Layout dialog box, as shown Figure 17-2.

After you start customizing your DVD menus, you may decide that you don't like the DVD template that you originally chose. Not a problem! Simply click Change Template in the DVD Layout window and choose a new template.

Figure 17-2: DVD menus are automatically generated from the Premiere Elements templates.

Customizing DVD menus

When you create DVD menus using a Premiere Elements DVD template, the template inserts some default text and links that you may want to edit. The default text is usually something generic and it may or may not be relevant to your movie project. For example, in Figure 17-2 the main menu bears the title `World Travels`. That title is perhaps a little too ambitious for a movie that is about travels to a single part of the world, a little-known national monument in North America. The following sections show you how to customize your DVD menus.

Changing menu text

To change text in a menu, simply double-click it. A Change Text dialog box appears, as shown in Figure 17-3. Simply enter some new text and click OK. The new text appears in the menu, as shown in Figure 17-4.

Figure 17-3: Enter new text for DVD menus here.

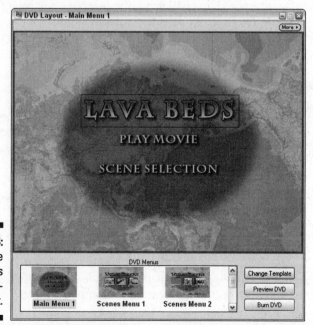

Figure 17-4: Personalize your menus with customized text.

Unfortunately, Premiere Elements doesn't allow you to change the size or alignment of text, so you'll have to be careful to not enter too much text on the Change Text dialog box. If you enter too much text, the words will flow off the screen or possibly obscure other elements on the menu.

Modifying scene selection menus

You should also take a look at your scene menus, which are the menus that will be used by viewers to select specific scenes in the movie. The number of scene menus for your project depends on

- **How many DVD markers are in your Timeline.** Premiere Elements considers each DVD scene marker the beginning of a new scene. If you have eight scenes as I do in my "Lava Beds" project, the template will be set up for seven scenes.

- **How many scenes per page are supported by the template.** When you created your DVD menus from a template, the DVD Templates dialog box (refer to Figure 17-1) showed how many scenes would appear on each scene's menu screen. The template I chose for my Lava Beds project allows three scenes per page, and since my project has seven scenes total there will be two pages with links to three scenes each, and one page with a lone link to the final scene.

Customizing your scenes menus is an important part of the DVD creation process because when Premiere Elements first creates your scene selection menus they probably aren't set up perfectly. The main problems are that scene links often overlap, and the thumbnail images shown for each scene are often less than ideal. To view your scene selection menus, simply click one at the bottom of the DVD Layout window. You may need to scroll down in the menu selection area to see all of your menu pages.

Correcting overlapping links

Overlapping links cause usability problems on the DVD, and should be studiously avoided. To see if you have overlapping titles, click the More button in the upper-right corner of the DVD Layout window and choose Show Overlapping Menu Buttons. Red outlines appear around overlapping links, as shown in Figure 17-5.

Unfortunately, there is only one thing you can do to resolve overlapping links: Shorten your scene titles. The Premiere Elements DVD Layout window doesn't allow you to move links or change text sizes. You can't even make scene titles wrap to multiple text lines, a feature I find extremely frustrating. To shorten a title, double-click the link. When you double-click a link, a DVD marker dialog box appears, as shown in Figure 17-6. Type a shorter name for the scene; you may need to abbreviate. Revise all of the link names in each menu screen until you no longer see any red outlines indicating overlapping links.

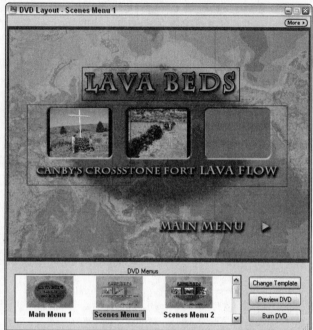

Figure 17-5:
Overlapping
links must
be resolved
before you
try to burn
your DVD.

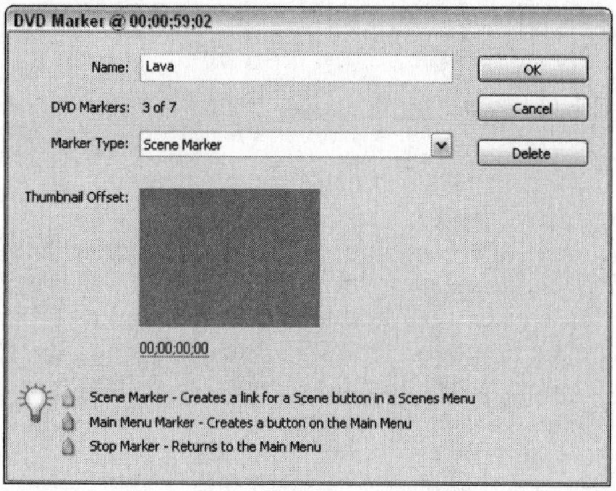

Figure 17-6:
Shorten
DVD marker
names to
eliminate
overlapping
links.

Changing link thumbnails

When you create DVD scene markers (see Chapter 8 for more on creating markers in the Timeline) you normally create them at the beginning of scenes. When Premiere Elements generates DVD menus based on a template, it automatically uses the first frame of each respective scene as a thumbnail image for the scene link. But as you can see in Figure 17-6, sometimes that thumbnail image doesn't properly illustrate the contents of the scene. In Figure 17-6 all that appears is a blank gray screen because this particular scene starts with a transition that has a gray background.

To change the thumbnail used for a scene marker, first double-click the scene in the DVD Layout window. In the DVD Marker window, click-and-drag left or right on the timecode under the Thumbnail Offset window. Keep dragging until you find a frame that you think would make a good thumbnail. In Figure 17-7 I have chosen a frame that is one second and three frames (00;00;01;03) ahead of the scene's first frame. Click OK to close the DVD Marker window when you have selected a good thumbnail frame.

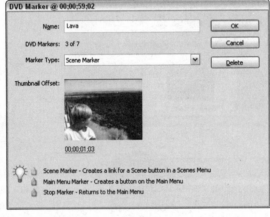

Figure 17-7: Use the DVD Marker dialog box to choose better scene link thumbnails.

Removing links

You may decide that some of your scene menu links are superfluous, especially if you created the DVD markers a long time ago. Don't worry, removing scene links from your menus is easy. Just double-click the offending link in the DVD Layout window, and click Remove in the DVD Marker dialog box that appears. The scene is removed from your DVD menus, and the DVD scene marker is removed from your project's Timeline, as well.

Adding a stop marker

Have you thought about what will happen when your movie ends? When your movie is over, ideally the DVD's main menu should appear. To make sure this happens automatically you should insert a stop marker at the end of your movie if you have not done so already. Adding a stop marker is easy:

1. **Click somewhere in the Timeline window to make it active.**

2. **Press the End key on your keyboard.**

   This moves the CTI to the very end of your project.

3. **Choose Marker⇨Set DVD Marker.**

   The DVD Marker dialog box appears.

4. **Choose Stop Marker in the Marker Type menu, as shown in Figure 17-8.**

5. **Click OK to close the DVD Marker dialog box.**

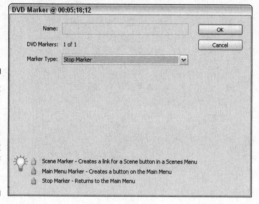

Figure 17-8:
Make sure
you place a
DVD stop
marker at
the end of
your project.

Previewing your DVD

When you have all of your DVD menus set up the way you want them, take a few moments to preview your DVD. To generate a preview of your DVD project, click Preview DVD in the DVD Layout window. A Preview DVD window appears, as shown in Figure 17-9. This window includes many of the same controls found on a typical DVD remote, and the menus and movie should provide a functional mock-up of how the final DVD should work.

When you preview your DVD, there are several important things you should check:

✔ Do the menus look as attractive as you'd hoped? If not, consider choosing a new DVD template.

✔ Click every scene link in the scenes menu. Does each scene seem to start at the correct place? If some of the scene links don't seem to link to the right places, you may need to move some DVD markers in your Timeline.

✔ Click the Play Movie link in the main menu, and then click the Next Scene button to jump to the next scene. Continue clicking Next Scene until you get to the end of the movie. Do the scenes seem to be spaced at appropriate intervals? You may find that you need to add or remove some DVD markers in the Timeline.

✔ Play the final scene in the movie until it ends. Does the movie return to the main menu when it ends? If not, make sure you've placed a DVD stop marker at the end of the movie, as described in the previous section.

Figure 17-9:
Preview
your DVD
project to
make sure
all links
function
properly.

When you are done previewing your DVD, click the Close (X) button in the upper-right corner of the Preview DVD window to close it. If you make any more changes to your project, make sure that you perform another complete preview of the revised project.

Burning your DVD

When you have previewed your DVD and you're certain that it's ready to go, you are ready to move on to the final step. You are ready to — drum roll, please — burn the DVD. Don't worry, you don't need matches and a burning permit from the county for this kind of burn! The term *burn* is often used in place of "record" when you record stuff onto CDs or DVDs.

Before you start burning your DVD, keep in mind that the burning process usually takes a long time. The process can literally take hours, so I usually like to burn DVDs near the end of a workday. You can click Burn and let the disc burn overnight, when you don't need to use the computer for anything else. DVD burning requires a lot of computer memory and processing resources, so make sure you close all non-critical programs before you start to burn a DVD.

To burn a DVD in Premiere Elements, follow these steps:

1. **Choose Timeline⇨Render Work Area.**

   It's a good idea to make sure that transitions, effects, titles, and other edits in the Timeline are rendered before you try to burn a DVD.

2. **When rendering is complete, click Burn DVD in the DVD Layout window.**

   The Burn DVD dialog box appears.

3. **Choose whether you want to burn to a disc or to a folder.**

   Most of the time you will want to burn to a disc, but you can also create a DVD movie disc image in a folder on your hard drive, which you can then record onto a DVD later using other software such as Roxio Easy CD Creator or Nero Burning ROM.

   If you want to make a VCD or SVCD, you must burn the movie to a folder and then create the VCD or SVCD in a program like Nero Burning ROM.

   If you find that DVD burns frequently fail while burning directly from Premiere Elements, try burning to a folder. Then use other DVD burning software to record the DVD later.

4. **Enter a name for the disc in the Disc Name field.**

5. **If you have more than one burner on your computer, make sure that the correct burner is selected in the Burner Location menu.**

   If you have an external DVD burner connected to your computer's USB or FireWire port, but the burner doesn't show up in the Burner Location menu, make sure that the external burner is properly connected and that the power is turned on. Wait several seconds and then click the Rescan button.

6. **Insert a blank recordable DVD disc in your DVD burner drive.**

   If you see a yellow asterisk icon and the words Media Not Present next to the Status indicator, make sure you have inserted your blank DVD disc and click Rescan. After several seconds you should see Ready next to the Status indicator.

7. **If you want to test the integrity and available write speed of the blank DVD disc, place a check mark next to Test Media Before Burning.**

8. **Choose how many copies you want to burn.**

   You may want to burn a single test disc first, and then burn multiple copies later when you know that the first DVD burned just fine.

9. **Choose a quality setting.**

   In general I recommend that you just leave the Fit Contents to Available Space option checked. Premiere Elements automatically detects how much space is available on the DVD and burns your movie at the highest quality that will fit on the disc.

   If you wish, you can disable this option and manually choose a quality level using the Video Quality slider. Lower bitrates give lower video quality, but they also allow more video to fit on a single disc.

   Pay attention to what is listed next to the Space Required indicator. If you are burning to a folder, make sure that the amount of space shown in the Space Required indicator will fit on whatever kind of media you plan to use when you finally burn the movie onto a disc.

10. **Choose a TV standard.**

    Choose NTSC or PAL, depending on the equipment used by your local audience. See Chapter 4 for more on TV standards.

11. **When you are ready to burn the DVD, click Burn.**

    The Burn DVD Progress window appears. As I said, the burning process can take a long time. The longest part of the process is encoding, which is where the movie is converted into the file format used by DVD players.

12. **When the burn process is complete, click Close to close the Burn DVD Progress dialog box.**

    When the DVD burning process is complete, make sure you test your DVD in as many DVD players as possible.

Some DVD players won't play certain DVDs. If you find that your DVDs often don't play in your DVD players, try a different brand of blank DVD discs, or try burning the DVD using different software such as Nero Burning Rom or Roxio Easy CD Creator.

Chapter 18

Recording Movies on Tape

In This Chapter

▶ Getting your movie ready for analog playback

▶ Making sure your tape contains a timecode

▶ Exporting your movie to videotape

Chances are you will probably share a lot of your movie projects in digital format, whether as files over the Internet or as files recorded onto DVDs. But there's a good chance that you may need to share your movies on good old-fashioned analog videotape as well. Although analog video may seem old fashioned, it is still a very common way to share video. It's also pretty reliable. When you share movies on the Internet, you have to worry about your possible users' mishmash of bandwidth capabilities — and whether they have the right playback software. And some DVD players simply refuse to play some discs. But you can trust in the fact that your VHS videotapes will play reliably in almost any VHS tape deck. You also know that virtually every human being in your target audience already owns at least one VHS tape deck and a TV.

This chapter helps you prepare your movies for playback on videotape. After your movie is ready, I show you how to export it from Adobe Premiere Elements to videotape.

Getting Ready for Analog Playback

Exporting video to an analog source is actually a far less complicated process than exporting for a digital source. The main difference is that you don't have to worry about codecs and player software (see Chapter 16). Your only real concern is that you have the right hardware for export, and that your computer runs well enough to export without dropping frames or causing other problems. Generally speaking, if your computer meets the system requirements for running Adobe Premiere Elements (see Chapter 2) and you can capture video successfully, you won't have any trouble exporting to tape.

Getting your movie ready for tape

Before you export your movie to tape, you should make sure that your movie is actually ready. Naturally, you should review the project and all of your edits. Because any movie you export to tape will be viewed primarily on broadcast-style TVs, you should also check the following:

✔ **Does the movie need any broadcast-style elements?** If your movie is going to a broadcast outlet — even a local public-access cable channel — you may need to provide color bars and tone at the beginning or end of the tape. There is also a (remote) possibility that the broadcaster wants a counting leader at the beginning of the tape. Contact the broadcaster and ask for specific requirements. I show you how to generate and use counting leaders and bars and tone in Chapter 15.

✔ **Is the movie compatible with the appropriate broadcast standard?** See Chapter 4 for more on video standards. Review settings in the General Project Settings (Project⇨Project Settings⇨General).

If your movie is standard size (not widescreen) and is to be viewed on NTSC TVs, these are the settings you should have:

- **Frame size:** 720 x 480
- **Display Format:** 30 fps Drop-Frame Timecode
- **Pixel Aspect Ratio:** NTSC (0.9)

For standard size PAL video, these are the settings you should have:

- **Frame size:** 720 x 576
- **Display Format:** 25 fps
- **Pixel Aspect Ratio:** PAL (1.067)

✔ **Have you previewed your project on a TV monitor yet?** Previewing your movie on a real TV monitor can help you identify problems such as weird colors or titles that get cut off at the edge of the screen. (See Chapter 15 for more on previewing your movie on an external monitor.)

Setting up your recording hardware

Though DVDs are quickly becoming the standard for video exchange, VHS videotapes are still a common video medium. If your ultimate plan is to put your video on a VHS tape, you can use one of three methods:

✔ **Export directly to a VHS deck connected to your computer.** Remember, Adobe Premiere Elements can only export video directly to a FireWire port. If your computer has an analog video capture card, Premiere Elements can't use it. However, if you have an external video converter (see Chapter 21 for more on video converters) you can connect the external converter to your FireWire port and connect your VHS deck to the analog outputs on the converter.

If you want to connect a video deck directly to analog ports on your analog capture card, you'll have to export an MPEG or AVI file from Premiere Elements (see Chapter 15) and then import that file into another program that can use your analog capture card. A few newer, professional-style S-VHS decks now have FireWire ports, making the process of connecting the VCR to your computer much, much easier, but these decks tend to be very expensive. I describe high-end video decks in Chapter 21.

✔ **Export video through the analog outputs on your digital camcorder.** With your camcorder connected to your FireWire port, the camcorder can serve as a digital-to-analog converter between your computer and the VHS deck. Some camcorders do not allow analog output and FireWire input at the same time, so you'll have to experiment with your own camcorder to see if this is a viable option. Also, when using this method, Premiere Elements' device control can only control the camcorder, not the analog deck.

✔ **Export video to your digital camcorder, and then dub it to the analog deck later.** This approach works even with the cheapest digital camcorder. If your camcorder doesn't allow simultaneous digital input and analog output, simply export the video to a DV tape in the camcorder and then later dub it to a VHS tape using the camcorder's analog outputs.

Blacking and coding a tape

If you plan to export your movie to a tape in a DV device (such as a digital camcorder), Premiere Elements assumes that there is already timecode on the videotape to which you are about to export. But if you are using a brand-new tape that you just peeled out of its plastic shrink-wrap, the tape has no timecode yet. You can rectify this situation by doing what video pros call *blacking and coding* the tape — recording black video and timecode onto the tape before you record anything else.

The easiest way to black and code a tape is to simply put your DV camcorder in a dark, quiet room and press Record with the lens cap on. Come back in an hour or so when the tape is full. Voilà! Your tape now has black video and timecode recorded on its entire length. Another way to black and code a tape is to create a project in Premiere Elements that contains nothing but black video (with *no* audio), and then export that project to the tape. You might be tempted to just black and code the first minute or two of a tape, but I have found that with some devices this can cause a recording glitch when the export reaches the end of the original timecode.

Preparing your computer to export video

Remember back when you were getting ready to capture video into your computer? That was ages ago, at the beginning of your project. As I suggest in Chapter 6, you probably spent some time preparing your system to ensure that you didn't drop any frames during capture. As with capturing, exporting video is also resource-intensive, and you must carefully prep your computer to ensure there aren't any dropped frames as you lay the movie down on tape. Before you export a movie to tape, perform the following tasks:

- ✔ **Turn off extra programs.** Make sure all unnecessary programs are closed, including your e-mail program, MP3 jukebox, and Web browser. Every open program uses up memory and processor resources that should be devoted to video export.

- ✔ **Disable programs that run in the background.** Disable memory-resident programs such as antivirus programs and any programs that have icons in the Windows system tray (the area in the lower-right corner of the screen, next to the clock). You should be able to close or disable most of these items by right-clicking them and choosing Close, Disable, or Exit from their respective menus. (Just don't forget to turn that antivirus program back on when you're done exporting!)

- ✔ **Disable screen savers and power-management settings to ensure they don't kick on in the middle of a long export operation.** If you're working on a laptop, make sure it's plugged in to wall power so that it doesn't hibernate or run out of battery power in the middle of export.

- ✔ **Defragment your hard drive.** A recently defragmented drive is important to ensure efficient operation during video capture and export.

Exporting Your Movie

After you have prepared your movie, computer, and recording deck for export to tape, you're ready to begin the actual export process. The steps you follow vary a little bit depending on whether you are exporting with or without device control. How do you know? If you are exporting to a DV device (a digital camcorder or a DV deck) that is connected directly to your FireWire port, Premiere Elements can probably control that device using the same FireWire connection that actually transfers the video. If you have an analog video deck connected to an external video converter, you won't be able to control the deck using device control even though the converter is connected to your FireWire port.

If you don't have device control, you'll have to juggle your hands as you manually press Record on your tape deck while beginning export in Premiere Elements. The following sections show you how to export video with and without device control.

Exporting to tape with device control

Years ago, when computer manufacturers introduced Plug and Play hardware, many old-timers scoffed. "Plug and *pray*," it was often called, especially when something went wrong. Thankfully, years of development have made Plug and Play — combined with device control — a crucial asset of IEEE-1394 (FireWire) technology. Connect a digital camcorder to your FireWire port, turn it on, and within seconds, you're in the driver's seat, controlling camcorder functions using your computer. I've been using digital video equipment for a few years now, and it still amazes me every time I click Play in Premiere Elements and the tape in my *camcorder* starts to roll. In fact, thanks to device control, you may discover (as I have) that you have *more* control over the camcorder in Premiere Elements than you do when you try to manipulate the buttons on the camcorder itself.

Generally speaking, a DV tape only has timecode on it if somebody (probably you) manually added the timecode through a process called *blacking and coding*. I describe this process earlier in this chapter. I suggest getting the blacking and coding process out of the way well *before* you get to this point.

Device control makes exporting video to tape really easy. If you are exporting to a device that has device control (such as a digital camcorder), follow these steps:

1. **Connect your recording device (your camcorder or DV deck) to your computer and turn it on.**

   Make sure the camcorder is turned on to VTR (Player) mode, and not to Camera mode.

2. **After you make sure that the sequence you want to export is active and currently in front in the Timeline window, press Enter to make sure everything in the sequence is rendered.**

3. **Choose File➪Export➪Export to Tape.**

   The Export to Tape Settings dialog box appears, as shown in Figure 18-1.

4. **Make sure a check mark is placed next to the Activate Recording Device option.**

   The only time you would disable this option is if you're exporting video through a video converter connected to your computer's FireWire port. (I describe video converters in Chapter 21.)

5. **If the tape already has a timecode on it, select the Assemble at Timecode option and specify a timecode where you want recording to begin.**

   Start the recording at about the one-minute mark on your tape.

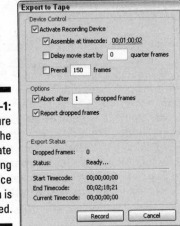

If you are exporting NTSC video, you might notice that you can't choose the timecode 00;01;00;00. You need to choose the timecode 00;01;00;02 (see Figure 18-1). The reason for this is that NTSC video uses drop-frame timecode — which skips frames 00 and 01 at the beginning of every minute, except at every tenth minute. (See Chapter 4 for more on how drop-frame timecode works.)

6. **Enter the number of quarter frames, if any, that you want to delay before the movie starts playing.**

   Some devices need a delay between receiving the *record* command and the actual movie.

7. **Enter the number of frames that you want to preroll the tape in the Preroll field.**

   Preroll allows the reels in the tape deck to spin up to the correct speed before recording begins. I recommend at least five seconds (150 frames for NTSC video, 125 frames for PAL video) of preroll.

8. **Place a check mark next to Abort after.**

   Of course, you can tell Premiere Elements to stop export only after 2 or 3 or 50 frames have been dropped, but even one dropped frame is an unacceptable quality problem. If you have trouble with dropped frames during capture, review the earlier sections of this chapter and Chapter 2 to make sure your computer is ready and that it meets the specs for running Premiere Elements.

9. **Click Record.**

   Your movie is recorded on the tape.

Steps 5 through 7 above require that there is already timecode on the tape to which you are exporting. Although you can often get away with skipping those three options — especially if you already placed a section of black video at the beginning of your movie — I recommend that you black and code your tapes before exporting to them.

Exporting to tape without device control

Exporting to tape without device control is a tad clumsy, but it is possible. You basically just use your own magic flying fingers to press Record on the tape deck *as you click Play* in Premiere Elements. Here's how:

1. **Connect your hardware and cue the tape to the point at which you want to start recording.**

2. **Click the Timeline window to make it active.**

3. **Make sure that the yellow work area bar at the top of the Timeline covers your entire movie.**

   If the work area bar (described in Chapter 8) doesn't cover the entire movie, click-and-drag the ends of the work area bar to expand it.

   If the work area bar doesn't encompass the entire project, some effects and edits might not be rendered.

4. **Press Enter to ensure that everything in the sequence has been rendered.**

   When the Timeline is done rendering, the CTI automatically moves to the beginning of the Timeline and starts to play. Make sure that the movie plays on your external monitor or camcorder display.

5. **When you are sure that your movie is playing on your external monitor, stop playback.**

6. **Place the CTI at the beginning of the Timeline.**

7. **Press Record on the tape deck or camcorder you are using to record.**

8. **Click Play in the Monitor window to play the movie.**

   Steps 4 and 5 not only ensure that the Timeline is rendered, but also serve as a test to make sure your hardware setup is going to work. This test is crucial because if you don't see the video from the Timeline playing out on the external hardware, you can bet that nothing is getting recorded onto your tape either.

Part V
The Part of Tens

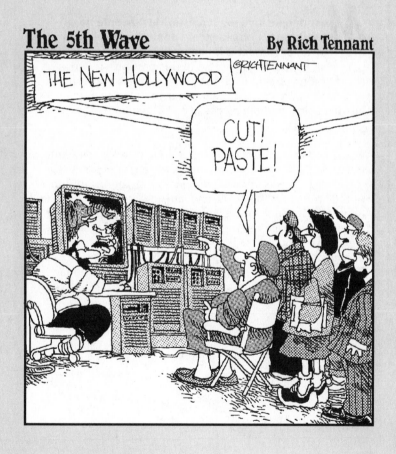

The 5th Wave   By Rich Tennant

THE NEW HOLLYWOOD   @RICHTENNANT

CUT! PASTE!

In this part . . .

Most people love top ten lists. Most people have ten fingers. Coincidence? I don't think so. If you've ever read a For Dummies book before, you know what this part is all about. The chapters in this part provide top-ten lists to help you find useful stuff by tens — ten advanced editing techniques in Premiere Elements, ten secrets of moviemaking, and ten pieces of software and hardware you just won't want to do without.

At the end of this part is an appendix. Unlike the appendix that is part of the human anatomy, the appendix of *Adobe Premiere Elements For Dummies* serves an important function. Throughout this book, and indeed through your entire adventure in video editing, you will encounter an entirely different language refering to video editing and technologies. You encounter new terms like *interlacing* or *pixel aspect ratio* and countless acronyms like NTSC and NLE. Thus, I've provided this glossary to serve as a dictionary of videography lingo.

Chapter 19

Ten Advanced Premiere Elements Techniques

Adobe didn't design Premiere Elements for professional video editors. Premiere Elements is primarily aimed at video hobbyists, people who have digital camcorders and want to spend some time turning their raw video into fun, personalized movies. But Premiere Elements brings a level of pro-caliber video-editing capabilities heretofore unseen in affordable video-editing programs, and I think it's only natural that you'll want to use this better software to make better movies.

Moviemaking is an art, and as with any art there's no single formula or magic technique to guarantee a great movie. One of the great things about a powerful program like Premiere Elements is that your creativity is not likely to be limited by the software. Premiere Elements has so many features and capabilities that you will probably come up with editing tricks and techniques all your own. But if you lack inspiration at the moment or just want to learn some more advanced techniques, this chapter is for you. Here I've collected some (okay, 10) great advanced editing techniques that didn't quite seem to fit in anywhere else in the book.

Now You See Him, Now You Don't

Think of all the special effects you've ever seen in movies and TV shows. I'll bet one of the most common effects you've seen is where a person or thing seems to magically appear or disappear from a scene. Sometimes a magician snaps his finger and blinks out of the picture. Other times people gradually fade in or out, as when crews on *Star Trek* use the transporter.

Believe it or not, this is one of the easiest special effects you can ever do. All you need is a camcorder, a tripod, and Adobe Premiere Elements. Basically you just position the camcorder on the tripod and shoot *before* and *after* scenes. The subject should only appear in one of the scenes.

When you've finished recording your "before" and "after" clips and captured them into Premiere Elements (see Chapter 6 for details), edit them into the Timeline, one after the other. If you don't use a transition between the clips, the subject will appear to "pop" into or out of the scene. If you want the subject to fade into the scene, apply a Cross Dissolve transition between the two clips (see Chapter 9 for more on using transitions). In Figure 19-1, my subject (Soren) is fading into the scene.

Figure 19-1:
Make your
subject
magically
appear (or
disappear)!

To effectively make a subject magically appear or disappear, follow these basic rules:

✔ **Use a tripod.** A tripod is absolutely mandatory to make this effect work. You won't be able to hold the camera steady enough by hand, and a jiggling camera ruins the results.

✔ **Don't move the camera between shots.** The camera must remain absolutely still between the before and after shots. If you have to reposition the camera, or if someone bumps it, re-shoot both scenes. If your camcorder has a remote control, use that to start and stop recording so that even the slight touch of your finger doesn't move the camera.

✔ **Shoot the "before" and "after" scenes quickly.** If you're shooting outdoors, shadows and lighting can change quickly. Even subtle light changes will be apparent when you edit the two scenes together later. So stop reading and start shooting. Now!

✔ **Don't disturb the rest of the scene.** If your subject moves a chair or picks up an object between the "before" and "after" shots, the scenes will appear inconsistent when edited together.

Seeing Double

Have you ever wondered if you have an evil twin somewhere in the world? With some simple videography tricks and Adobe Premiere Elements, you can easily make your evil twin a visual reality, as shown in Figure 19-2. Don't worry, no human cloning is necessary for this effect. Like the effect described in the previous section, this effect requires the use of a tripod. You shoot the two scenes quickly, and then edit them together as a single scene in Premiere Elements.

Figure 19-2: Are you really seeing double?

To make this effect work, you first shoot one half of the image, and then shoot the other half. This gives two clips that will be combined to make a single scene. As you can see in Figure 19-3, one clip is placed in track Video 1, and the other clip — we'll call it the *overlay clip* — is placed in track Video 2. You then apply the Crop effect to the overlay clip so it only covers half the screen. Notice in Figure 19-4 that I have cropped 50% off the right side of my overlay clip. To apply the Crop effect, follow these steps:

1. **Choose Window⇨Effects to open the Effects window.**

2. **Open the Video Effects folder, and then open the Transform subfolder.**

3. **Click-and-drag the Crop effect from the Effects window to an overlay clip in the Timeline.**

   An overlay clip should be in track Video 2 or higher.

4. **Click the overlay clip in the Timeline to select it.**

5. **Choose Window⇨Effect Controls to open the Effect Controls window.**

6. **Click the Crop effect under Video Effects in the Effect Controls window to select it.**

   When you select the Crop effect, handles appear around the corners of the video image in the Monitor.

7. **Click-and-drag a corner of the video image to crop it.**

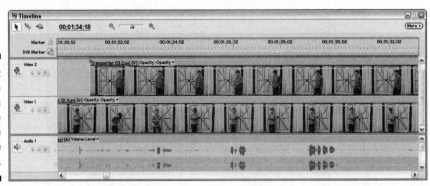

Figure 19-3:
You can use overlays in the Timeline to provide creative illusion.

When you crop a video image in an overlay track, video images in underlying tracks show up in the cropped area.

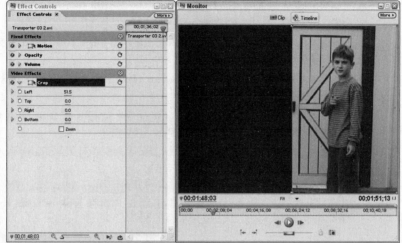

Figure 19-4:
I used the
Crop effect
to remove
half of the
overlay clip.

Freeze-Framing Video

Have you ever watched those old "Road Runner" cartoons where Wile E.
Coyote attempts to chase down the Road Runner? You probably remember a
scene that appeared early in each cartoon — Road Runner would momentarily freeze, and its scientific name (*Acceleratii Incredibilus* or something along
those lines) would appear on the screen.

You can add momentary freeze-frames to your video as well. To momentarily
freeze a frame of video in the middle of a clip, and then make it play again,
follow these steps:

1. **In the Timeline, move the CTI to the frame that you want to freeze.**

   You can use the left and right arrow keys to move back and forth a single
   frame at a time.

2. **Click the clip in the Timeline that you want to freeze to select it.**

3. **Choose Timeline⇨Razor at Current Time Indicator.**

   The clip splits into two.

4. **Choose File⇨Export⇨Frame.**

5. **In the Export Frame dialog box that appears, give the exported frame
   a file name and click Save.**

   The exported frame now appears in your Media window as a still image.

6. **Click-and-drag the still image from the Media window and drop it on the Timeline at the location of the CTI.**

   The still image is inserted between the two clips you created when you split the original clip in step 3.

7. **Click the inserted still image in the Timeline to select it, and choose Clip⇨Time Stretch.**

8. **In the Time Stretch dialog box, enter the length of time that you want the frozen frame to appear next to Duration.**

   If you want the frame to freeze for three seconds, for example, enter 00;00;03;00.

9. **If an empty space now appears in the Timeline after the still clip, right-click the empty space and choose Ripple Delete from the menu that appears.**

Your Timeline will end up looking similar to the Timeline shown in Figure 19-5. When you play the Timeline, the frame appears to freeze momentarily.

Figure 19-5:
Frames of video can be momentarily frozen.

Working in the Golden Age of Cinema

Motion pictures have been around for well over a century now. You may want to pay homage to the history of cinema by using some "old" (or at least old-*looking*) footage in your movie projects. Thankfully, creating footage that looks old does not require a trip to some dank film vault deep beneath a Hollywood movie studio. You can simulate an old-fashioned look with your own video by following these steps:

- ✔ **Beware the anachronism!** Pay attention to your subjects and the scene. Cowboys of the Old West didn't carry cell phones at their hips, for example; nor was the sky filled with white condensation trails left by jet airplanes. Remove objects from the scene that don't fit the period you are trying to simulate, and shoot carefully so that the background doesn't depict modernity.

- ✔ **Remove color from the clip.** Perhaps the easiest way to convert a color image to grayscale is to use the Black & White filter in the Image Control subfolder of the Video Effects folder (Window⇨Effects), although I prefer to use the Color Balance (HLS) effect. Adjust the saturation level to –100, which essentially makes the clip grayscale.

  One advantage of using the Color Balance (HLS) effect is that you can use keyframes to change the effect in the middle of a clip.

  Grayscale is just a fancy way of saying black and white. Grayscale is a more technically accurate term because black-and-white video images are actually made using various shades of gray.

- ✔ **"Weather" the video image.** Film tends to deteriorate over time, so if you're trying to simulate old footage, you should simulate some of that deterioration. Use the Noise effect under Stylize to add some graininess to the video image.

- ✔ **Reduce audio quality and if possible use a mono setting.** Audio recordings made 75 years ago did not use 16-bit stereo sound, I assure you. To reduce quality, reduce the sampling rate of the audio when you export your movie (see Chapters 15 and 16 for more on movie export settings).

  Alternatively, you may want to go for the "silent movie" effect and not record any audio at all. Just use an appropriate musical soundtrack and insert title screens for dialogue.

- ✔ **Speed up the clip.** Older film often plays back at a faster speed, so speed up the clip by selecting it, choosing Clip⇨Time Stretch, and increasing the Speed percentage in the Time Stretch dialog box that appears.

A Long Time Ago. . .

. . .In a galaxy far, far, away, there was a filmmaker with a singular vision that would forever change the way we think about movies. That filmmaker was George Lucas, of course, and his great vision was to make titles that floated off into space, drifting farther and farther away until finally disappearing into infinity.

Mr. Lucas had other great visions, of course, but for now we're concerned with that really cool thing he did with the titles at the beginning of each *Star Wars* movie. I'm going to show you how to do that using the Adobe Title Designer and some simple effects in Premiere Elements. Follow these steps:

1. **Choose File⇨New⇨Title to open the Adobe Title Designer.**

2. **In the Adobe Title Designer, click More⇨Roll/Crawl Options to open the Roll/Crawl Options dialog box.**

3. **Choose Roll in the Motion menu, place a check mark next to Start Off Screen, and click OK to close the Roll/Crawl Options dialog box.**

4. **Enter and style the text for your rolling title.**

   See Chapter 14 for more on creating and styling title text.

5. **When you're done creating your title, click Save Title As to save your title, and then close the Adobe Title Designer.**

6. **Add your title to the Timeline, as described in Chapter 14.**

7. **Choose Window⇨Effects to open the Effects window.**

8. **Open the Perspective submenu under Video Effects, and click-and-drag the Basic 3D effect to your title clip in the Timeline.**

9. **Click the title clip in the Timeline to select it.**

10. **Choose Window⇨Effect Controls to open the Effect Controls window.**

11. **In the Effect Controls window, click the arrow next to Basic 3D to expand the controls for that effect, as shown in Figure 19-6.**

12. **Adjust the Tilt angle to –55.0 degrees.**

    You may want to experiment with the exact angle a bit, but I find that –55.0 degrees provides a good balance of readability and coolness in this effect.

That's it! Preview your effect and fine-tune as necessary. You may need to change the playing time of the title to get the desired effect, or make other adjustments.

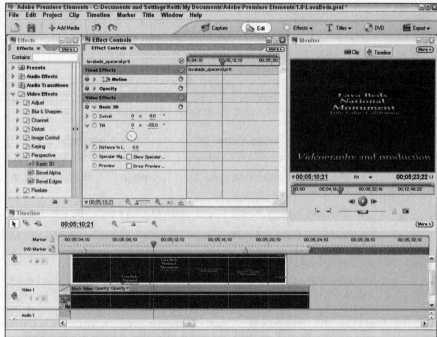

Figure 19-6:
Combine
rolling titles
with the
Basic 3D
effect to
make *Star
Wars*-style
titles.

The Ken Burns Effect

Ken Burns is one of the most renowned documentarians to ever make, er, documentaries. He has the uncanny ability to make fascinating movies about historical subjects for which there is little or no original film or video footage. For example, Burns' documentary film series' on the American Civil War and the Oregon Trail were put together mainly using spoken interviews and still photographs from the period.

The tricky part about what Ken Burns does is to make his work come across as interesting movies instead of just slide shows with music and narration. Burns and other documentary filmmakers do this by panning or zooming on still images as they appear on the screen. This technique adds a sense of motion and action to the movie that would otherwise be lacking in a simple slide show.

Apple iMovie includes an effect called the Ken Burns Effect, and basically what this effect does is slowly pan or zoom on a still image. You can do the same thing with Premiere Elements, although Premiere Elements doesn't use Ken Burns' name.

Even if you're not doing a documentary film without much video footage, using the Ken Burns technique works especially well. Say, for example, you're making a movie about a road trip. You can periodically pan and zoom across a still image of a map that details the progress.

To pan or zoom on a still image, choose Window➪Effects to open the Effects window and then open the Presets folder. The Presets folder contains four subfolders that you can use on your still images:

- **Horizontal Image Pans:** These presets pan horizontally left-to-right or right-to-left across the image.

- **Horizontal Image Zooms:** These zoom in or out on the image along a horizontal plane.

- **Vertical Image Pans:** These presets pan vertically up or down the image.

- **Vertical Image Zooms:** These zoom in or out on the image along a vertical plane.

Simply drag-and-drop an image pan or zoom preset to a still image in the Timeline, just like any other effect. These presets modify the Motion settings for the clip. As with most effects, you'll probably have to experiment a bit to get just the desired effect. And of course, preview your edits carefully. Pans and zooms on still images are most effective if they move slowly and in only one direction. Panning back and forth might make some audience members sea sick!

Working with Mattes

TV screens are usually rectangular, and so most video images are rectangular, as well. But you can make a video image of virtually any shape you want using *mattes.* Matte is simply a fancy name for a solid-colored screen or a screen with a monochrome shape.

Here's how:

1. **In a graphics program such as Photoshop Elements, create an image file with the shape you want to use for your matte.**

   I recommend creating a matte with just two contrasting colors (black and white provide the best contrast). Also, follow the guidelines I give in Chapter 6 for creating still images for use in movies. If your video uses NTSC video, the final image size should be 720 x 534 pixels. If you are using PAL video, the image size for the matte should be 768 x 576 pixels. Save the image as a PSD (Photoshop Document) file.

2. **Choose File⇨Add Media in Premiere Elements and import the matte image.**

   I describe how to import media into Premiere Elements in Chapter 6.

3. **Add the matte image to an overlay track in the Timeline.**

   Overlay tracks are tracks Video 2 or higher. In Figure 19-7 I have inserted a matte image that is shaped like a snowflake.

4. **Choose Window⇨Effects to open the Effects window.**

5. **In the Effects window, open the Keying subfolder of the Video Effects folder.**

6. **Click-and-drag the Track Matte Key to the matte image in the Timeline.**

7. **Click the matte in the Timeline to select it, and then choose Window⇨ Effect Controls to open the Effect Controls window.**

8. **Click the arrow next to Track Matte Key in the Effect Controls window to expand the controls as shown in Figure 19-8.**

9. **Next to Matte, choose the video track that includes the matte image.**

   I placed my matte image in Video 2, so I've selected Video 2 in the Matte menu.

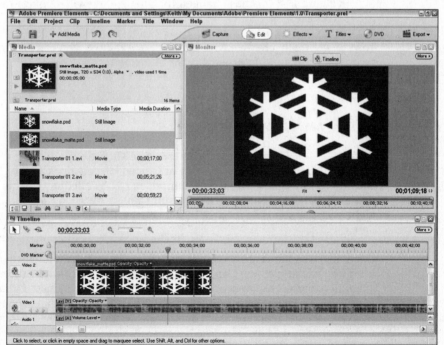

Figure 19-7:
This snow-flake matte has been added to track Video 2.

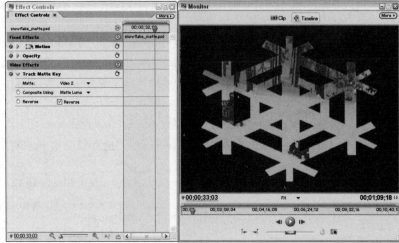

Figure 19-8:
The shape
of the video
image is
now deter-
mined by
the matte
image.

10. **Choose Matte Luma in the Composite Using menu.**

    Part of the video image in the underlying video track should show through.

11. **If desired, place a check mark next to Reverse.**

    In Figure 19-8 this has changed the shape of my video image to a snowflake.

You can get really creative with mattes. For example, you can create a lot of neat video effects with, especially for title screens.

Adding a Lens Flare

Camera lenses, whether in still cameras or camcorders, are made of glass and are designed to collect light. Despite advanced lens coatings, those glass lenses can still reflect light when they're supposed to be collecting it. This phenomenon is especially common when the sun shines directly onto a camera's lens. Light from the sun is so intense that it causes sharp reflections called lens flares.

Generally, lens flares are to be avoided. But in some cases a lens flare can be used for dramatic effect. Consider many recent movies that feature computer animation. Faux lens flares are often used to make the animated image appear more real. And in real video images that are washed out from too much sun, you can add manufactured lens flares to accentuate color and detail. Or you may want to add a lens flare to a properly lit desert scene simply to draw attention to the fact that the sun is blazing brightly overhead. To add a lens flare, follow these steps:

1. **In the Timeline, move the CTI to a frame where the sun appears or where you would otherwise like the sun to *appear* to appear.**

2. **Choose Window⇨Effects to open the Effects window.**

3. **Open the Render subfolder of the Video Effects folder, and then click-and-drag the Lens Flare effect to a clip to which you want to add a lens flare.**

   The Lens Flare Settings dialog box appears as shown in Figure 19-9.

Figure 19-9: Specify the center of your lens flare here.

4. **Under Flare Center, click the spot in the image where you want the center of the flare to appear.**

5. **Adjust the brightness of the flare using the Brightness slider.**

6. **Choose a lens type at the bottom of the Lens Flare Settings dialog box.**

   Each lens type gives a slightly different lens flare appearance. Experiment with each one, as well as with the Brightness slider and the flare center to achieve just the right look.

7. **Click OK to close the Lens Flare Settings dialog box.**

   If the clip is a static clip, you are done adding your lens flare. If the clip pans, continue with the following steps.

8. **Choose Window⇨Effect Controls to open the Effect Controls window, and click the clip in the Timeline to select it.**

9. **In the Effect Controls window, click the arrow next to Lens Flare to expand the Lens Flare controls, as shown in Figure 19-10.**

10. **Click Toggle Animation next to Center X, Center Y, and Brightness under the Lens Flare controls.**

    Keyframes appear in the keyframes viewer, as shown in Figure 19-10.

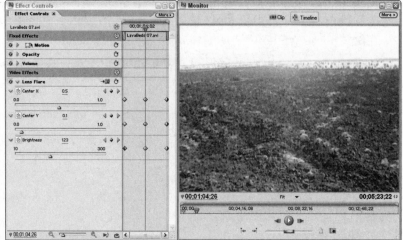

Figure 19-10:
Fine-tune
lens flare
settings in
the Effect
Controls
window.

11. **In the Effect Controls window, move the CTI to the beginning of the clip and then click Reset at top of the Lens Flare controls.**

To move the CTI to the beginning of the clip, press the Page Up key on your keyboard. Press Page Down to move to the end of the clip. See Chapter 12 for more on working with the Effect Controls window.

12. **Now move the CTI to the end of the clip and click Reset again.**

You now have a lens flare that appears to move with the lens. Depending on the direction of the pan you may need to experiment a bit with the Center X, Center Y, and Brightness settings. In the video image shown in Figure 19-10, the camera pans from left to right. Table 19-1 lists the settings I used at the clip's In point, middle, and Out point. These settings give the appearance that the sun is in the middle of the clip, and the lens flare stays near the top of the image as it pans.

Table 19-1	Lens Flare Settings		
Setting	*In Point*	*Middle*	*Out Point*
Center X	1.0	0.5	0.0
Center Y	0.0	0.0	0.0
Brightness	10	100	10

Removing Audio Hums

As I point out in Chapter 13, audio is too often overlooked when editing video. One common editing problem is constant-frequency humming that sometimes occurs in audio recordings. The humming may be caused by interference from a fluorescent light or other electric device, or a flaw in the microphone or recording device.

Whatever the cause, if you have an audio recording with an annoying hum, Premiere Elements has a tool that may help you remove that hum. That tool is the Notch effect, which can be found in the Audio Effects folder in the Effects window (Window⇨Effects). The Notch effect removes all audio at or near a given frequency within the clip. Here's how to use it:

1. **Click-and-drag the Notch effect to the humming clip, and then choose Window⇨Effect Controls to open the Effect Controls window.**

2. **Adjust the Center slider until you find the frequency that is causing the hum.**

   If the hum comes from a poorly shielded power cord, adjust the Center slider to 60 Hz if you live in an area that uses NTSC video, or 50 Hz if video equipment in your area uses PAL.

3. **Adjust the Q slider to broaden the frequency range of the sound that is removed.**

   Be careful not to broaden the range too much or the audio quality will diminish considerably.

A Zoom with a View

As I mention in Chapter 20, zooming in and out too much on a video image with the zoom lens is one of the most common mistakes that amateur videographers make. But sometimes zooming can have a desirable dramatic effect, especially when you want to show that the emphasis of the scene is suddenly shifting to a single point. Often, the realization that a zoom effect might actually be called for only comes *after* you've already shot your video and are using Premiere Elements to edit and fine-tune the project.

Adobe Premiere Elements can come to your rescue! Using the Camera View effect you can quickly zoom in on a specific point in a video image. The Camera

View effect is located in the Transform subfolder of the Video Effects folder (Window⇨Video Effects). Here's what you do to zoom in:

1. **Click-and-drag the Camera View effect to a clip, and then adjust the Zoom slider in the Effect Controls window (Window⇨Effect Controls).**

   The default zoom level on the slider is 10.

2. **To zoom in, drag the Zoom slider to the left.**

   Use keyframes (see Chapter 12 for more on controlling video effects using keyframes) to change the level of zoom as the clip plays.

You can zoom out on video images as well using the Camera View effect, but keep in mind that as you zoom out the edges of the video screen will become empty. Choose a fill color for the empty areas using the Fill Color control. Black works best most of the time.

Chapter 20

Ten Videography Tips and Secrets

*H*ave you ever watched a movie and wondered, "How did they do that?" Moviemakers have been perfecting their art and developing new techniques for over a century, and they've gotten pretty good at what they do. If you watch a "Making of. . ." documentary, you may get the impression that modern moviemaking is all about fancy computer animation effects and massive budgets, but even the biggest blockbuster projects still rely on many time-honored and proven techniques.

In this chapter I show you ten tips and secrets of videography that won't break the bank or require you to get a degree in computer animation. Here I show you how to make realistic sound effects with everyday objects, create special visual effects with simple camera tricks, give your scenes better lighting, and more.

Making Realistic Sound Effects

Believe it or not, some professional videographers will tell you that sound is actually more important than video. The reasoning goes like this: A typical viewing audience is surprisingly forgiving of minor flaws and glitches in the video picture. Viewers can easily tune out visual imperfections, which partially explains why cartoons are so effective. However, poor sound has an immediate and significant effect on the viewer. Poor sound gives the impression of an unprofessional, poorly produced movie.

Great sound doesn't just mean recording good-quality audio. Another key aspect of your movie's audio is the sound *effects*. I don't just mean laser blasts or crude bathroom noises, but subtle, everyday sounds that make your movie sound much more realistic. These effects are often called *Foley sounds*, named for sound-effects pioneer Jack Foley. Here are some easy sound effects you can make:

- **Breaking bones:** Snap carrots or celery in half. Fruit and vegetables can be used to produce many disgusting sounds. When you're done you have a healthy snack ready for your video crew.

- **Buzzing insect:** Wrap wax paper tightly around a comb, place your lips so that they are just barely touching the paper, and hum so that the wax paper makes a buzzing sound.

- **Fire:** Crumple cellophane or wax paper to simulate the sound of a crackling fire. This is much safer than the real thing.

- **Footsteps:** Hold two shoes and tap the heels together, followed by the toes. Experiment with different shoe types for different sounds. This may take some practice to get the timing of each footstep just right.

- **Gravel or snow:** Use cat litter to simulate the sound of walking through snow or gravel. I strongly recommend that you use clean cat litter for this effect.

- **Horse hooves:** This is one of *the* classic sound effects. The clop-clop-clopping of horse hooves is often made by clapping two halves of a coconut shell together.

- **Kiss:** Pucker up and give your forearm a nice, big smooch to make the sound of a kiss.

- **Punch:** Punch a raw piece of steak or a raw chicken. Of course, make sure you practice safe food-handling hygiene rules when handling raw foods: Wash your hands and all other surfaces after you're done.

- **Thunder:** Shake a large piece of sheet metal to simulate a thunderstorm.

- **Town bell:** To replicate the sound of a large bell ringing, hold the handle of a metal stew pot lid, and tap the edge with a spoon or other metal object. Experiment with various strikers, lids, or other pots and pans for just the right effect.

Tricking the Camera Eye with Forced Perspective

We humans perceive the world as a three-dimensional space. When you look out upon the world you see color and light, and you can tell which things are close to you and which things are farther away. This is called *depth perception*.

Bats use a sort of natural radar to perceive depth and distance, which is fine for winged creatures that flap in the night; but we humans perceive depth using *stereoscopic vision*. That's a fancy way of saying we have two eyes.

Our eyes focus on objects, sending the data to our brains; our brains then interpret the difference between what each eye sees to provide depth perception. Without two eyes, the world would look like a flat, two-dimensional place, and activities that require depth perception (say, a game of catch) would be very difficult, if not impossible.

A video camera only has one eye, so it has no depth perception — which is why video images appear as two-dimensional pictures. You can use two-dimensionality to your advantage because you can make objects look like they're right next to each other when they're actually very far apart. Video professionals use this trick often, and call it *forced perspective*.

Consider the video image in Figure 20-1. It looks like a locomotive and train cars parked in a train yard, but looks are deceiving in this case. As you can see in Figure 20-2, the locomotive in the foreground is a relatively tiny scale model, and the train cars in the background are real and about 50 yards away.

To make forced perspective work, you must

✔ **Compose the shot carefully.** The illusion of forced perspective works only if the scale looks realistic for the various items in the shot. You'll probably have to fine-tune the position of your subjects and the camera to get just the right visual effect.

✔ **Focus.** If objects are very far apart, getting both of them in focus may be difficult.

Figure 20-1:
A typical industrial scene?

Figure 20-2:
Not quite.
The camera's eye
is easily
deceived.

Both composing a forced-perspective shot and then getting your camera to properly focus are complicated tasks. Because I can't be there with you to help design your set, I will stick to giving you some camera techniques that can help you control focus. Follow these steps for professional results:

1. **Set the zoom lens at the widest setting by pressing the zoom control toward "W" on the camcorder.**

   The lens zooms all the way out.

2. **Turn off the auto-focus feature on your camera.**

   If you're not sure how to do this, consult the manual that came with your camcorder.

3. **Set the focus to Infinity.**

   Some manual-focus controls have an Infinity setting. If your camcorder does not, manually adjust the focus so objects that are 20 or more feet away are in focus.

4. **Position the camera five to ten feet away from the closer subject in your forced-perspective shot.**

5. **Make final adjustments manually.**

   Check carefully to make sure everything is in focus before you shoot; move the camera if necessary.

With most camcorders, everything beyond a distance of about five feet will probably be in focus when you zoom out and set focus to Infinity.

In Figures 20-1 and 20-2, I show you how a small object in the foreground blends well with a large object in the background. But forced-perspective camera techniques can also work the other way around. In fact, model-railroad enthusiasts often use forced perspective to make their train layouts seem bigger than they really are. Mountains, trees, and buildings in the background are made smaller to provide the illusion that they are farther away.

Managing Ambient Noise

Ambient noise is the general din that we don't usually think much about because it surrounds us constantly. Ambient noise might come from chirping birds, an airplane flying overhead, chattering bystanders, passing cars, a blowing furnace, the little fans spinning inside your computer, and even the tiny motor turning the tape reels in your camcorder or tape recorder. Although it's easy to tune out these noises when you're immersed in them, they can be very loud and ugly when they are captured in your audio recordings.

If you're recording outdoors or in a public gathering place, you probably can't do much to eliminate the actual sources of ambient noise. But wherever you are recording, you can take some basic steps to manage ambient noise:

- ✔ **Use a microphone:** I know, this is about the millionth time I've said it, but a microphone placed close to your subject can go a long way toward ensuring that the sound you actually *want* to record is not totally overwhelmed by ambient noise.

- ✔ **Wear headphones:** Camcorders and tape recorders almost always have headphone jacks. If you plug a set of headphones into the headphone jack, you can listen to the audio that is actually being recorded, and possibly detect potential annoyances at the beginning of shooting — before they become actual problems.

- ✔ **Record and preview some audio:** Similar to the idea of wearing headphones to hear and eliminate ambient noise before it ruins your movie, taping a little bit of audio, and then playing it back can be a good preemptive strategy. This might help you identify ambient noise or other audio problems.

- ✔ **Shield the camcorder's mic from wind:** A gentle breeze may seem almost silent to your ear, but the camcorder's microphone may pick it up as a loud roar that overwhelms all other sound. If nothing else, you can position your hand to block wind from blowing directly across the screen on the front of your camcorder's mic.

- ✔ **Try to minimize sound reflection:** Audio waves reflect off any hard surface, which can cause echoing echoing in a recording recording. Hanging blankets on walls and other hard surfaces will significantly reduce reflection.

✔ **Turn off fans, heaters, and air conditioners:** Air rushing through vents creates a surprising amount of unwanted ambient noise. If possible, temporarily turn off your furnace, air conditioner, or fans while you record your audio.

✔ **Turn off cell phones and pagers:** You know how annoying it is when someone's cell phone rings while you're trying to *watch* a movie; just imagine how bothersome it will be when you're *making* a movie! Make sure that you and everyone else on the set turns those things off. Even the sound of a vibrating pager might be picked up by your microphones.

✔ **Shut down your computer:** Obviously this is impossible if you are recording using a microphone that is connected to your computer, but computers do tend to make a lot of noise, so shut yours down if you can.

✔ **Warn everyone else to be quiet:** If anyone else is in the building or general area, ask them to be quiet while you are recording audio. Noises from the next room may be muffled, but they still contribute to ambient noise. Likewise, you may want to wait until your neighbor is done mowing his lawn before recording your audio.

Dealing with the Elements

You may, at times, deal with extremes of temperature or other weather conditions while shooting video. No, this section isn't about making sure the people in your movies wear jackets when it's cold (although it's always wise to bundle up). I'm more concerned about the health of your camcorder right now, and several environmental factors can affect it:

✔ **Condensation:** If you quickly move your camera from a very cold environment to a very warm environment (or vice versa), condensation can form on or even inside the lens. Avoid subjecting your camcorder to rapid, extreme temperature changes.

✔ **Heat:** Digital tapes are still subject to the same environmental hazards as old analog tapes. Don't leave your camcorder or tapes in a roasting car when it's 105 degrees out. Consider storing tapes in a cooler (but *not* the one holding your lunch). Your videotape cooler shouldn't contain any food or liquids. Simply placing the tapes in an empty cooler helps insulate them from temperature extremes.

✔ **Water:** A few drops of rain can quickly destroy the sensitive electronic circuits inside your camcorder. If you believe that water may be a problem, cover your camcorder with a plastic bag, or shoot your video at another time, if possible.

✔ **Wind:** Even a gentle breeze blowing across the screen on your camcorder's microphone can cause a loud roaring on the audio recording. Try to shield your microphone from wind unless you know you'll be replacing the audio later during the editing process.

Another environmental hazard in many video shoots is the sun — that big, bright ball of nuclear fusion that crosses the sky every day. The sun makes plants grow, provides solar energy, and helps humans generate Vitamin D. But like all good things, the sun is best enjoyed in moderation. Too much sunlight causes skin cancer, fades the paint on your car, and overexposes the subjects in your video. Natural skin tones turn into washed-out blobs, and sunlight reflecting directly on your camcorder's lens causes light flares or hazing in your video image. Follow these tips when shooting outdoors in bright sunlight:

✔ **Use filters.** Later in this chapter, I describe how lens filters can improve the video you shoot. Neutral-density and color-correction filters can reduce overexposure and improve color quality.

✔ **Shade your lens.** If sunlight reflects directly on your lens, it can cause streaks or bright spots called *lens flares*. Higher-end camcorders usually have black hoods that extend out in front of the lens to prevent this. If your camcorder doesn't have a hood, you can make one, using black paper or photographic tape from a photographic-supply store. (Check the video image to make sure your homemade hood doesn't show up in the picture!) There are times when you may actually want to have a lens flare — and even create one using Premiere Elements. If so, check out Chapter 19, which shows you how to play with lens flares.

✔ **If possible, position your subject in a shaded area.** Shade allows you to take advantage of the abundant natural light without overexposure.

✔ **Avoid backlit situations.** Even if your subject is in shade, you can have problems if you shoot video at such an angle that the background is very bright. This is the recipe for creating a severely backlit situation; your subject will appear as a black shadow against a brightly glowing background. Shoot subjects against a more neutral or dark background whenever possible.

✔ **Wear sunscreen.** Your video image isn't the only thing you should protect from the sun!

Rehearse!

Everybody knows what rehearsal is, but in most cases, you probably don't have a script to memorize. So what is there to rehearse? You should carefully consider and plan every aspect of your video shoot. For example, if you plan to move the camera while you shoot, practice walking the path of travel to make sure there aren't any obstacles that might block you. If you're using a tripod, practice panning to make sure you can do it effectively. Other things to check and rehearse beforehand include

- **Testing sound:** If your camcorder has an audio meter, check the sound levels before you start recording. Have your subjects speak; check the levels of their speech.

- **Marking where everything and everyone should be located:** Have subjects go through the motions of the shoot, and then coach them on how to stand or move so they show up better in the video.

- **Testing focus:** Check your camera's focus. If objects in the foreground cause your camcorder's auto-focus feature to "hunt" for the correct focus, turn off auto-focus and adjust your focus manually.

- **Testing lighting and exposure:** Check to see whether the shot is overexposed. On some higher-end camcorders, any overexposed shot shows up as a zebra-stripe pattern in the viewfinder or LCD display. If your camera doesn't have a warning bell like this, you'll have to make a careful judgment and adjust exposure as necessary. Read your camcorder's documentation to see whether it lists any special exposure settings that may help you out.

Reflecting and Diffusing Light

When you record video you're actually recording light. But more light isn't always better light. Consider a scene shot in bright sunlight, where colors wash out and the faces of your subjects become white blobs as they reflect the blazing sun. If you want to record high-quality video, you'll have to record high-quality light.

As the sun shows, shining a bright light directly on your subject usually isn't the best way to properly light that subject. Video professionals often prefer to bounce light onto the subject, which helps diffuse the light so that it isn't so harsh. You can bounce light using a reflector. You can make reflectors out of various materials:

- **Poster board:** White poster board is a good, cheap material that you can find just about anywhere. Try to choose thicker, corrugated poster board so that it doesn't flop around and is easier to work with. Paint one side of a poster board gold and the other side silver, and experiment with each side to gain different lighting effects.

✔ **Aluminum foil:** Crumple a large sheet of foil, and then spread it out again and tape it to a backing board. Crumpled foil provides a more diffuse — yet still highly effective — light reflection.

✔ **Black plastic garbage bag:** Despite the relatively dark color, black plastic garbage bags can reflect a fair amount of light. Tape the bag to a backing board so it's easier to handle and doesn't create ambient noise as it flutters in the wind. Black plastic garbage bags also come in handy when it's time to clean up the video shoot scene.

✔ **Cheesecloth or light gels:** You can also diffuse light by placing something directly over a light to filter it. You can make light filters from cheesecloth, or using translucent plastic in a variety of colors. Translucent plastic light filters are called *gels* by video pros.

Lights tend to get very hot. To avoid fire hazards, you must use extreme care when placing gels or cheesecloth in front of lights. *Never* attach filters directly to lights. Position your filters some distance away from the lights so that they don't melt or catch on fire, and check the condition of your lights and filters regularly. Read and heed all safety warnings on your lights before using them.

Seeing Stars

So you want to shoot your own science-fiction epic? All you need is a script, some willing actors, a few props from the local toy store, and you're ready to make your futuristic movie.

Well, you're *almost* ready. No sci-fi movie would be complete without a scene of spaceships flying through space, and that means you'll have to create a field of stars to serve as a backdrop. You can put stars behind your spaceships using one of two methods:

✔ **Add it later.** Most professional moviemakers shoot their spaceship models in front of a blue or green screen. The video image of the spaceship is then composited over a picture of a star-filled sky during the editing process. Professionals use this method because they can use more realistic looking star fields, and, well, just because they can. See Chapter 11 for more on compositing.

✔ **Create a star-field backdrop.** If you don't have the time or patience to build a bluescreen studio and composite your video, just shoot the spaceships in front of a star-field backdrop that you create. The best way to create a star field is to sew different-sized sequins onto black velvet. The velvet will absorb virtually all light that falls on it, while the sequins reflect brightly.

Sequins sewn to a velvet backdrop will also tend to twinkle slightly. Of course, any sci-fi geek will tell you that twinkling stars are technically inaccurate, for the same reason that spaceships and explosions don't actually make noise in the vacuum of space. The twinkling of stars that we Earth-bound humans witness is an effect caused by our atmosphere. I doubt that the Galactic Overlord will come and vaporize you over this minor technicality, but be prepared for scoffs from a few space-opera fanatics.

Using Video Filters

Say you're making a movie showing the fun people can have when they're stuck indoors on a rainy day. Such a movie wouldn't be complete without an establishing shot to show one of the subjects looking out a window at the dismal weather. Alas, when you try to shoot this scene, all you see is a big, nasty, glaring reflection on the window.

Reflections are among the many video problems you can resolve with a lens filter on your camcorder. Filters usually attach to the front of your camera lens, and change the nature of the light passing though it. Different kinds of filters have different effects. Common filter types include

- **Polarizing filter:** This type of filter often features an adjustable ring and can be used to reduce or control reflections on windows, water, and other shiny surfaces.

- **UV filter:** This filter reduces UV light and is often used to protect the lens from scratches, dust, or other damage. I never use my camcorder without at least a UV filter in place.

- **Neutral-density (ND) filter:** This filter works kind of like sunglasses for your camcorder. It prevents overexposure in very bright light conditions, reducing the amount of light that passes through the lens without changing the color. If you experience washed-out color when you shoot on a sunny day, try using an ND filter.

- **Color-correction filters:** You have as many choices in color-correction filters as your heart desires. These filters help correct for various kinds of color imbalances in your video. Some filters can enhance colors when you're shooting outdoors on an overcast day; others reduce the color cast by certain kinds of light (such as a greenish cast that comes from many fluorescent lights).

- **Soft filter:** A soft filter softens details slightly in your image. This filter is often used to hide skin blemishes or wrinkles on actors who are more advanced in age.

- **Star filter:** Creates star-like patterns on extreme light sources to add a sense of magic to the video.

Many more kinds of filters are available. Check with the manufacturer of your camcorder to see whether the company also offers filters specially designed for your camera; check the camcorder's documentation to see what kinds of filters can work with your camcorder. Many camcorders accept standard 37mm or 58mm threaded filters, regardless of the manufacturer.

Tiffen, founded in 1938, is an excellent manufacturer of filters; its Web site (www.tiffen.com) has photographic samples that show the effects of various filters on your images. To see these samples, visit www.tiffen.com and click the <u>Tiffen Filters & Lens Accessories</u> link for information on Tiffen filters. Then locate and click the <u>Tiffen Filter Brochure</u> link. This online brochure provides detailed information on the filters offered by Tiffen.

Using (But Not Abusing) the Zoom Lens

If every camcorder owner makes a single mistake, it's zoom-lens abuse. On most camcorders, the zoom feature is easy and fun to use, encouraging us to use it more than is prudent. The effect of constantly zooming in and out is a disorienting video image that just looks, well, amateur. Here are some general zoom lens guidelines to follow on any video shoot:

- If possible, avoid zooming in or out *while* you're recording. It's usually best to adjust zoom *before* you start recording.

- If you must zoom while recording, try to zoom *only once* during the shot. This will make the zoom look planned rather than chaotic.

- Consider the merits of actually moving the camera closer to your subject instead of zooming in or out.

- Prevent *focus hunting* (where the auto-focus feature randomly goes in and out of focus) by using manual focus. Auto-focus often hunts while you zoom, but you can easily prevent this. Before you start recording, zoom in on your subject. Get the subject in focus, *and then turn off auto-focus.* This technique enables you to lock focus on the subject once and for all — as long as you're steady with your filming. Now, zoom out and begin recording. With focus set to manual, your subject remains in focus as you zoom in. On most camcorders, anything farther than about ten feet away will probably be in focus if you set the camera's focal control to the Infinity setting.

- Practice using the zoom control gently. Zooming slowly and smoothly is usually preferable, but it takes a practiced hand on the control.

If you have a difficult time using the zoom control smoothly, try taping or gluing a piece of foam to the zoom-slider button on your camcorder. The foam can help dampen your inputs on the control.

Video Shoot Checklist

Two problems always seem to plague me when I go on a video shoot. One, I usually forget something. Two. . . Well, I can't remember what the second problem is right now; but the first problem is easily avoided by simply running down a checklist of things that are needed on a video shoot. At the very least, you should always have the following:

- Camcorder, owners manual, and remote control (if your camcorder has one)
- Extra *charged* batteries and spare *blank* tapes
- Lens cleaner and lens filters
- Tripod
- Duct tape

I usually keep all of these items in my camcorder bag so that if I have my camcorder, I have all of my filters and spare batteries too. If you're going on a more formal video shoot, you may also want to bring several items:

- Lights, extension cords, reflectors, clamps, and backdrops
- Clothes/wardrobe for the cast (or at least, make sure your cast is dressed appropriately for the shoot), make-up and hair-care items
- Stool (useful for interviews)
- AC adapter and/or battery charger for your camcorder
- Microphones and headphones
- Slate, script, and scene list

Chapter 21

Ten Essential Extras for Moviemaking

I don't know about you, but I consider myself a gadget hound. As such, videography is a great hobby to pursue because there are definitely lots of video-related gadgets to play with — and new technologies are being developed every day. There are fancy camcorders and accessories, cool multimedia programs, and even some nifty add-ons for your computer. But I don't want to kid you — digital photography, editing, and multimedia technologies are among the more expensive technologies out there, so you have picked a rewarding, yet expensive hobby to pursue.

If you have some money burning a hole in your pocket and you want to find out what kind of gear you need to be a more serious video enthusiast, this chapter is for you. In this chapter I show you hardware and software that helps you create, edit, and share video more effectively — and more expensively.

Adobe Premiere Pro

I know what you're thinking. This is a book about Adobe Premiere Elements, and I'm already trying to talk you into using a different editing program. Not really; Adobe Premiere Elements is a great program, especially considering its very low price. But at some point you may decide that you need even more capabilities than those offered by Premiere Elements. And if you decide to turn your videography hobby into a profession, you may find that you need more advanced time-saving and editing features than those offered by Adobe Premiere Elements.

Adobe Premiere Pro is your next logical step up, for two important reasons. First, because Premiere Elements is based on Premiere Pro you won't have a steep learning curve if you upgrade to Premiere Pro. If you know how to use Premiere Elements, you can get right to work in Premiere Pro. Also, Adobe usually offers upgrade discounts, so as a registered Premiere Elements user you can probably get a better price on Premiere Pro than you could if you switch to a competing program like Apple Final Cut Pro or Avid Xpress (both of which are also great programs, by the way).

What does Premiere Pro offer over the basic Premiere Elements? Here are a few key features:

- ✔ **Multiple Timelines:** The Premiere Pro Timeline allows you to create and use multiple sequences. Each sequence is like a separate timeline. You can use these multiple timelines to create alternate versions of a project, or use them to manage subsections of large projects. Sequences can be linked together in a process called *nesting*.

- ✔ **Advanced Color Corrector:** Premiere Pro incorporates an advanced, professional-grade color correction tool that gives you precision control over the color and light in your video images. Also included are broadcast-style video scopes such as a waveform monitor, vectorscope, and YCbCr parade. These scopes help you more precisely measure the color and light in your video images.

- ✔ **Audio Mixer:** The more you work with video, the more you realize the importance of great audio. Premiere Pro incorporates an advanced audio mixer to give you greater control over your audio. Premiere Pro supports 5.1 channel surround sound audio tracks, and you can easily pan 5.1 audio using the Premiere Pro audio mixer.

- ✔ **Batch Capture:** Video capture can be a time-consuming process, but in Premiere Pro you can create *batch lists* which automate much of this process.

- ✔ **Broad Format Support:** Premiere Elements is designed to work almost exclusively with DV-format video, but Premiere Pro can handle analog formats as well as new professional digital formats such as HD and 24p.

- ✔ **Integration with After Effects and Encore DVD:** Premiere Pro works seamlessly with other professional-grade video products from Adobe, including Adobe After Effects and Adobe Encore DVD. After Effects is the industry standard for advanced visual effects editing, and Encore DVD is a professional-grade DVD authoring program which gives you far more creative control over menus and other DVD features than what is found in Premiere Elements.

Adobe Premiere Pro offers other advantages over Premiere Elements as well, including even more effects and transitions, and additional output options. If you decide to move up to Premiere Pro, make sure you also move up to *Adobe Premiere Pro For Dummies*, by Little Old Me (Wiley).

Audio Recorders

I know, I know, your camcorder records audio along with video, and it's already perfectly synchronized. So what's the point of a dedicated audio recorder? Well, you may need the capabilities of an audio recorder in many situations. Take, for example, these three:

- ✔ You may want to record a subject who is across the room — in which case, have the subject hold a recorder (or conceal it so it's off-camera), and attach an inconspicuous lavalier microphone. (See the section on microphones later in this chapter.)

- ✔ You may want to record only a special sound, on location, and add it to the soundtrack later. For example, you might show crashing waves in the distant background, but use the close-up sound of those waves for dramatic effect.

- ✔ You can record narration for a video project, tweak it till it suits you, and then add it to the soundtrack of your movie.

You also need a slate

If you use a secondary audio recorder, one of the biggest challenges you may face is synchronizing your separate audio and video recordings. Professionals ensure synchronization of audio and video by using a *slate* — that black-and-white board that you often see production people snapping shut on camera just before the director yells "Action!"

The slate is not just a kitschy movie prop. The snapping of the slate makes a noise that can be picked up by all audio recorders on-scene. When you are editing audio tracks later, this noise will show up as a visible spike on the audio waveform. Because the slate is snapped in front of the camera, you can later match the waveform spike on the audio track with the visual picture of the slate snapping closed on the video track. If you're recording audio with external recorders, consider making your own slate to ease audio-video synchronization.

Recording decent audio used to mean spending hundreds or even thousands of dollars for a DAT (digital audio tape) recorder. However, these days I think the best compromise for any moviemaker on a budget is to use a MiniDisc recorder. MiniDisc player/recorders can record CD-quality audio in WAV format. Pop the MiniDisc into your computer's CD-ROM drive and you can easily import it into a Premiere Elements project. Countless MiniDisc recorders are available for less than $200 from companies that include Aiwa, Sharp, and Sony.

Microphones

Virtually all digital camcorders have built-in microphones with 48-bit stereo sound-recording capabilities, but you'll soon find that the quality of the audio you record is still limited primarily by the quality of the microphone you use. Therefore, if you care even a little about making great movies, you *need* better microphones than the one built into your camcorder.

Your camcorder should have connectors for external microphones, and your camcorder's manufacturer may offer accessory microphones for your specific camera.

One type of special microphone you may want to use is a *lavalier* microphone — a tiny unit that usually clips to a subject's clothing to pick up his or her voice. You often see lavalier mics clipped to the lapels of TV newscasters. Some lavalier units are designed to fit inside clothing or costumes, although some practice and special shielding may be required to eliminate rubbing noises. You may also need to coach your subjects to sit still so that the lavalier mics can pick up their voices more effectively.

You might also use a condenser microphone to record audio. Some *prosumer* (or *professional-consumer*) camcorders come with large, boom-style condenser mics built in. Although these are nice, if you want to record the voice of a subject speaking on camera such mics may still be inferior to a handheld or lavalier mic.

Microphones are generally defined by the directional pattern in which they pick up sound. The three basic categories are *cardioid* (which has a heart-shaped pattern), *omnidirectional* (which picks up sound from all directions), and *bidirectional* (which picks up sound from the sides).

If you're in the market for a new mic, here's where you should look:

✔ A good place to look for high-quality microphones is a musicians' supply store. Just make sure that the connectors and frequency range are compatible with your camcorder or other recording device (check the documentation).

- ✔ You may also want to check with your camcorder's manufacturer; it may offer accessory microphones specially designed to work with your camcorder.

- ✔ The Internet is always a good resource as well. One especially good resource is `www.shure.com`, the Web site of Shure Incorporated. Shure sells microphones and other audio products, and the Web site is an excellent resource for general information about choosing and using microphones.

Digital Camcorders

If you recently purchased your first digital camcorder, you're probably impressed by the image quality it produces, especially compared to older consumer technologies like 8mm, Hi8, and S-VHS. Most digital camcorders are also packed with features that were considered wildly advanced just a few years ago.

But you know how the old saying goes: The grass is always greener, and all that. As impressive and wonderful as your camcorder may seem, you'll soon find even better products out there. As you get more serious about moviemaking, one of the first things you should do is upgrade to a really serious camera. High-end (yet somewhat affordable) DV camcorders are becoming so advanced now that even the pros are using them.

When you're ready to step up to the next level of DV camcorder, look for the following features that make some digital camcorders better than others:

- ✔ **CCD:** The *charged-coupled device* is the unit in a camcorder that captures a video image from light. Most consumer-grade camcorders have one CCD, but higher-quality units have three, one for each of the standard video colors (red, green, and blue). Three-CCD cameras — also called *three-chip* cameras — capture much sharper, more color-saturated images.

- ✔ **Progressive scan:** Many cheaper camcorders capture only interlaced video. This can create a variety of problems — such as the *interlacing jaggies* that I discuss in Chapter 15 and elsewhere in this book — especially if you're editing a project for distribution on DVD, HDTV, or the Web. Higher-quality camcorders usually offer a progressive-scan mode.

- ✔ **Resolution:** Okay, this one can get confusing; resolution is defined and listed in many different ways. Some spec sheets emphasize a camcorder's resolution capabilities by telling you how many *thousands* of pixels the camcorder can record, but a large number of pixels isn't always a good indication of ultimate video quality in and of itself. Instead, I recommend that you use horizontal resolution lines as the litmus test for quality resolution. A high-quality digital camcorder should capture at least 500 lines of resolution.

✔ **Audio:** Many high-end DV camcorders have big, condenser-style microphones attached to their outsides — a definite improvement in audio quality compared to the built-in mics on cheaper camcorders. But don't just look for a big mic. Check for external audio connectors so you can use a remote microphone if you need to. For external audio, I recommend XLR-style (also called *balanced audio*) microphone connectors.

✔ **Lens:** Any digital camcorder still needs a good old-fashioned analog glass lens to collect and focus light. A bigger, higher-quality lens produces better video images. Make sure that any camcorder you get accepts filters on the lens. Some more expensive cameras offer interchangeable lenses.

✔ **Zebra pattern:** Most professional-grade camcorders display a zebra-stripe pattern in the viewfinder on overexposed areas of a shot. This pattern can be extremely helpful, especially when you're adjusting exposure manually.

✔ **Manual control rings:** Although many cheaper digital camcorders have manual focus, exposure, and zoom controls, they also often make these controls small and difficult to access. You know what I mean if you already own such a camcorder — the controls consist of lilliputian dials or slider switches that are difficult to use (provided you can *find* the things). Try to get a camera with large, easy-to-use control rings around the lens for focus, zoom, and exposure.

Before you buy any video gear, make sure it matches the video-broadcast standard (NTSC, PAL, or SECAM) that you are using before placing your order. This is especially important when purchasing camcorders via mail order or the Internet. (For more on broadcast standards, see Chapter 4.)

Getting a high-quality camcorder used to mean spending about $2,000 or more (usually, a *lot* more), but prices are dropping rapidly and new, affordable 3CCD camcorders like the Panasonic PV-GS200 are making pro-quality video downright affordable. Table 21-1 lists a few high-end camcorders you may want to consider.

Table 21-1	Dream Camcorders	
Manufacturer	*Model*	*Street Price (U.S. Dollars)*
Canon	GL2	$1,900–$2,700
JVC	GY-DV300U	$1,900–$2,900
Panasonic	PV-GS200	$800–1,000
Panasonic	PV-DV953	$1,300–$1,500
Sony	DCR-TRV950	$1,400–$2,000
Sony	DCR-VX2100	$2,000–$2,900

Musical Soundtracks

I probably don't have to tell you how important good music is for your movie projects. And if you've spent time trying to locate and get permission for good music, I probably also don't have to tell you how expensive good music can be. Thankfully, a company called SmartSound has come to your rescue with affordable programs that help you generate a wide variety of soundtrack music. The music can be of almost any length, comes in a wide variety of styles, and — best of all — you can use it royalty-free!

Music programs are available for as little as $50, with professional-oriented programs starting at around $300. Additional royalty-free music is always being added to the SmartSound online libraries. Find out more at www.smartsound.com.

Multimedia Controllers

Manipulating some of the playback and editing controls in Premiere Elements using a mouse isn't always easy. Sure, there are keyboard shortcuts for most actions, and you may find yourself using those keyboard shortcuts quite a bit. In particular, I find that controlling playback with the J, K, and L keys is a lot easier than using the mouse; and using the arrow keys to frame forward or back is vastly superior to clicking the Next Frame and Previous Frame buttons in the Monitor window.

Useful though the keyboard may be, there is an even better way. You can also control Premiere Elements with an external multimedia controller, such as the ShuttlePro from Contour A/V Solutions or ShuttlePRO v. 2 from Contour Design. The ShuttlePro, shown in Figure 21-1, costs about $100 and features 13 buttons and a two-part dial control in an ergonomically designed housing. The overall design of the ShuttlePro is based on professional video-editing controllers. The dials can be used to shuttle forward and back in your video, and the various buttons control various other program features. The unit plugs into a USB port, which can be found on virtually any modern computer. If you do a lot of video editing, you can save a lot of time and effort by using a multimedia controller. Find out more about multimedia controllers online at

www.contouravs.com
www.contourdesign.com

A less expensive version of this controller, the SpaceShuttle A/V, which I discuss in Chapter 7, is also available from Contour A/V Solutions. The SpaceShuttle A/V is about half the price of the ShuttlePro and also works great.

Figure 21-1:
Ergonomic
multimedia
controllers
make
editing in
Premiere
Elements
fun and
easy.

Tripods and Other Stabilization Devices

The need for image stabilization will probably become apparent the first time you watch your footage on a large TV screen. No matter how carefully you try to hold the camera, some movement is going to show up on the image. Of course, there are plenty of times when handheld is the way to shoot, but there are plenty of other times when a totally stable image is best. To get that stability, you need a tripod.

Tripods are generally available for as low as $20 at your local department store. Alas, as with so many other things in life, when you buy a tripod you get what you pay for. High-quality video tripods incorporate several important features:

- ✔ **Dual-stanchion legs and bracing:** This gives the tripod greater stability, especially during panning shots. Braces at the base or middle of the tripod's legs also aid stability.

- ✔ **High-tech materials:** You'll soon get tired of lugging a 15- to 20-pound tripod around with your camera gear. Higher-quality tripods usually use high-tech materials (including titanium, aircraft-quality aluminum, and carbon fiber) that are both strong and lightweight, making the gear less cumbersome to transport and use.

✔ **Bubble levels:** Built-in bubble levels help you ensure that your camera is level, even if the ground underneath the tripod isn't.

✔ **Fluid heads:** High-quality tripods have fluid heads to ensure that pans will be smooth and jerk-free.

✔ **Counterweights:** The best tripods have adjustable counterweights so the head can be balanced for your camera and lens (telephoto lenses, for example, can make the camera a bit front-heavy). Counterweights allow smooth use of the fluid head while still giving you the option of letting go of the camera without having it tilt out of position.

For a tripod with all these features, you can expect to spend a couple of hundred dollars (if not *many* hundreds of dollars). If that kind of money isn't in your tripod budget right now, try to get a tripod that incorporates as many of these features as possible.

Tripods aren't the only stabilization devices available. You may also want to keep a *monopod* handy for certain occasions. As the name suggests, a monopod has only one leg (just as tripods have three legs, octopods have eight, and . . . never mind). Although by definition (and by design) a monopod inevitably allows some camera movement — you have to keep the camera balanced on the monopod — you can still get more stability than you'd have if you simply hold the camera without any stabilization device.

For moving shots, you may want to try a mobile stabilizer such as a Steadicam (www.steadicam.com). Devices like the Steadicam use a system of weights and harnesses to keep the camera remarkably stable even as the operator moves around a scene.

Video Converters

You have a computer with a FireWire (IEEE-1394) port, and you want to capture some analog video. What are you going to do? You have many, many solutions, of course. You could install a video capture card, but a good one is expensive and installing it means tearing apart your computer. Plus, Premiere Elements can't capture video using an analog capture card, meaning you'll have to use different software with your analog video capture card.

A simpler solution may be to use an external *video converter* — usually a box that connects to your computer's FireWire port. The box includes analog inputs so you can connect an analog VCR or camcorder to the box. The unit itself converts signals from analog media into DV-format video, which is then captured into your computer — where you can easily edit it using Premiere Elements.

If you have worked with analog video a lot, you're probably aware that each time you make a copy of the video some quality is lost. This is called *generational loss* (see Chapter 4 for more on this subject). Video converters like the ones described here don't present any more of a generational-loss problem than a standard video capture card: After the signal is converted from analog to digital, generational loss is no longer a problem until you output the video back to an analog tape again.

Most converter boxes can also be useful for exporting video to an analog source. You simply export the DV-format video from Premiere Elements, and the converter box converts it into an analog signal that you can record on your analog tape deck. Among other advantages, this method of export saves a lot of wear and tear on the tape-drive mechanisms in your expensive digital camcorder. Features to look for in a video converter include

- ✔ Analog output
- ✔ Broadcast standard support (NTSC or PAL)
- ✔ Color-bar output
- ✔ Multiple FireWire and analog inputs/outputs

Video converters typically range in price from $250 to $300 or more. Table 21-2 lists a few popular units.

Make sure you choose a video converter that works with a FireWire port! Many mass-market video converters available today work only with a USB 2.0 port, but Premiere Elements can only capture video from FireWire ports.

Table 21-2	Video Converters		
Manufacturer	*Model*	*Street Price*	*Web Site*
ADS Technologies	PYRO A/V Link	$200	www.adstech.com/
Canopus	ADVC-55	$200–$230	www.canopuscorp.com/
Data Video	DAC-100	$200	www.datavideo-tek.com/
Pinnacle	Studio MovieBox DV	$250	www.pinnaclesys.com/

Video Decks

Because it's so easy to simply connect a FireWire cable to your camcorder and capture video right into your computer, you may be tempted to use your digital camcorder as your sole MiniDV tape deck. If you're on a really tight budget, you may not have much of a choice, but if you have a bit of extra money, I recommend that you spend it on a high-quality video deck.

A video deck not only saves wear and tear on the tape drive mechanisms in your expensive camcorder, but it can also give you greater control over video capture and export back to tape. Professional video decks are expensive, but if you do a lot of video editing, they quickly pay for themselves — both in terms of the greater satisfaction and quality you're likely to get from your finished movie and in less money spent on camcorder maintenance. Table 21-3 lists some decks to consider.

Table 21-3		DV Video Decks	
Manufacturer	*Model*	*Formats*	*Street Price*
JVC	HR-DVS3	MiniDV, S-VHS	$750
Panasonic	AG-DV1000	MiniDV	$900–$1,000
Sony	GVD-1000 VCR Walkman with 4-inch LCD screen	MiniDV	$1,200–$1,400

When shopping for a professional-grade MiniDV deck, you can also look for decks that support the DVCAM or DVCPRO tape formats. In general, decks that support these more robust, professional-grade DV-tape formats also support MiniDV.

Web Space

The Internet seems like a natural place to share your movies with others, but video files are often very big, and that means problems if you're trying to find an online home for your movies. If you want others to be able to view your movies, you'll have to put the movie files on a Web server that other Internet users can access. Your Internet Service Provider (ISP) may provide free Web site space, but usually the only provide about 10 or 20MB, which isn't enough to host very many movies.

Fortunately, many low-cost Web hosting options are now available. For example, as of this writing GoDaddy.com (`www.godaddy.com`) offers a Web hosting plan which provides 1,000MB of Web server space and 15GB of monthly data transfer for about $10 per month. This type of account offers enough space and bandwidth to support typical online movie hosting.

When looking for online Web space, consider the following features:

- **Storage space:** Get a lot more space than you think you'll need. 100MB of server space is a good start, but 500MB or more allows you to host more movies.

- **Bandwidth:** Usually listed as "monthly data transfer," the bandwidth is just as important as the total space. If you put a 50MB movie online and it is downloaded by ten people, those downloads will use up 500MB of bandwidth. Make sure you have more than enough monthly bandwidth, and read the fine print to find out whether and how you will be charged for exceeding your monthly bandwidth allotment (believe me — you will be charged). While you're reading that fine print, see if there are daily bandwidth limits as well as monthly limits.

- **Cost:** Some Web sites offer free storage space, but these so-called "free" sites also usually also require visitors to view annoying ads and pop-up windows. Pay sites usually don't have ads or pop-ups, because you have to, um, pay for the site. Review the plan details carefully to make sure that your pay plan doesn't also subject users to pop-up windows and ads. If the site charges setup fees or lots of other obscure service fees, consider looking elsewhere because there are lots of choices.

- **Reliability:** Is the site reliable? Will you be stuck with hidden charges? Will the site fold in a few days or weeks? Talk to friends about Web hosting services they use, and check Web sites such as `www.webhosting ratings.com/`, `www.tophosts.com/`, or `www.findmyhosting.com/` for consumer reviews and feature-by-feature comparisons of various Web hosting services.

- **Extras:** Does the service include extra e-mail addresses or affordable domain name registration? Can you upload movie files using a simple Web browser page, or will you have to learn how to use FTP software and other Internet technologies?

Appendix

Glossary

· ·

alpha channel: A channel or layer used to define any transparent areas in a digital image.

analog: Technology that records data as waves with infinitely varying values. Analog recordings are usually electromechanical, so they often suffer from generational loss. *See also* digital, generational loss.

aspect ratio: The shape of a video image as determined by its proportions (width compared to height). Traditional television screens have an aspect ratio of 4:3, meaning the screen is four units wide and three units high. Some newer HDTVs use a "widescreen" aspect ratio of 16:9. Image pixels can also have various aspect ratios. *See also* HDTV, pixel.

bars and tone: A video image that serves the function of the "test pattern" used in TV broadcasting: Standardized color bars and a 1-kHz tone are usually placed at the beginning of movie projects. The test pattern created with bars and tone helps broadcast engineers calibrate video equipment to the color and audio levels of the video presentation. The format for color bars is standardized by the SMPTE. Adobe Premiere Elements can generate bars and tone. *See also* SMPTE.

bit depth: A unit of measurement for color and sound quality. The amount of data that a single piece of information can hold depends upon how many bits are available. Bit depth usually measures color or sound quality. A larger bit-depth number means a greater range of color or sound.

black and code: The process of recording black video and timecode onto a new camcorder tape. Recording black and code helps prevent timecode breaks. *See also* timecode, timecode break.

Bluetooth: A wireless networking technology common in cell phones, wireless keyboards, and wireless mice. Some camcorders claim to incorporate Bluetooth technology, although it is of little value for video capture or editing because Bluetooth is not fast enough for video transfer.

capture: The process of recording digital video or other media from a camcorder or VCR tape onto a computer's hard drive.

CCD (charged-coupled device): The unit in camcorders that interprets light photons and converts the information into an electronic video signal. This signal can then be recorded on tape. CCDs are also used by digital still cameras.

chrominance: A fancy word for color. *See also* luminance.

clip: One of various segments making up the scenes of a video project. You edit individual clips into the Premiere Elements Timeline to form complete scenes and a complete story line. *See also* Timeline.

coaxial: Cables used to carry a cable TV signal. Coaxial connectors are round and have a single thin pin in the middle of the connector. Coaxial cables carry both sound and video. Although most TVs and VCRs have coaxial connectors, digital camcorders usually do not. Coaxial cables usually provide inferior video quality when compared to component, composite, and S-Video cables. *See also* component video, composite video, S-Video.

codec: A scheme used to compress, and later decompress, video and audio information so that it can be passed more efficiently over computer cables and Internet connections to hard drives and other components.

color gamut: The total range of colors a given system can create (by combining several basic colors) to display a video image. The total number of individual colors that are available is finite. If a color cannot be displayed correctly, it is considered *out of gamut.*

color space: The method used to generate color in a video display. *See also* color gamut, RGB, YUV.

component video: A high-quality connection type for analog video. Component video splits the video signal and sends it over three separate cables, usually color-coded red, green, and blue. Component video connections are unusual in consumer-grade video equipment, but they provide video quality that is superior to coaxial, composite, and S-Video connections. *See also* analog, coaxial, composite video, S-Video.

composite video: A connection type for analog video, typically using a single video-connector cable (color-coded yellow). The connector type is also sometimes called an *RCA connector,* which is usually found paired with audio cables that have red and white connectors. Composite video signals are inferior to S-Video or component video because they tend to allow more signal noise and artifacts in the video signal. *See also* analog, coaxial, component video, S-Video.

DAT (digital audio tape): A digital tape format often used in audio recorders by professional video producers.

data rate: The amount of data that can pass over a connection in a second. The data rate of DV-format video is 3.6MB (megabytes) per second.

device control: A technology that allows a computer to control the playback functions on a digital camcorder (such as play, stop, and rewind). Clicking Rewind in the program window on the computer causes the camcorder tape to actually rewind.

digital: A method of recording sound and light by converting them into data made up of discrete, binary values (expressed as ones and zeros). *See also* analog.

Digital8: A digital camcorder format that uses Hi8 tapes. *See also* digital, DV, MicroMV, MiniDV.

DIMM (Dual Inline Memory Module): A memory module for a computer. Most computer RAM today comes on easily replaced DIMM cards. *See also* RAM.

driver: Pre-1980, the person in control of a car or horse-drawn carriage. Post-1980, a piece of software that allows a computer to utilize a piece of hardware, such as a video card or a printer.

drop-frame timecode: A type of timecode specified by the NTSC video standard, usually with a frame rate of 29.97 fps (frames per second). To maintain continuity, two frames are dropped at the beginning of each minute, except for every tenth minute. *See also* timecode.

DV (Digital Video): A standard format and codec for digital video. Digital camcorders that include a FireWire interface usually record DV-format video. *See also* codec, FireWire.

DVCAM: A professional-grade version of the MiniDV digital-tape format developed by Sony. DVCAM camcorders are usually pretty expensive. *See also* digital, DVCPro, MiniDV.

DVCPro: A professional-grade version of the MiniDV digital-tape format developed by Panasonic. Like DVCAM camcorders, DVCPro camcorders are usually very expensive. *See also* digital, DVCAM, MiniDV.

DVD (Digital Versatile Disc): A category of disc formats that allows capacities from 4.7GB (gigabytes) up to 17GB. DVDs are now the most popular format for distributing movies. Recordable DVDs (DVD-Rs) are also becoming a common among hobbyists.

EIDE (Enhanced Integrated Drive Electronics): The interface used by most modern PCs to connect to their hard drives. For digital video, you should try to use EIDE disks with a speed of 7200 rpm (revolutions per minute).

field: One of two separate sets of scan lines in an interlaced video frame. Each field contains every other horizontal resolution line. Immediately after one field is drawn on the screen, the other is drawn in a separate pass while the previous frame is still glowing, resulting in a complete image. *See also* frame, interlacing.

FireWire: Also known by its official designation IEEE-1394, or by other names such as i.Link, FireWire is a high-speed computer peripheral interface standard developed by Apple Computer. FireWire is often used to connect digital camcorders, external hard drives, and some other devices to a computer. The speed of FireWire has contributed greatly to the affordability of modern video editing. To use Premiere Elements you *must* have a FireWire port. Premiere Elements can't capture video directly from a USB port or analog video capture card.

frame: A single still image in a sequence of many that make up a moving picture. *See also* frame rate.

frame rate: The speed at which the frames in a moving picture change, measured in frames per second (fps). Video images usually display 25 to 30 fps, providing the illusion of movement to the human eye. Slower frame rates save storage space, but can produce jerky motion; faster frame rates produce smoother motion but use up more space in the recording medium for storage and presentation.

gamut: *See* color gamut.

gel: A translucent or colored sheet of plastic or other material that is placed in front of a light to diffuse the light or otherwise change its appearance.

generational loss: A decrease in the quality of an analog recording with every generation (copy) of the recording that is made. Generational loss is jocularly defined as signal-to-noise ratio (less signal, more noise). Every time an analog recording is copied some values are lost in the copying process. Each copy (especially if it's a copy of a copy) represents a later, lower-quality *generation* of the original. *See also* analog.

grayscale: The proper name of a black-and-white picture or video image. Black-and-white images are actually made up of varying shades of gray.

HDTV (High-Definition Television): A set of broadcast-video standards that incorporates resolutions and frame rates higher than those used for traditional analog video. *See also* NTSC, PAL, SECAM.

IEEE-1394: *See* FireWire.

i.Link: *See* FireWire.

interlacing: The production of an image by alternating sets of scan lines on-screen. Most video images are actually composed of two separate fields, drawn on consecutive passes of the electron gun in the video tube. Each field contains every other horizontal resolution line of a video image. Each field is drawn so quickly that the human eye perceives a complete image. *See also* progressive scan, field.

jog: *See* scrub.

lavalier: A tiny microphone designed to clip to a subject's clothing. Lavalier mics are often clipped to the lapels of TV newscasters.

lens flare: A light point or artifact that appears in a video image when the sun or other bright light source reflects on a camera lens.

luminance: A fancy word for brightness in video images. *See also* chrominance.

MicroMV: A small digital camcorder tape format developed by Sony for ultra-compact camcorders. *See also* digital, Digital8, DV, MiniDV.

MiniDV: The most common tape format used by digital camcorders. *See also* digital, Digital8, DV, MicroMV.

moiré pattern: A wavy or shimmering artifact that appears in video images when tight parallel lines appear in the image. This problem often occurs when a subject wears a pinstriped suit or coarse corduroy.

NLE (nonlinear editor): A computer program that can edit video, audio, or other multimedia information without confining the user to an unchangeable sequence of frames from beginning to end. Using an NLE, you can edit the work in any order you choose. Adobe Premiere Elements is one example of a video NLE program.

NTSC (National Television Standards Committee): The broadcast-video standard used in North America, Japan, the Philippines, and elsewhere. *See also* PAL, SECAM.

online/offline editing: A differentiation in editing that is based primarily on the quality of the captured video. When you edit using full-quality footage, you are performing *online* editing. If you perform edits using lower-quality captures and intend to apply those edits to the full-quality footage later, you are performing *offline* editing.

overscan: What happens when a TV cuts off portions of the video image at the edges of the screen. Most standard TVs overscan the video image to some extent.

PAL (Phase Alternating Line): The broadcast-video standard used in Western Europe, Australia, Southeast Asia, South America, and elsewhere. *See also* NTSC, SECAM.

PCI (Peripheral Component Interconnect): A standard type of connection for computer expansion cards (such as FireWire cards). Any new PCI expansion card must be placed in an empty PCI slot on the computer's motherboard.

pixel: The smallest element of a video image, abbreviated from *picture element*. Still images are usually made up of grids containing thousands, even millions, of pixels. A screen or image size that has a resolution of 640 x 480 is 640 pixels wide by 480 pixels high.

Plug and Play: A hardware technology that allows you to easily connect devices such as digital camcorders to your computer. The computer automatically detects the device when it is connected and turned on.

progressive scan: A scan display that draws all the horizontal resolution lines in a single pass. Most computer monitors use progressive scan displays. *See also* interlacing.

RAM (random access memory): The electronic working space for your computer's processor and software. To use digital video on your computer, you need lots of RAM.

render: To produce a playable version of an altered video image. When you apply an effect, speed change, or transition to a video image, your video-editing program must figure out how each frame of the image should look after the change. Rendering is the process of applying these changes. Usually, the rendering process generates a preview file that is stored on the hard drive. *See also* transition.

RGB (red-green-blue): The color space (method of creating on-screen colors) used by computer monitors; all the available colors result from combining red, green, and blue pixels. *See also* color space, YUV.

sampling rate: The number of samples obtained per second during a digital audio recording. When audio is recorded digitally, the sound is sampled thousands of times per second. 48-kHz audio has 48,000 samples per second.

scrub: To move back and forth through a video project, one frame at a time. Some video-editing programs have a scrub bar located underneath the video preview window (also called the *jog control*). *See also* shuttle.

SECAM (Sequential Couleur Avec Memoire): Broadcast video standard used in France, Russia, Eastern Europe, Central Asia, and elsewhere. *See also* NTSC, PAL.

shuttle: To roll video images slowly forward or back, often to check a detail of motion. Professional video decks and cameras often have shuttle controls. Some video-editing programs also have shuttle controls in their capture windows. *See also* scrub.

slate: The black-and-white hinged board that moviemakers snap closed in front of the camera just before action commences. The noise made by the snapping slate is used later to synchronize the video and audio recordings, which are made by separate machines.

SMPTE (Society for Motion Picture and Television Engineers): The organization that develops standards for professional broadcasting equipment and formats. Among other things, the SMPTE defines standards for bars and tone, counting leaders, and timecode.

S-VHS: A higher-quality version of the VHS videotape format. S-VHS VCRs usually have S-Video connectors. *See also* S-Video.

S-Video: A high-quality connection technology for analog video. S-Video connectors separate the color and brightness signals, resulting in less signal noise and fewer artifacts. Most digital camcorders include S-Video connectors for analog output. Analog capture cards and S-VHS VCRs usually have S-Video connectors as well. *See also* analog, capture, coaxial, composite video, component video, S-VHS.

timecode: The standard system for identifying individual frames in a movie or video project. Timecode is expressed as hours:minutes:seconds:frames (as in 01:20:31:02 or 1 hour, 20 minutes, 31 seconds, and 3 frames). This format has been standardized by the SMPTE. Non-drop-frame timecode uses colons between the numbers; drop-frame timecode uses semicolons. *See also* drop-frame timecode, SMPTE, timecode break.

timecode break: An inconsistency in the timecode on a camcorder tape. *See also* timecode.

Timeline: The working space in most video-editing programs, including Adobe Premiere Elements. Clips are arranged along a line that represents the duration of the movie project. The left side of the Timeline represents the beginning of the movie and the right side represents the ending. The Timeline may include multiple video tracks, multiple audio tracks, transitions, effects, titles, and other features. *See also* clip.

title: Text that appears on-screen to display the name of the movie, or to give credit to the people who made the movie. A *subtitle* is a special type of title, often used during a video project to show translations of dialogue spoken in foreign languages.

transition: The method by which one clip ends and another begins in a movie project. A common type of transition is when one clip gradually fades out as the next clip fades in. *See also* clip, render.

USB (Universal Serial Bus): A computer-port technology that makes it easy to connect a mouse, printer, or other device to a computer. Although USB often isn't fast enough for digital-video capture, some digital camcorders have USB ports. Connected to a computer's USB port, these cameras can often be used as Web cams. Most computers built after Spring, 2002 use a newer, faster version of USB called USB 2.0. Adobe Premiere Elements *cannot* capture video from a camcorder or other device that is connected to a USB port.

vectorscope: A professional video tool that monitors the color of a video image.

video card: This term can refer to either of two different kinds of devices inside a computer: The device that generates a video signal for the computer's monitor; or the card that captures video from VCRs and camcorders onto the computer's hard drive. Some hardware manufacturers refer to FireWire cards as video cards because FireWire cards are most often used to capture video from digital camcorders. *See also* capture, FireWire.

waveform: A visual representation of an audio signal. Viewing a waveform on a computer screen allows precise synchronization of sound and video.

waveform monitor: A professional video tool that displays brightness information for a video image.

YCbCr: An alternative acronym for the YUV color space. *See also* YUV.

YUV: The acronym for the color space used by most TVs and digital camcorders. For some obscure reason, YUV stands for *luminance-chrominance*. *See also* chrominance, color space, luminance, RGB.

zebra pattern: An overexposure-warning feature that is used by some high-end camcorders. A striped pattern appears in the viewfinder over areas of the image that will be overexposed unless the camcorder is adjusted to compensate.

Index

• *W* •